IMAGES
of America

GLENNVILLE

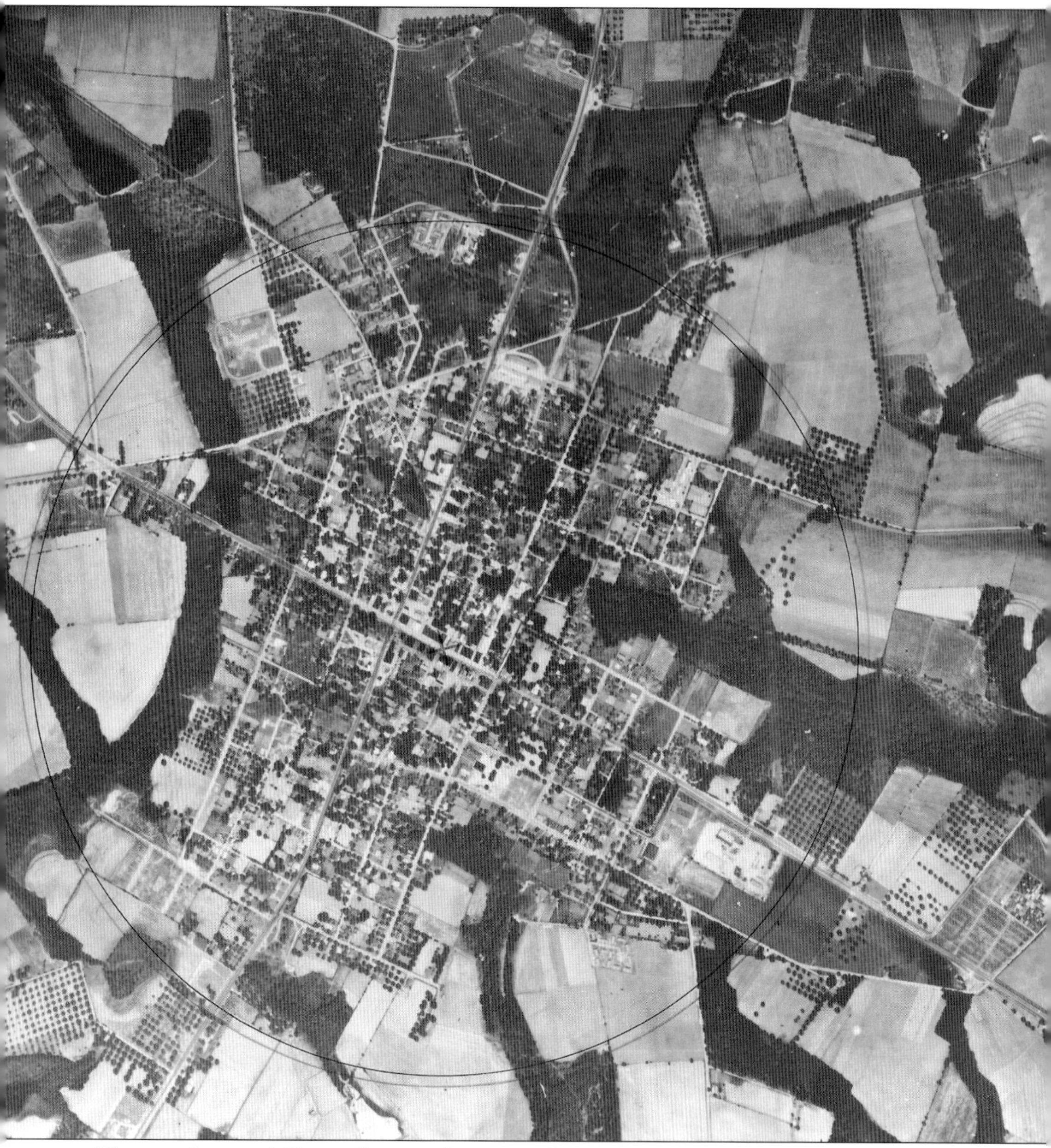

This aerial view of Glennville was taken around 1957. (Courtesy of the City of Glennville.)

ON THE COVER: In this c. 1949–1950 photograph, a tomato parade features the Fort Stewart marching band on Barnard Street. Standing from right to left in front of Central Pharmacy are Dr. J.M. Hughes Sr. (wearing a hat), Virginia Hughes Howard, Olivia Dubberly Hughes, unidentified, Frances Hughes Evers, and more unidentified. In front are two men propping their feet on the rear bumper of a car. They are M.E. "Boby" Curry (left) and John Arthur Dasher (right). To Curry's left is his wife, Lois Kicklighter Curry, and to their left, the boy wearing a striped shirt is Joseph Marcus Hughes III. Standing in the door of the United 5 & 10 Cent Store is owner Brantley Denmark "B.D." Blitch (wearing a white shirt). (Courtesy of the Glennville-Tattnall Museum.)

IMAGES
of America

GLENNVILLE

Glennville-Tattnall Museum

ARCADIA
PUBLISHING

ISBN 978-1-4671-1616-9

Published by Arcadia Publishing
Charleston, South Carolina

Printed in the United States of America

Library of Congress Control Number: 2015952221

For all general information, please contact Arcadia Publishing:
Telephone 843-853-2070
Fax 843-853-0044
E-mail sales@arcadiapublishing.com
For customer service and orders:
Toll-Free 1-888-313-2665

Visit us on the Internet at www.arcadiapublishing.com

Dedicated to the memory of Edythe Collins Phillips,
without whose love for and knowledge of Glennville's history
the present work would not have been possible.

Contents

Acknowledgments

After the founding of the Glennville-Tattnall Museum in 1994, the museum's board of directors began amassing a large collection of photographs pertaining to Glennville's history. Some of these images were incorporated into the museum's exhibits; however, most have remained hidden from view and inaccessible to the general public. With the publication of *Glennville*, however, that has changed.

Most of the images that appear in the present volume are courtesy of the Glennville-Tattnall Museum (GTM). A substantial portion is courtesy of the Perkins Collection (Perkins), which was the work of the late Marvin Perkins and was bequeathed to the late Lee Woodcock, who expanded the collection and conducted extensive research on many of the images. We are greatly indebted to Deneb Causey for generously allowing us the use of these priceless photographs.

It must be noted that this book is not a documented work. While we have striven to be as accurate and scholarly as possible, most of the information presented here is the result of oral history, tradition, and recollections by various local residents. Although we as authors have attempted to be as objective as possible, history is often subjective and may be remembered differently by various individuals. As a result, this book may contain various factual errors. These are solely the responsibility of the authors.

Throughout the course of this project, numerous individuals, businesses, and organizations have provided much assistance, without which this project would not have been a success. We would like to extend special thanks to the City of Glennville, Pam Waters and the staff of the *Glennville Sentinel*, the *Tattnall Journal*, Connie Rogers and the Glennville Bank, Brent Walker, Bobby Kicklighter, Edythe Phillips, Wayne Dasher, and Bobby and Vicki Nelson. Special thanks are also due to Patty Wilson of the Glennville Public Library for allowing the use of the library's facilities throughout this project, as well as for the use of the library's collection of Glennville High School annuals, from which many of the images contained herein were taken.

Lastly, on behalf of the board of directors of the Glennville-Tattnall Museum, we would like to thank the entire community of Glennville and Tattnall County for being so supportive of this worthwhile project. The images contained in *Glennville* tell the story of a town and its people, and it is our sincere hope that this collection will be treasured by generations to come.

Introduction

Over two centuries have passed since the first settlers arrived at what is now Glennville. One of the first settlers to the Glennville vicinity was Matthew Beard, for whom Beards Creek is named. Little reference is made to Beard in our local history other than his acceptance of a land grant in the western end of St. Andrew's Parish in 1774. In 1773, the Creek Nation ceded a large amount of territory between the Altamaha and Ogeechee Rivers to the Colony of Georgia. The western boundary of this new land was a straight line from the mouth of Beards Creek north toward present-day Manassas. Thus, in 1773, the southeastern portion of present-day Tattnall County was opened for settlement.

During the American Revolution, St. Andrew's Parish was combined with St. John's Parish to form Liberty County, of which the Glennville vicinity formed the far western section. In 1784, the remainder of present-day Tattnall County, which had until then been considered Creek territory, became part of the newly created Washington County and, in 1793, part of Montgomery County. In 1801, our own glorious Tattnall became the 25th county of Georgia.

A majority of Tattnall County was carved out of Montgomery; however, the area around modern Glennville remained part of Liberty County until 1811. In that year, the boundary line between old Liberty County and new Tattnall County was moved east to Beards Creek, and thus present-day Glennville became a permanent part of Tattnall County.

The land surrounding Glennville had already been open to settlement for 28 years by the time Tattnall County was created. Despite the early availability of land, access presented a problem. Indian raids were frequent, and few were willing to settle in this frontier area until around 1800. After Matthew Beard, there came Matthew Jones in 1805, who built the Lumber Bridge over Beards Creek at what is now Highway 301 South. In 1809, another settler, Thomas Hall, established the area's largest plantation a few miles southeast of the present-day city limits near Hall's Bridge; his main crop was long staple sea island cotton, which could only be grown up to about 60 miles inland.

While these planters are relevant to our history, the origins of Glennville itself stem from the intersection of two important roads. The earliest and most traveled was Hencart Road, sometimes referred to as "Handcart Road." The road began at Kings Ferry on the Ogeechee River near present-day Richmond Hill and made its way inland through present-day Fort Stewart. It crossed Beards Creek, passed through Glennville, crossed the Ohoopee River at Cowford, and proceeded to an area near what is now Hawkinsville. This road was one of the most vital trade routes into the Creek Nation and was well-traveled by 1800. The second road came along several years later and ran from what is now Reidsville to the train depot at Johnston's Station (now Ludowici). The Hencart Road and the Reidsville–Johnston's Station Road intersected at the location now known as "Hilltop" in Glennville. It was there that settlers began to flock. The ensuing village came to be known as Philadelphia Crossroads.

The earliest settlers to Philadelphia were Rev. Seth Knight and Elijah Padgett, who received land grants in the 1820s. They were immediately followed by the families of Joseph Dubberly,

John J. Baxter, Asa Barnard, Hardy DeLoach, Joshua Groover, Dempsey Griffin, and Gideon Poppell. Knight was one of the most prominent citizens of the area, serving as treasurer of Tattnall County and an inferior court justice. In 1845, he built a large plantation house facing the intersection at Philadelphia. His plantation comprised some 700 acres, the chief crops being sea island cotton and rice.

Philadelphia continued to see growth throughout the 1800s. The year 1850 brought the first school, and the first general store appears to have been established around 1855. A milestone year in the town's history was 1857, which saw the establishment of Philadelphia Baptist Church (now First Baptist Church). In 1854, due to the growth of the village, the old post office was moved from Stafford's Ferry (near Lane's Bridge) on the Altamaha River to Matlock Plantation just southwest of town. Matlock Plantation was originally owned by Stephen Matlock and later by the Tillman and Durrence families. By the 1850s, the plantation comprised over 3,000 acres and was worked by over 50 slaves, as was the previously mentioned Hall Plantation. However, these are examples of the more prosperous planters in the area. Most farmers only owned about 50 acres, while about six local farmers owned up to 150 acres worked by approximately 10 slaves. The days of prosperity and happiness were not to last, as war clouds loomed on the horizon.

In 1860, the vicinity of Philadelphia had 148 families, and the 144 slaves living in the area were owned by only 22 of those families. As the Southern states continually felt their rights infringed upon by the federal government, talk of states' rights reached a head. At the Secession Convention in Milledgeville in 1861, Tattnall County delegates Benjamin Brewton and Henry Solomon Strickland voted against secession but were forced to sign the Ordinance of Secession. The subsequent Civil War brought much hardship to Philadelphia, as young men marched off to battle to defend their beliefs and homes. As the war raged on, the Confederate lines gradually became exhausted, until there was nothing standing between the invading army of Gen. William T. Sherman and the port of Savannah. The citizens of Philadelphia could do nothing but wait for the true horror of war to reach home. They would not have to wait long.

On December 14, 1864, a band of Sherman's army under Col. Smith Atkins forced its way across the Canoochee River at Taylor's Creek and invaded Liberty and Tattnall Counties. The Yankee invaders forded Beards Creek and marched into defenseless Philadelphia, where they camped in the front yard of the Knight-Dubberly house. Seth Knight had passed away in 1853. On or around December 15, the troops awoke and awaited orders from Colonel Atkins. As they had already inflicted much damage in other parts of the county, Philadelphia seemed fit for the torch. Before ordering the destruction of the plantation and the surrounding village, Colonel Atkins entered the deserted Knight-Dubberly house, where he allegedly discovered a Masonic emblem displayed on the mantel. He allegedly received orders from General Sherman not to lay a hand on any property belonging to Masons, as Sherman himself belonged to the brotherhood. Atkins ordered his troops to leave the village, claiming that there was not much worth burning there anyway. Thus, the Knight-Dubberly house was the savior of the village.

It is interesting to note that on December 15, 1868, the fourth anniversary of the sparing of Philadelphia, the old Knight house came under new ownership—that of William Dubberly, the son of early settler Joseph Dubberly. With most of the original settlers of Philadelphia dead, the burden of leadership passed to William, who served as the local justice of the peace. A constable was selected, and law and order came to town. Dubberly used his home as a courthouse and held court there regularly until his death. Because he was the central authority in town, Dubberly earned the nickname "Squire," which denoted a lower-ranking nobleman or, in his case, a justice of the peace. The Knight-Dubberly house, now the oldest in Glennville, still stands solemnly at Hilltop as a sort of memorial to its former occupants, two of the founding fathers of Glennville.

With order restored after the war, Philadelphia again began experiencing growth—growth like it had not yet seen. Newer, more substantial buildings began to replace the older ones, and more settlers arrived and established farms and businesses. By 1889, there was a need for a closer post office than the one located two miles away at Matlock, so, with the assistance of local schoolteacher Glenn Thompson, a post office was established at Philadelphia. The name

"Glennville" was selected in honor of Thompson's hard work in securing the post office. Soon after, in 1891, the Tattnall Baptist Institute, forerunner of Glennville High School, was established, and a large frame schoolhouse was constructed. By 1894, the population and economy of Glennville made it impossible to refer to it as a village anymore. On October 6, 1894, Glennville was at last incorporated as a town after a petition was signed by 16 prominent local citizens.

The first half of the 20th century was a time of remarkable growth and prosperity for Glennville. By 1900, there were 234 people residing within the town limits, and this number would steadily increase. Another milestone of Glennville's history occurred in 1901—the first railroad. Though only a tram line of the Perkins Lumber Company in Hagan, it was a major advancement for the town, as it provided another link with the outside world. It became known as the Register & Glennville Railroad, and a depot was erected on East Barnard Street adjacent to the present-day Glennwanis Hotel.

In 1905, another railroad was established. This railroad would change hands and names several times. For several years, it was known as the Georgia Coast & Piedmont Railroad (often referred to as the Gopher, Coon & Possum), with six passenger trains running daily from Brunswick to Collins through Darien, Ludowici, Glennville, and Reidsville. After it was purchased for a second time in 1921 by D.M. Bradley (who had owned it previously), it became the Collins & Glennville Railroad, as it eventually ran between those towns via Reidsville and Mendes. It continued operating until it was finally dismantled in 1941. The depot was located between the Methodist church and Main Street (now Veterans Boulevard/Highway 301) and stood there until the early 2000s.

The second decade of the 20th century saw many brick buildings replacing older wooden ones, and Glennville began to take on a new appearance. Many of the present structures in downtown Glennville were built during this time of growth and prosperity. In 1911, after the old Tattnall Institute building burned, a two-story brick building topped with a cupola was built on the site. This school building, which served as Glennville High School and later Glennville Middle School, still stands and is now home to the Glennville-Tattnall Museum. In 1914, the old wooden Philadelphia Baptist Church building was replaced by the present brick sanctuary of the First Baptist Church. In addition to these more prominent landmarks, there were numerous brick stores constructed on Barnard Street, most of which still stand.

Perhaps the most impressive structure ever constructed in Glennville, however, came in 1926—the Glennwanis Hotel. After the old Hughes Hotel burned in 1920, there was a need for a new hotel in the community; therefore, a group of citizens helped to establish the Glennwanis Hotel—a large, stately brick building equipped with state-of-the-art technology. It was odd for such a small town to have such a large hotel; however, it was well used by the traveling salesmen known as "drummers," and tourists coming to relax and fish near Glennville. Later, a restaurant was added, which provided the hotel's guests as well as locals a place to dine.

Glennville's economy has always been agriculture-based. In the early plantation days, cotton was the primary crop, and this held true into the 20th century; however, the effects of the Great Depression combined with the dreaded boll weevil had very adverse effects on local farming. Many farmers still relied on tobacco, which provided a source of income, but a helping hand was needed.

In the 1930s, Glennville received that helping hand from the tomato. The rich soil around Glennville was well-suited for growing tomatoes, and they quickly became the new cash crop. Most of the present generation is unaware of a time when onions were not king in Glennville; however, tomatoes held the same level of importance during much of the early 1900s. They became so important to the local economy that an oversized tomato was placed on a pedestal at the corner of Barnard and Main Streets near First Baptist Church. The Glennville Tomato Festival was held annually in Glennville for several years to celebrate the crop. The economic boom provided by tomatoes eventually began to die out after newer, better varieties were discovered elsewhere.

Around the same time that tomatoes were on their way out, a new crop was on its way in—the sweet onion. The soil of Tattnall County was even better suited for the sweet onion than the tomato, and the onions continued to gain prominence throughout the 1900s. In 1976, the first

Glennville Sweet Onion Festival was held and has continued ever since. Onions continue to play a central role in the economy and society of Glennville and Tattnall County.

In the 1940s, Glennville received another economic boost in the form of Highway 301. As the Interstate 95 of its day, Highway 301 conveyed nearly all north-south travelers to and from their destinations, and as a result, Glennville's economy no longer depend solely on its local inhabitants. New motels and tourist shops began appearing in Glennville. Glennville selected as its slogan the "Accommodating City," which reflected not only the large number of accommodations but also the city's friendly atmosphere. After the completion of Interstate 95, Highway 301 began to lose importance, and the motels began disappearing. Despite the decline in its use, Highway 301 still remains heavily traveled by locals and those who want to avoid the hectic interstate and take a more scenic route, though it seems deserted when compared to the traffic of years gone by.

The rest of the 20th century brought many changes, but the chief aspects of Glennville remained the same. Businesses opened and closed with the cycling economy, and life carried on as it always had. A hallmark in Glennville's past came in 1994, when the town celebrated its centennial on October 6. Suddenly, the forgotten aspects of our local history again surfaced and became of interest to the newer generation as a centennial committee began to make plans for the upcoming celebration.

Prior to the centennial, the city council made plans to establish a museum after local artists Juliet Tarver and Socorro DeLoach offered to paint a large canvas mural depicting Glennville as it would have appeared in 1915. The mural and museum that would house it required a great deal of research, so a museum board was formed by area historians to oversee the process. Part of the old school building was restored to serve as the new Glennville-Tattnall Museum, which opened during the week of the centennial. A town history was compiled from the writings of D. Mark Baxter, Carroll L. Cowart, Joseph T. Grice, and Alec F. Thompson. The result was *Philadelphia to Glennville: A Backward Glance*. The centennial celebration was commemorated with historical tours of downtown, an old-fashioned parade, and various other festivities. It was the proudest day in Glennville's history since October 6, 1894.

The arrival of the 21st century created much fanfare throughout the world, and Glennville was no exception, although the transition brought no real noticeable changes to the community. Time inevitably brings change; however, that change in Glennville is gradual. When one compares the Glennville of the late 1800s with the present-day community, they appear to be two completely different places. Yet, when one considers the fundamental element of a community—its people—Glennville is virtually the same now as it was then. It is still home to an entrepreneurial, all-American, God-fearing citizenry, and that is one aspect of our town that will always remain the same.

One

ORIGINS

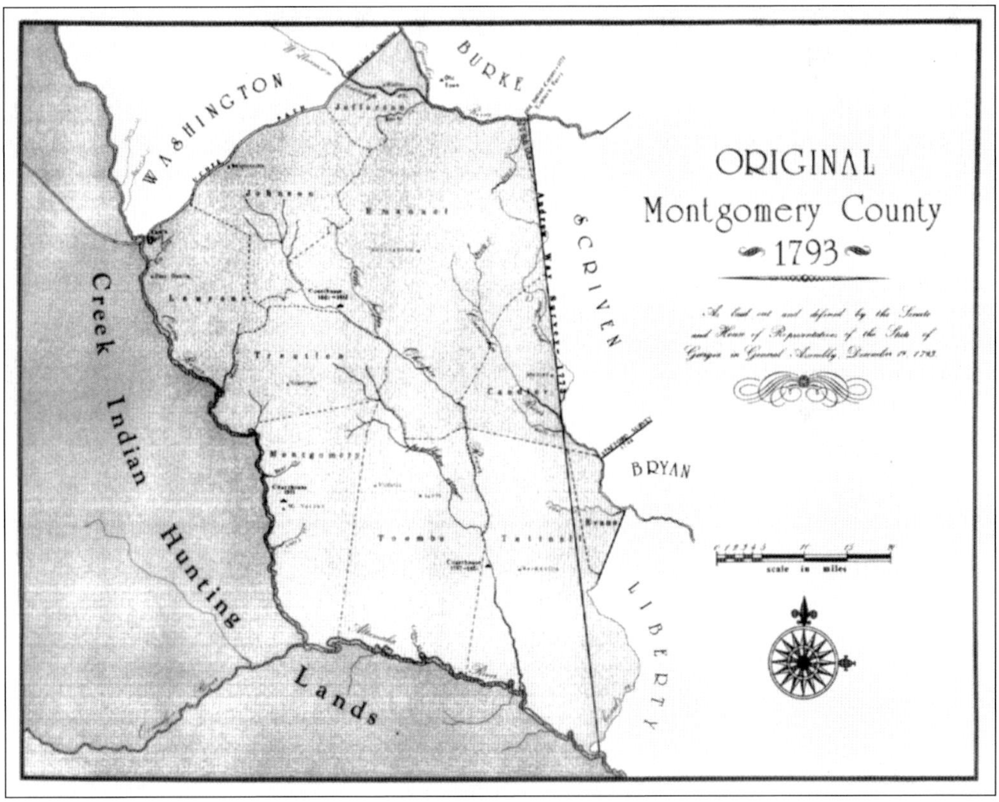

A diagonal line shows the 1773 Andrew Way Survey, which, from 1773 until the conclusion of the American Revolution, served as the Colony of Georgia's western boundary, which ran just west of what is now Glennville. The lightly shaded areas west of the line depict the original boundaries of Montgomery County, created in 1793. The area between the line and Beards Creek remained part of Liberty County until 1811. (GTM.)

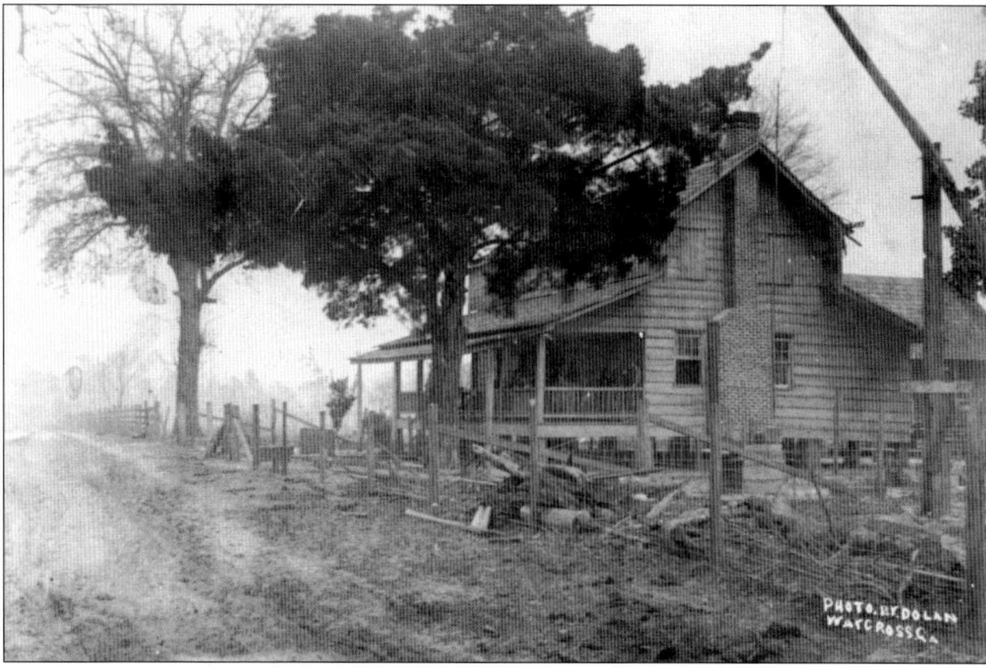

The Knight-Dubberly house, pictured above in 1906, was constructed in 1845 by Rev. Seth Knight at the center of Philadelphia Crossroads, facing the intersection. The house is a notable example of "plantation plain" architecture, which was the prevalent house type found on larger, wealthier plantations in southeast Georgia. In 1868, the house was purchased by William Dubberly and has remained in the Dubberly family ever since. Today, the Knight-Dubberly house still stands at Hilltop and is the oldest structure in the city limits of Glennville. The photograph below shows the house as it appeared in the 1990s. (Both, Perkins.)

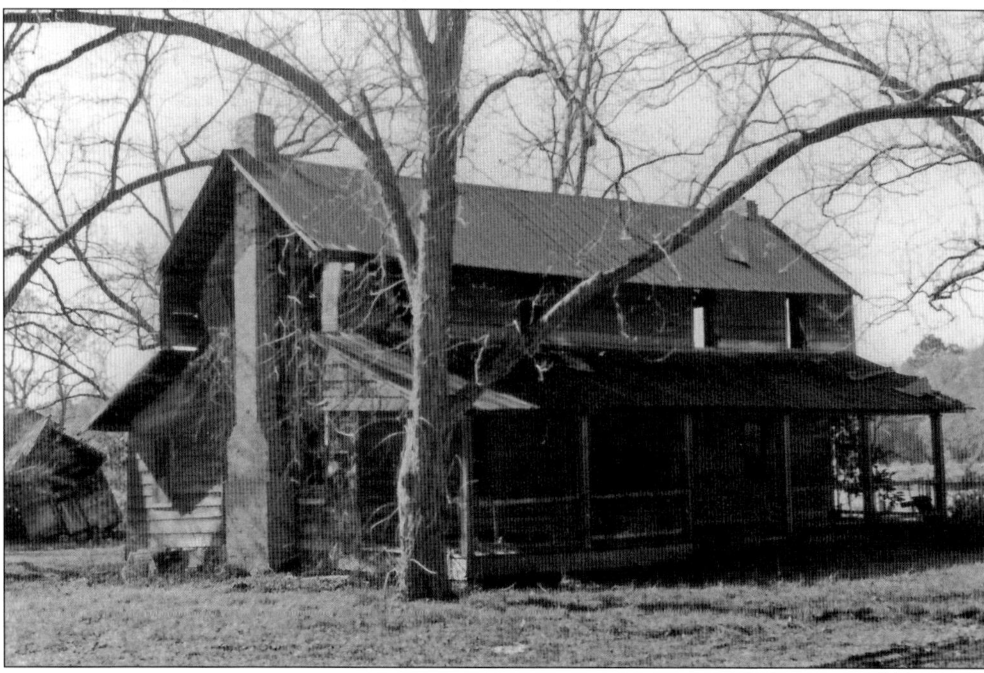

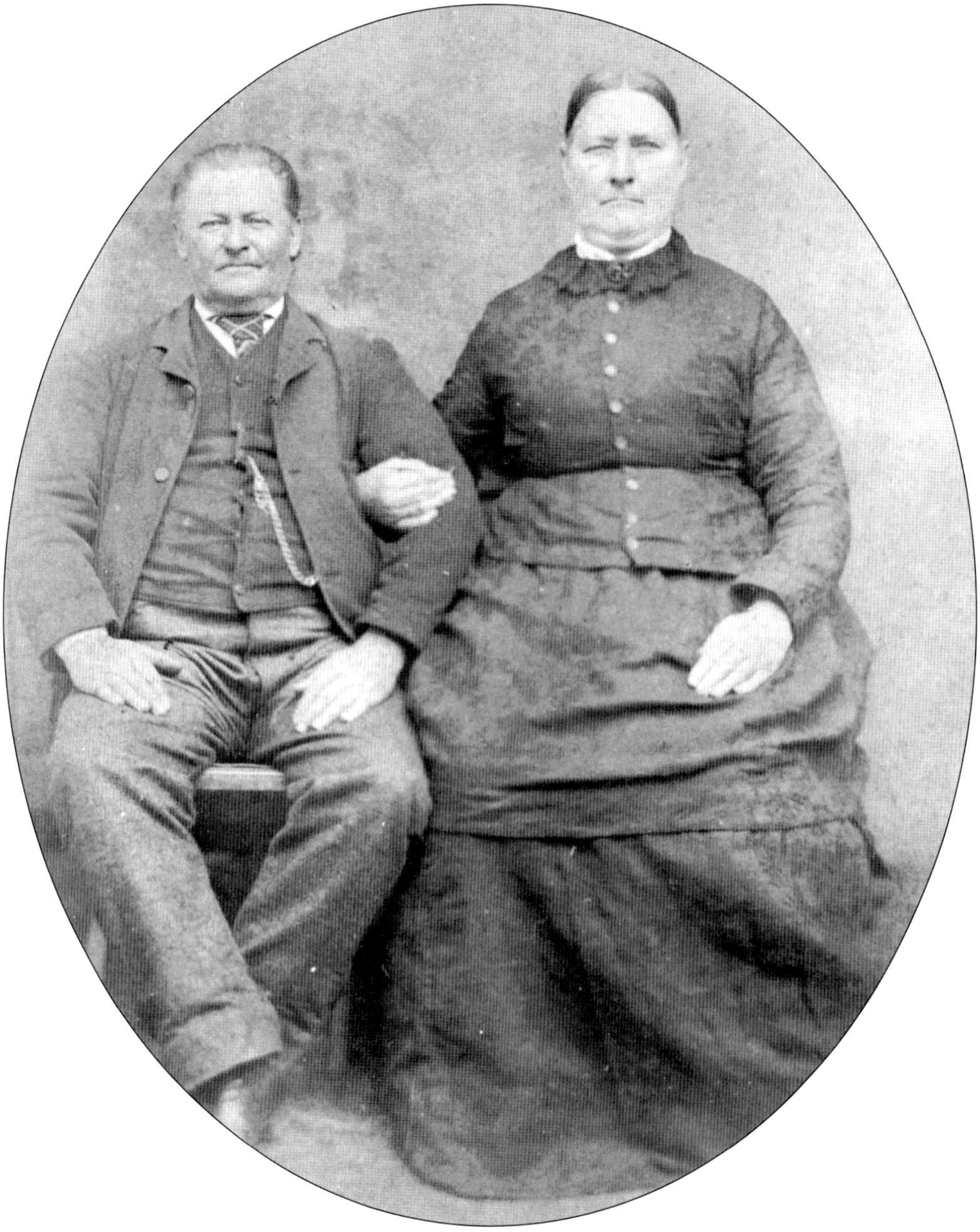

One of Glennville's most noteworthy founding fathers was William "Squire" Dubberly (1827–1895), who led the village of Philadelphia through some of its most formative early years during the Civil War and Reconstruction. Following the war, Dubberly served as justice of the peace, earning him the nickname "Squire" or "Squire Bill," and was the central authority in the village until Glennville was incorporated as a town in 1894. In 1868, he purchased the Seth Knight house, where he resided and held court regularly until his death. Dubberly was the son of two of Philadelphia's original settlers, Joseph and Holland Anderson Dubberly, and the grandson of Tattnall County pioneer and Revolutionary War veteran John Dubberly. Squire Dubberly is pictured here with his second wife, Mary Ellen Smiley Curry Dubberly (1832–1902). (Courtesy of B. Daniel Dubberly Jr.)

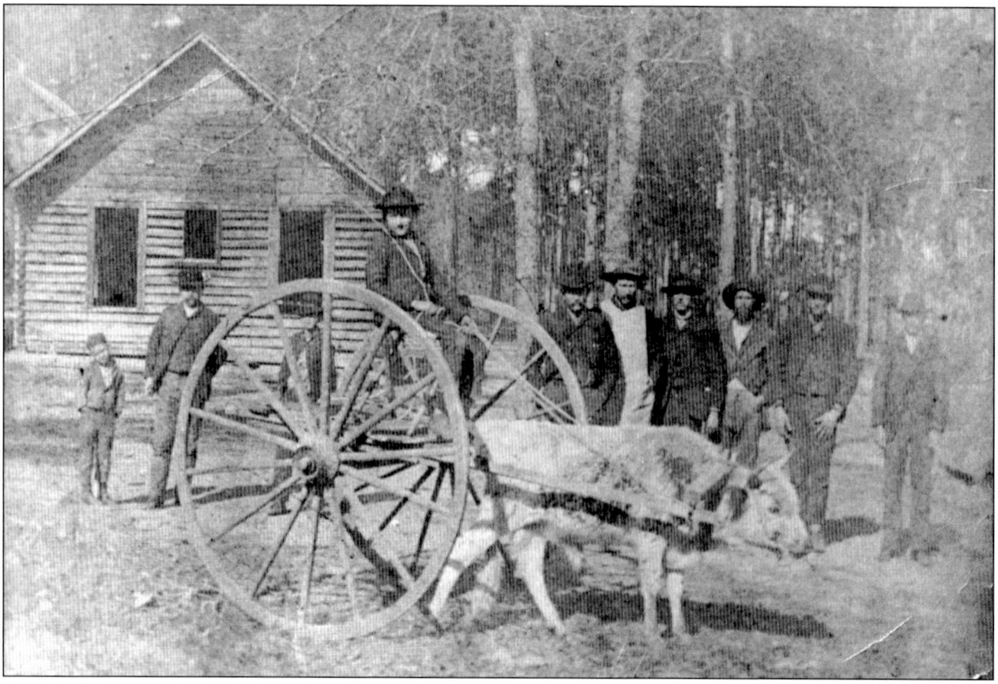

Established in 1857, Philadelphia Baptist Church (now Glennville First Baptist Church) was the backbone of the Philadelphia community during its formative years. Above, a group of men with an oxcart pose in front of the original log structure, most likely shortly after the Civil War. This building served the congregation until 1881, when a larger frame structure with an imposing steeple was constructed on the same site. This second sanctuary is pictured below in a 1906 photograph and served until construction of the present brick sanctuary in 1914. (Above, GTM; below, Perkins.)

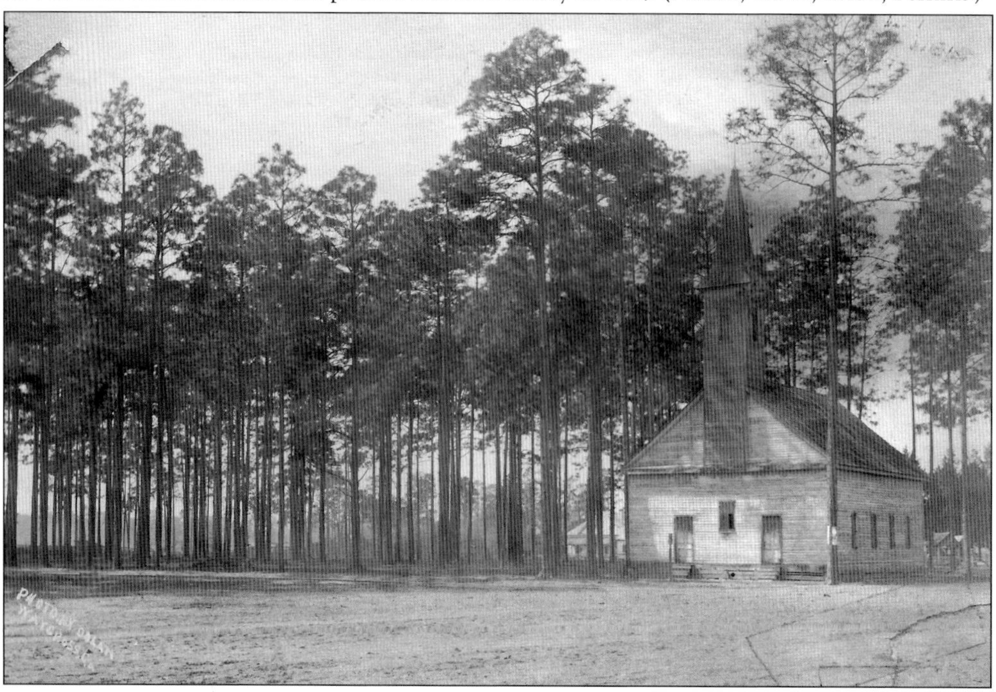

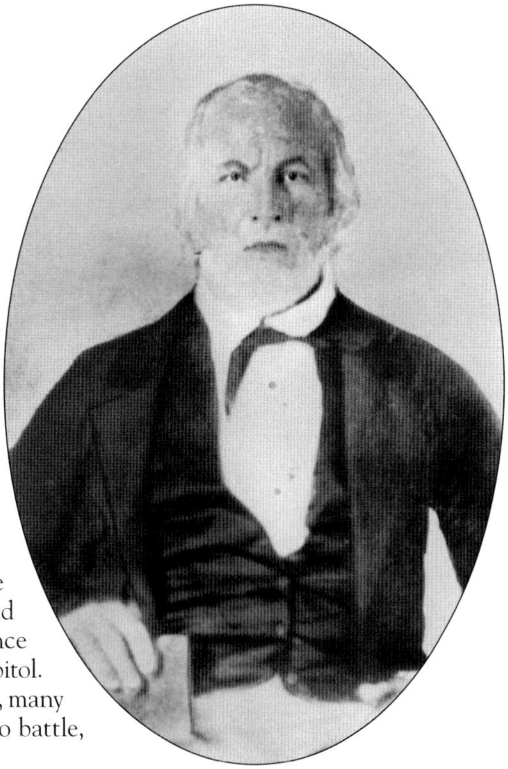

As talk of secession grew in the months leading up to the Civil War, Tattnall County remained solidly Unionist. Tattnall County's delegates to the state secession convention in Milledgeville, Henry Solomon Strickland (right) and Benjamin Brewton (below), represented two of the county's largest slaveholding families; however, both voted against secession at the convention. According to legend, after the secessionists carried the day, Strickland and Brewton were forced to sign Georgia's Ordinance of Secession before being allowed to leave the capitol. Despite Tattnall County's opposition to secession, many of the county's young men were proudly sent to battle, and many would never return. (Both, GTM.)

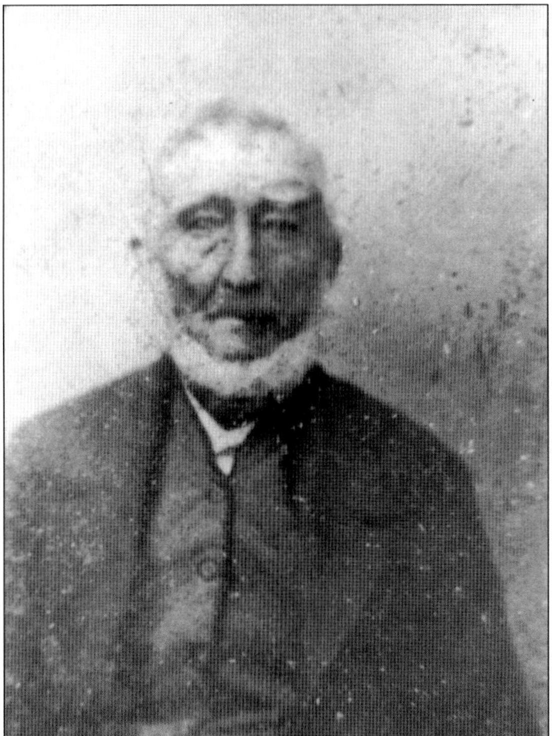

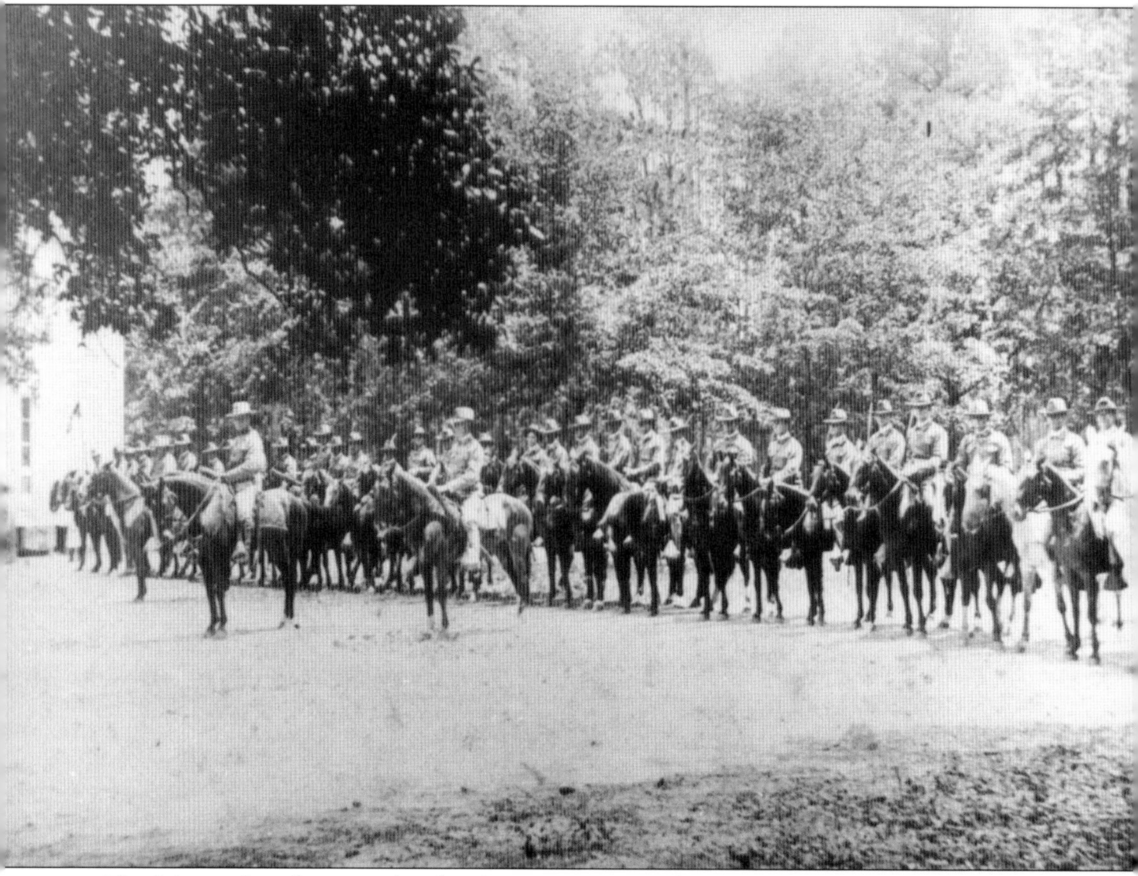

The Liberty Guards were a local militia unit organized in 1845 including men from southern Tattnall County and western Liberty (present-day Long) County. During the Civil War, the Guards were called into Confederate service under Capt. Joseph William Hughes Jr. as Troop D, 5th Georgia Cavalry, and served with great distinction in a number of battles. In this photograph from around 1900, the Liberty Guards stand at attention with sabers drawn at their parade ground at Jones Creek (in present-day Long County), with their armory at left. Joseph William Hughes III (front center) served as the last captain before the Guards disbanded between 1905 and 1910. The Liberty Guards, praised by their contemporaries as experts in horsemanship and cavalry tactics, are considered by many to be the forerunner to the current Glennville National Guard Armory. (GTM.)

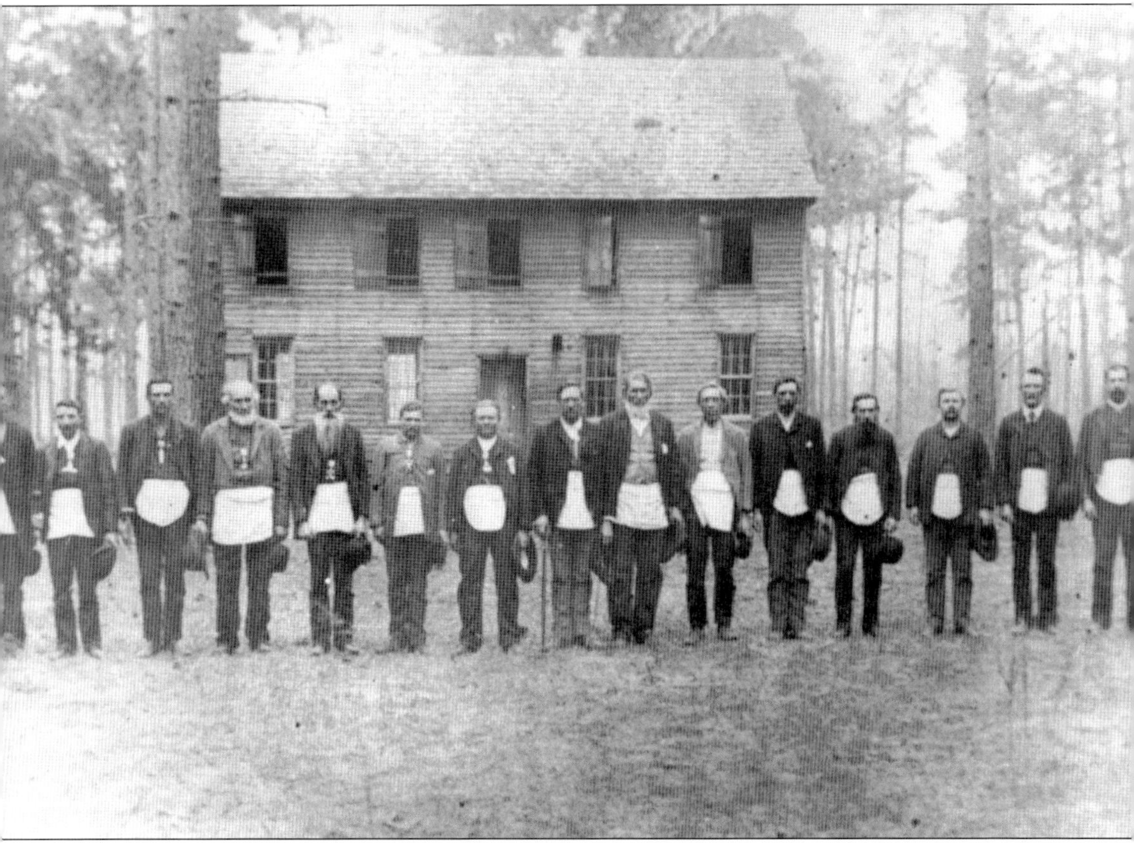

Following the Civil War, many Confederate veterans met in 1866 to organize Middleground Masonic Lodge just north of Ebenezer Baptist Church. As the village of Philadelphia continued to grow during Reconstruction, the Philadelphia Lodge was organized in 1886 to replace Middleground. In 1889, members of the new lodge erected a two-story frame structure, pictured here at some point prior to 1894, on the east side of South Caswell Street. The Masons met on the second floor, while the first floor housed the store of J.B. Caswell, for whom Caswell Street was named. From left to right are G. Godwin, J.J. Barnard, A.F. DeLoach, Edward Weathers, Aquilla Weathers, Edward Miles Dubberly, William "Squire" Dubberly, I.J. DeLoach, Jonathan Barnard, Asa Barnard, Jack DeLoach, Glenn Thompson, Joseph P. Collins, F.D. Griffin, and A.H. Prince. (GTM.)

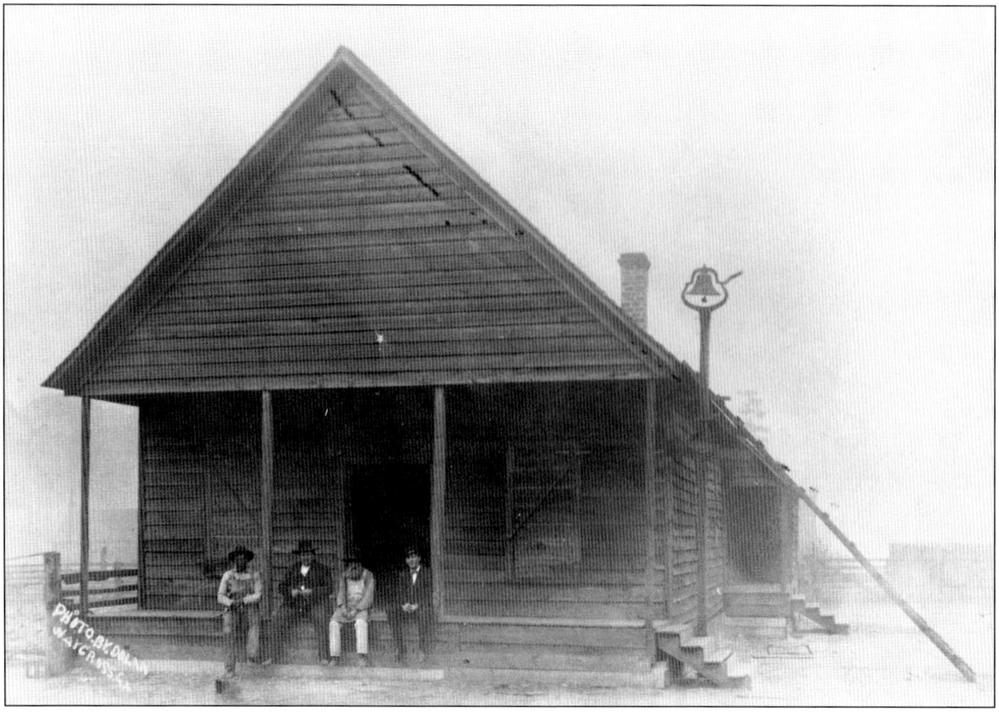

Beginning in 1854, the closest post office to Philadelphia was located at Matlock, about two miles from town on Hencart Road (now Highway 144 West). In 1889, a new post office was established at Philadelphia, which was renamed Glennville. The first post office building, pictured here in 1906, was constructed in 1889. Glennville was incorporated as a town in 1894. (GTM.)

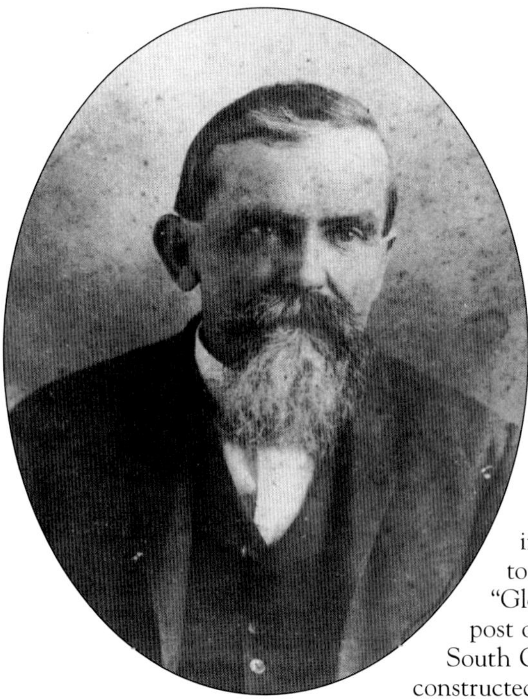

With the establishment of the village's first post office in 1889, Philadelphia was renamed Glennville after local pastor and schoolteacher Rev. Glenn J. Thompson (1853–1915). Thompson played a central role in securing the post office, and when prompted to select a name for their village, residents chose "Glennville" in honor of Thompson's efforts. The post office briefly occupied Thompson's home on South Caswell Street until the first post office was constructed. (GTM.)

Two

Growth of a Town

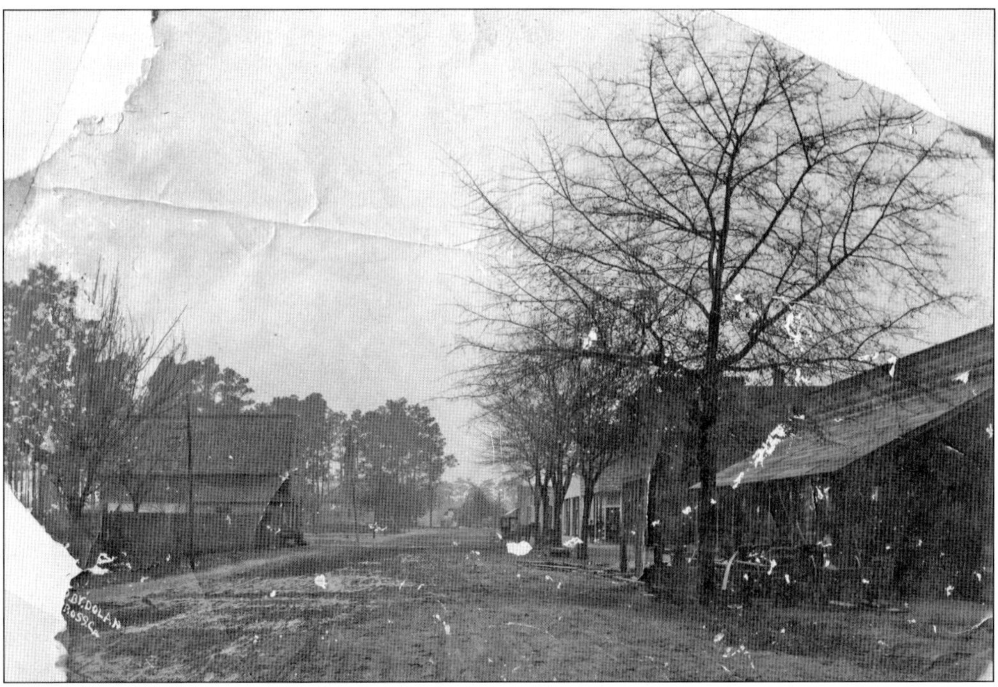

During the summer of 1906, a fire destroyed most of the south side of Barnard Street, pictured here that same year. This photograph was taken from the vicinity of Railroad Street, facing west toward First Baptist Church in the distance. At left is the store of Glenn Thompson, and at far right is the Weitman-Bazemore blacksmith. The Glennville Bank can be seen just beyond. (Perkins.)

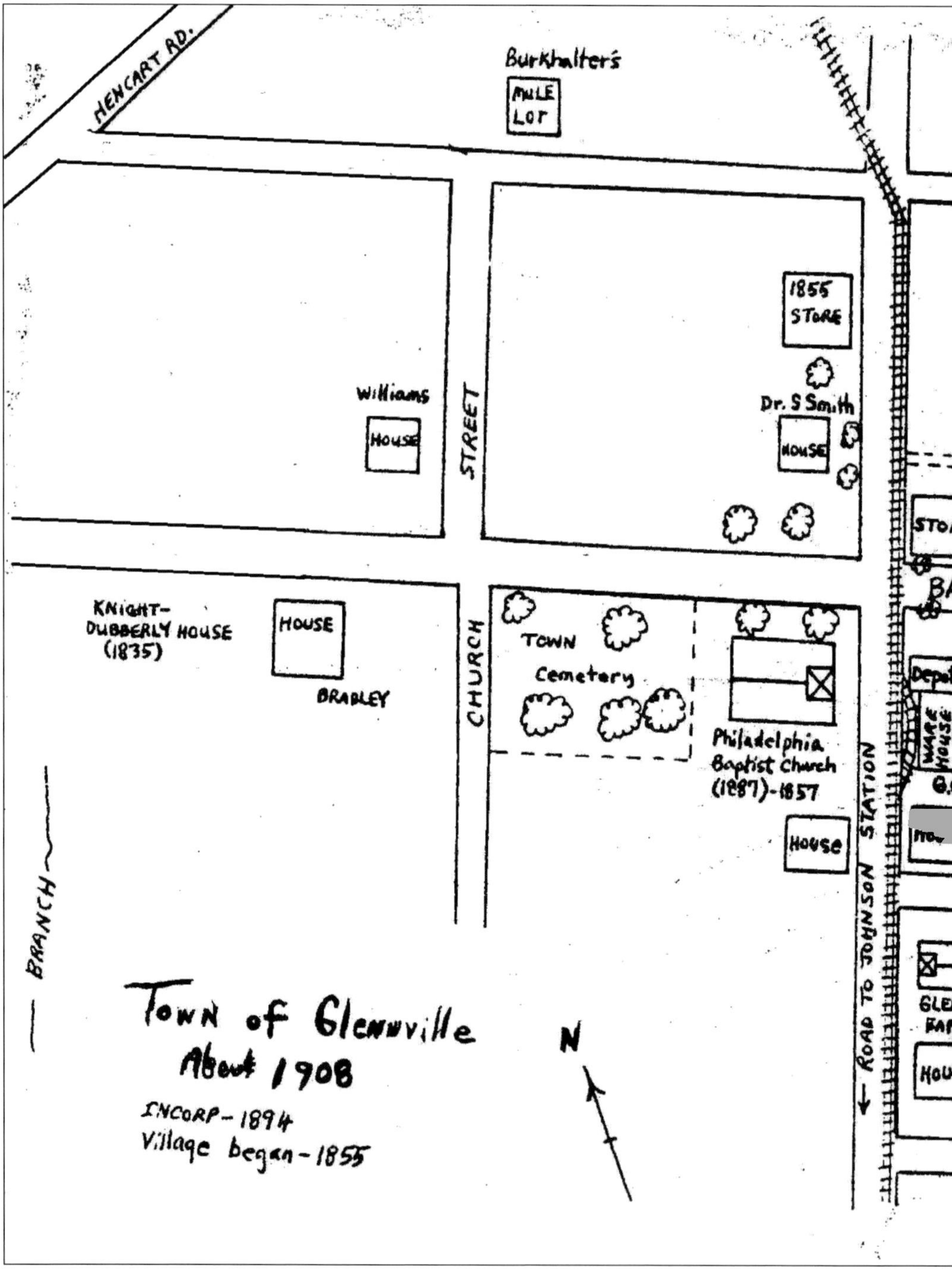

A contemporary map shows a thriving Glennville as it would have appeared around 1908. The artist included Tattnall Institute at the bottom right to show its general location; however, in actuality, it would have stood farther east on South Tillman Street, which is not shown. Also, the Knight-Dubberly house stood farther west. The Georgia Coast & Piedmont Railroad tracks

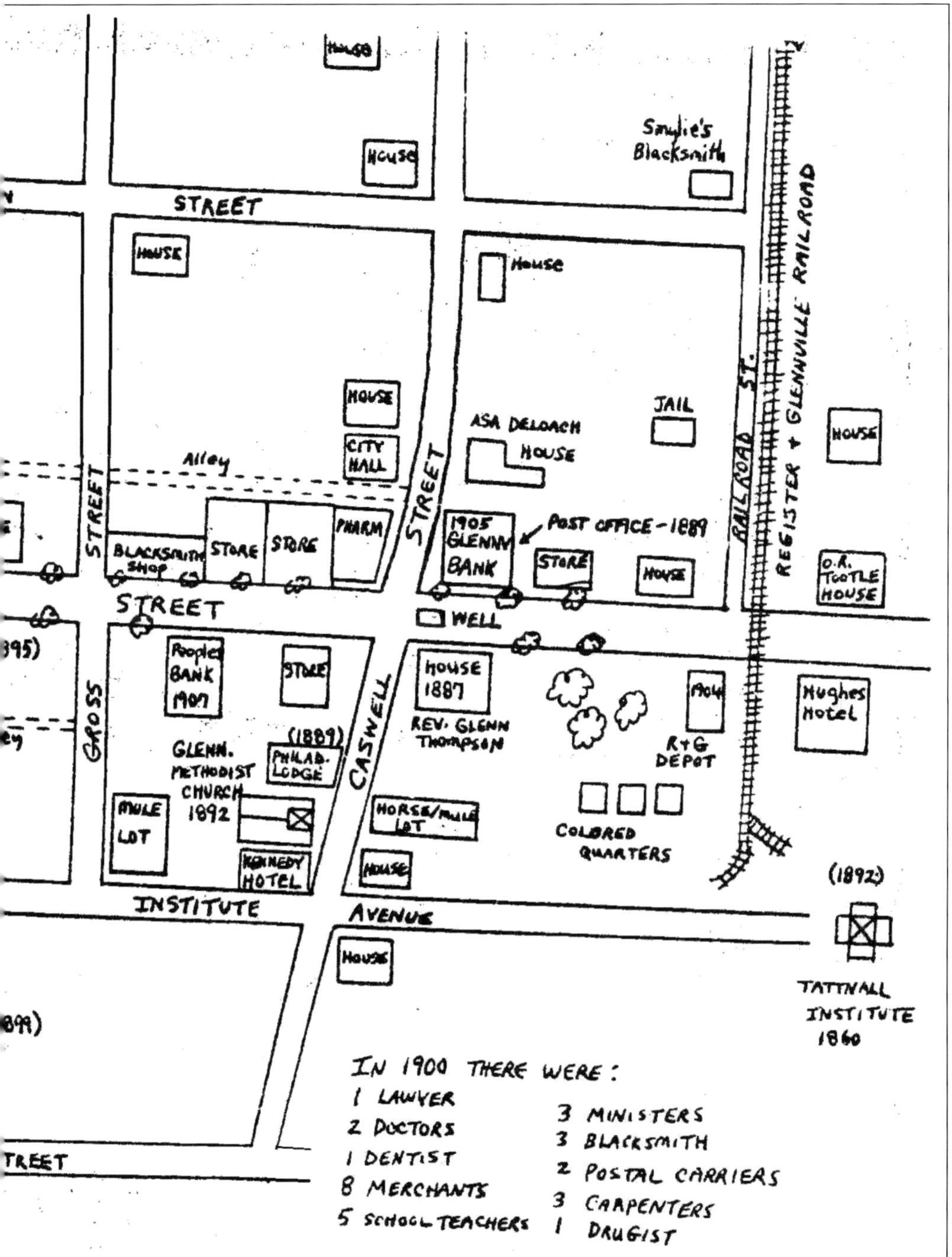

run parallel to Main Street, and the Register & Glennville runs parallel to Railroad Street. The artist noted that, in 1900, there were one lawyer, two doctors, one dentist, eight merchants, five schoolteachers, three ministers, three blacksmiths, two postal carriers, three carpenters, and one druggist. (Perkins.)

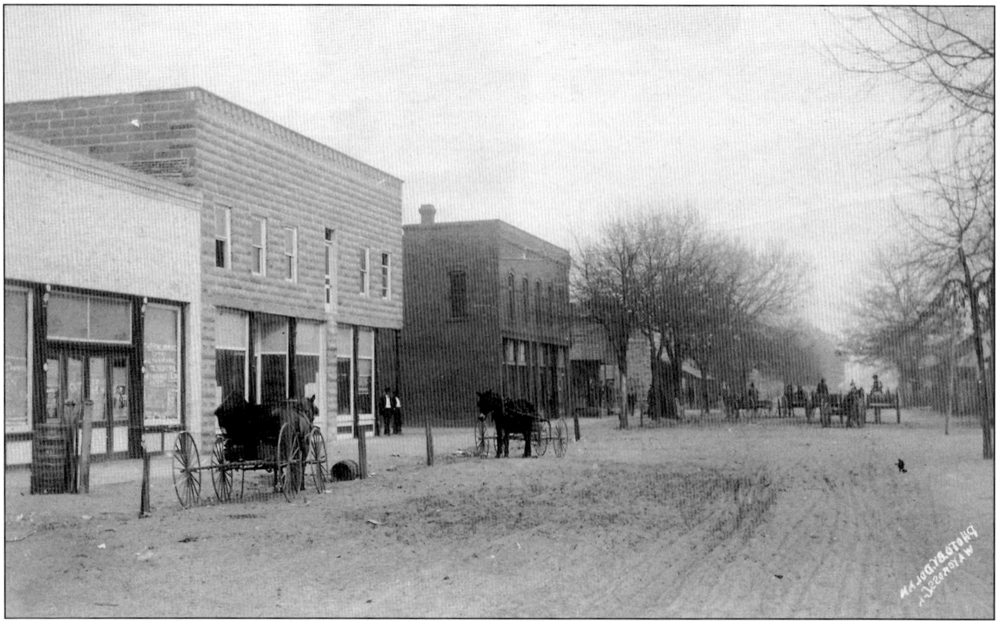

This 1906 photograph shows Barnard Street, facing east from Gross Street toward Caswell Street. At the time, the north side of Barnard Street boasted a row of fine, newly constructed brick and stone stores. The intersection of Caswell and Barnard Streets was the geographical center of town and is the dividing line between East and West Barnard and North and South Caswell Streets. (Perkins.)

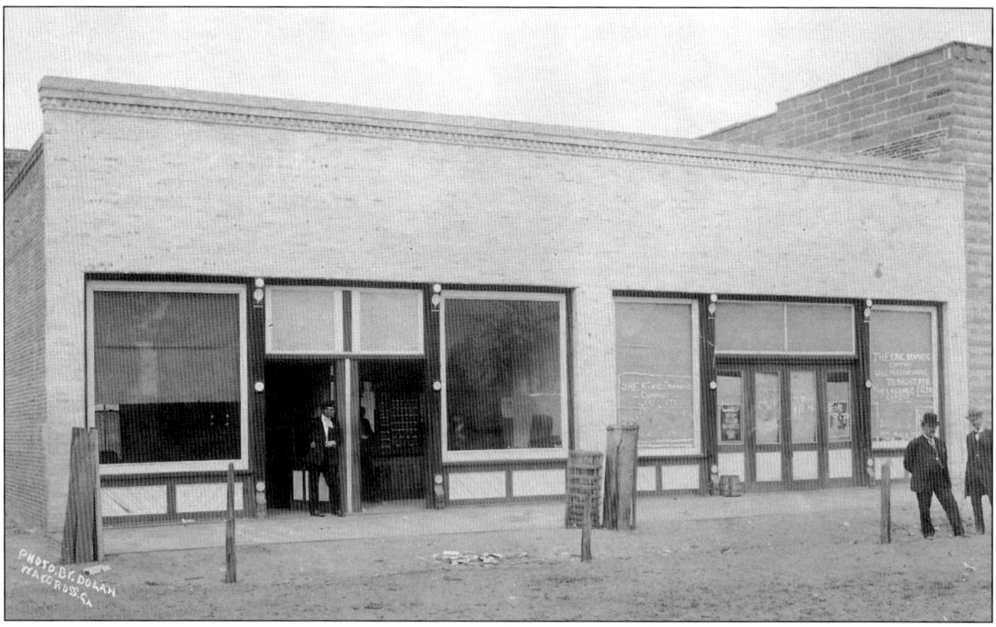

The eastern half of this building housed Glennville's first moving picture show. The sign on the window reads, "The King Dramatic Company will present here, tonight, Feb. 16th, The Laughable Comedy." Lipsitz Department Store was founded in 1897 by Jewish immigrant Joe Lipsitz. His business was originally located on the south side of Barnard Street but later occupied the building pictured here for many decades. (Perkins.)

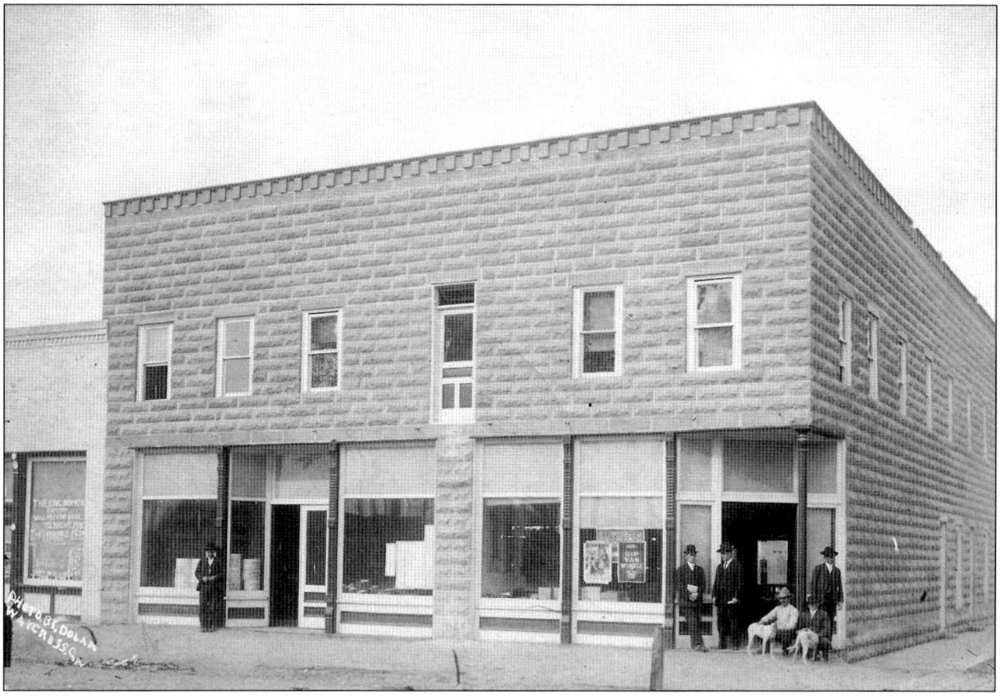

This building on the northwest corner of Barnard and Caswell Streets was built around 1906 by Asa W. DeLoach, whose Margurite Hotel occupied the second floor. Soon after, a two-story covered porch was added. The right side of the bottom floor was home to several pharmacies through the years, including Dent's, Smith's, and Central (Hughes) Pharmacies. The latter, most notable pharmacy, was owned by Joseph M. "Joe Boy" Hughes Jr. The angled corner entrance has since been bricked over. (Perkins.)

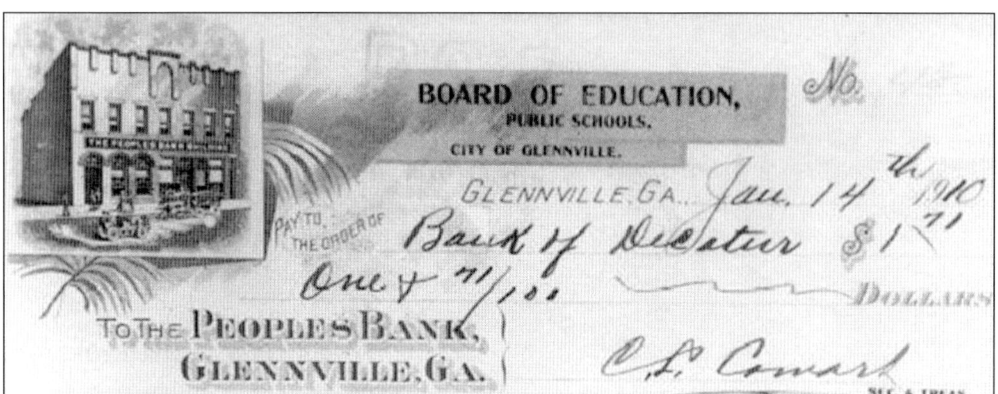

The People's Bank was organized in 1907 under S.J. Kicklighter, James V. Delk, D.M. Bradley, John D. Bradley, I.J. DeLoach, C.C. Padgett, H.C. Dubberly, Bob Purcell, and E.H. Bacon in a large brick building constructed on the south side of Barnard Street by D.M. Bradley. The People's Bank operated until 1932, when it was forced to merge with the Glennville Bank. (GTM.)

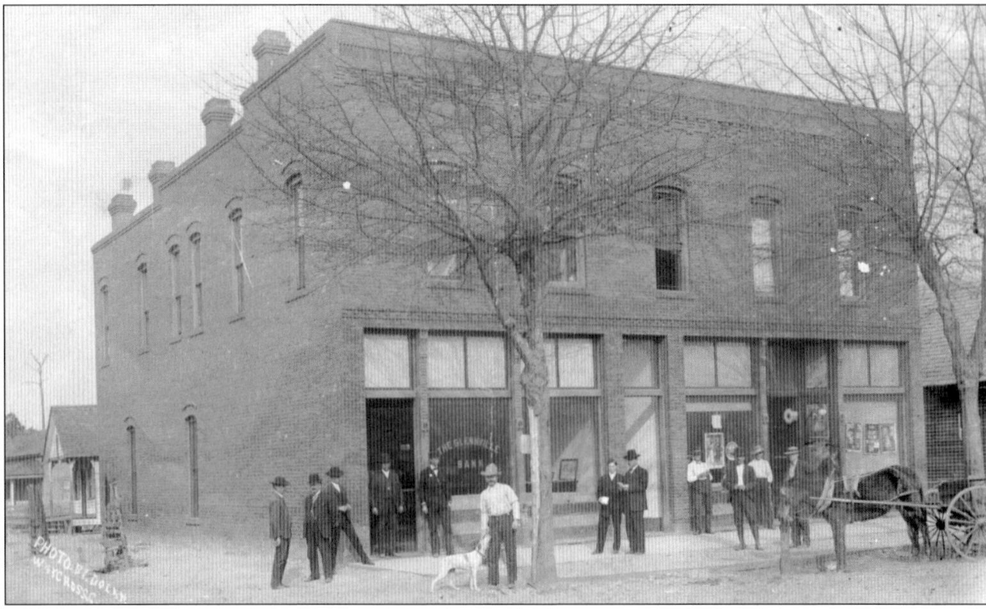

The Glennville Bank was organized in 1904 and formally incorporated in 1905, with Henry J. Banks as first president and E.C. Collins, Asa W. DeLoach, William A. Dubberly, and Jesse W. Durrence as directors. Stockholder and later bank president W.F. Durrence sold the bank this parcel of land at the northeast corner of Caswell and Barnard Streets for $250, and in 1905, the building pictured above and below was constructed, with the bank originally occupying the left side. This building housed the bank until 2004, when it was replaced by the current bank building. The Glennville Bank was the only local bank to weather the Great Depression and has remained at the center of Glennville, both physically and financially. (Both, courtesy of the Glennville Bank.)

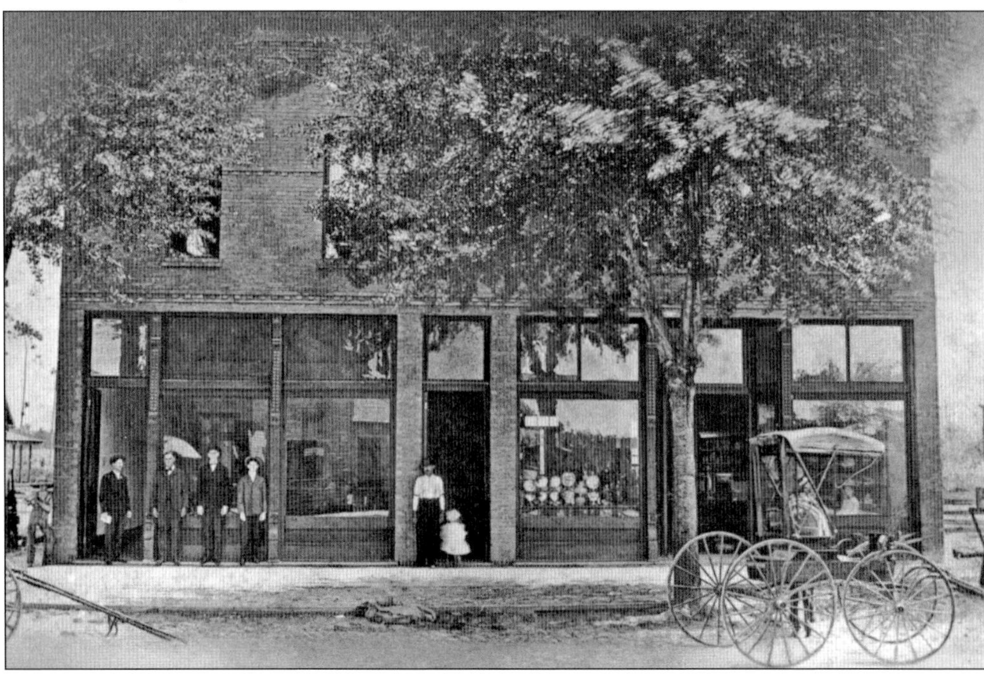

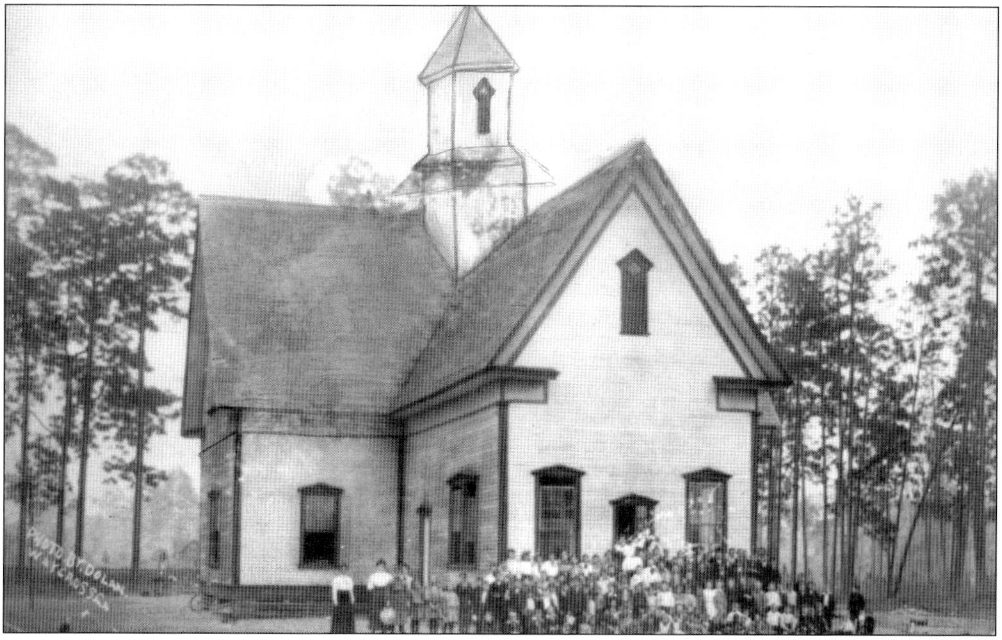

Philadelphia's first school was established around 1850 and occupied several different buildings. In 1891, J.J. Barnard donated a large tract of land between present-day Tillman, Bolton, Baker, and Howard Streets for the purpose of erecting a new school, Tattnall Baptist Institute. A frame building, pictured here in 1906, was constructed around 1892 and served the community until it burned in 1910. (Perkins.)

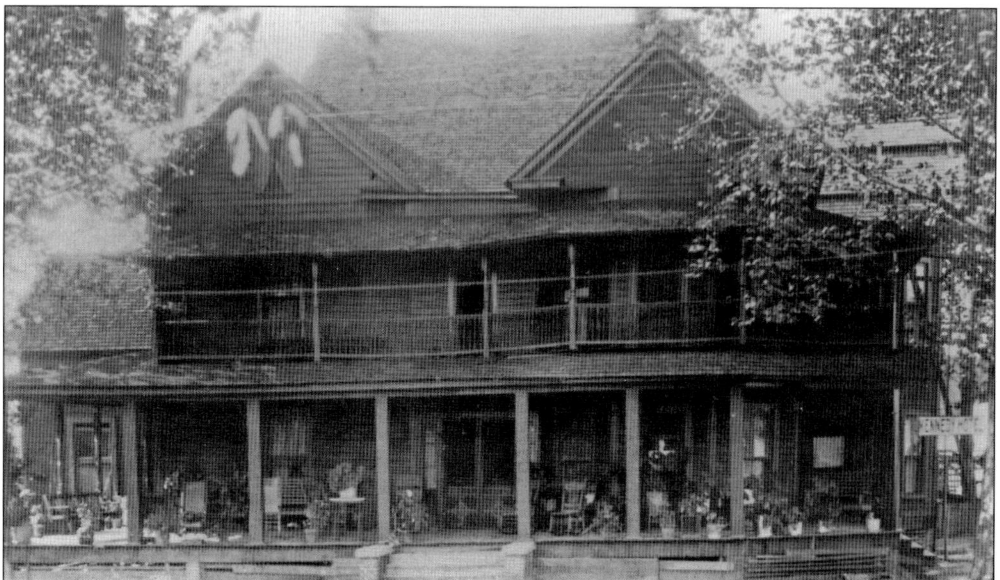

The Kennedy Hotel was built on South Caswell Street around 1905 by Carrie Easterling Padgett and later owned and operated by D. Milton Kennedy and Fleta Jones Kennedy. Despite its forlorn exterior, the Kennedy Hotel was a favorite among locals for its home-cooked meals. The hotel burned in 1929, and today the site is occupied by the social hall and parking lot of the Glennville United Methodist Church. (Courtesy of Nell Kirkland Avant.)

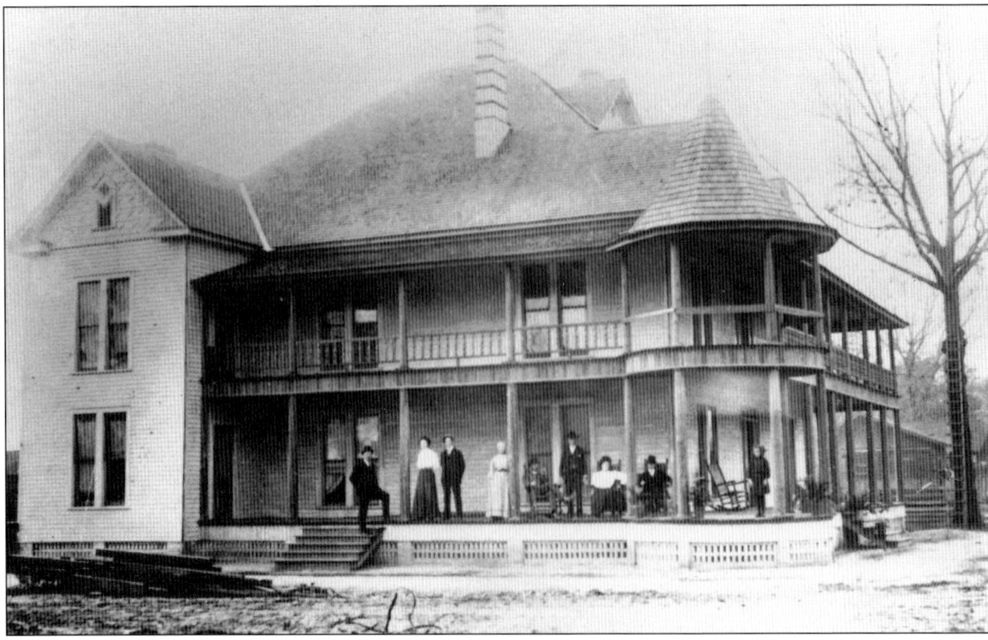

The Hughes Hotel, predecessor of the Glennwanis Hotel, was built around 1905 by Dr. Joseph Marcus Hughes Sr. of Jones Creek in Liberty (now Long) County. Dr. Hughes (1877–1962) was the son of Capt. Joseph William Hughes III of the Liberty Guards and was one of the area's most prominent physicians for many decades. The Hughes Hotel, pictured above in 1906, served as the center of community life until it fell victim to Roman candles on Christmas Eve 1920. The photograph below, taken in 1908, shows a large crowd assembled at the hotel to hear a speech delivered by Thomas Edward Watson. Tom Watson (1856–1922) was a lawyer, congressman, senator, publisher, and leader of the Populist Party in Georgia. He ran for president in 1904 and 1908 on the Populist ticket. (Both, Perkins.)

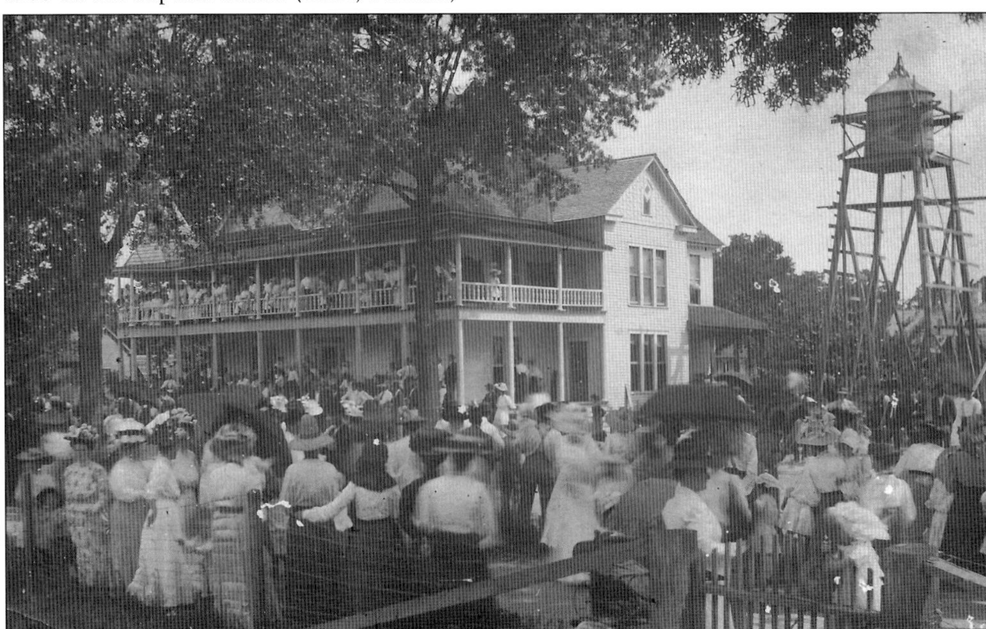

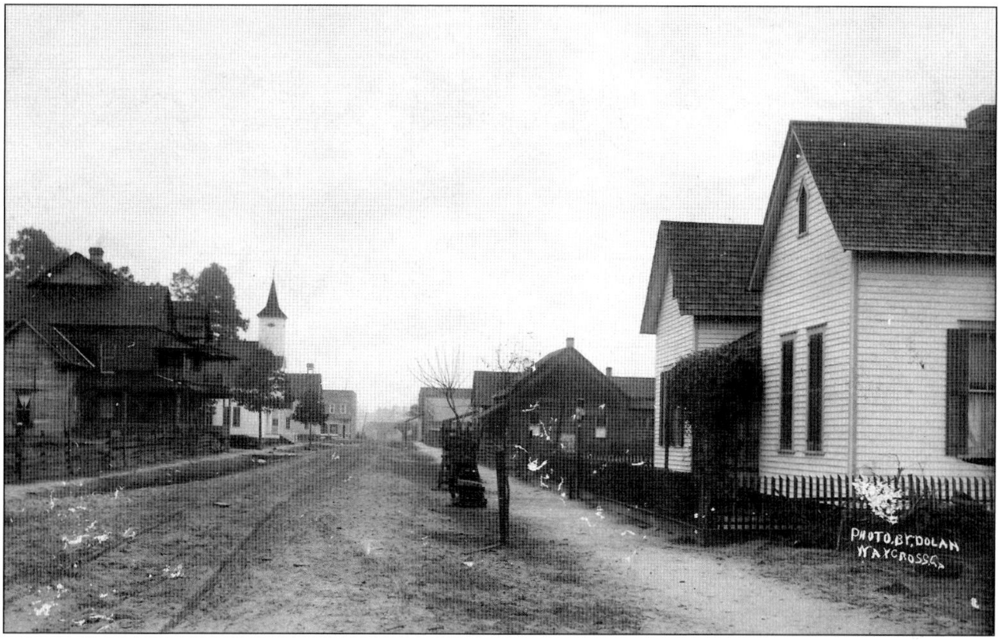

In this 1906 photograph of South Caswell Street, taken from Institute Street facing north, the Kennedy Hotel can be seen at far left. Directly adjacent was the Methodist church. The residence of Martha Emily Howard Easterling, widow of James O'Neill Easterling, located on the northeast corner of Caswell and Institute Streets, is at right. (Perkins.)

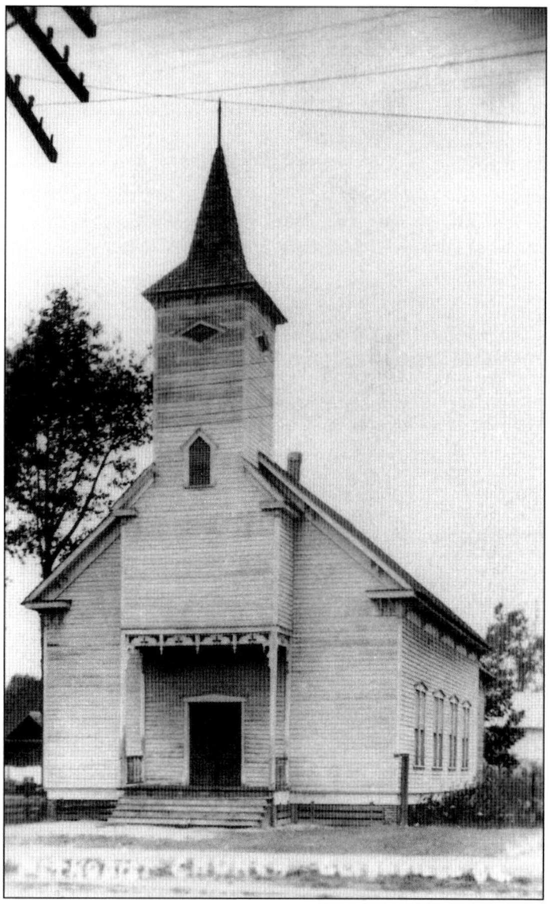

Following a revival service, resident James O'Neill Easterling organized the local Methodist congregation in 1891. The sanctuary, pictured here, was constructed in 1892 by Easterling and an assistant with lumber provided by Columbus S. Grice on land donated by Joseph P. Collins. The building was bricked in 1932 and renovated several more times throughout the 1900s to give it its present appearance. (Courtesy of the Glennville United Methodist Church.)

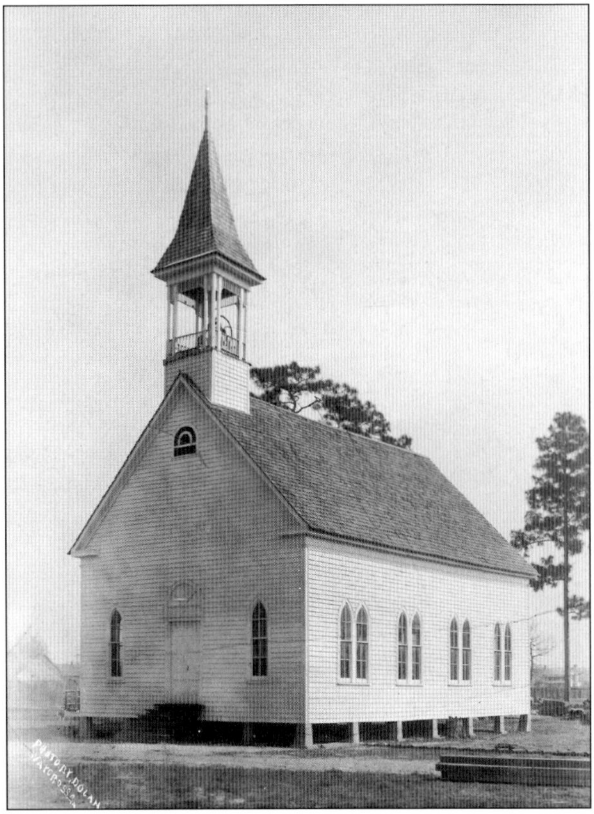

Glennville Free Will Baptist Church, pictured here in 1906, was organized in 1899, with E.L. St. Clair as the first pastor. The sanctuary was constructed in 1900 and remains standing as the church social hall, though it has been bricked and the steeple removed. (Perkins.)

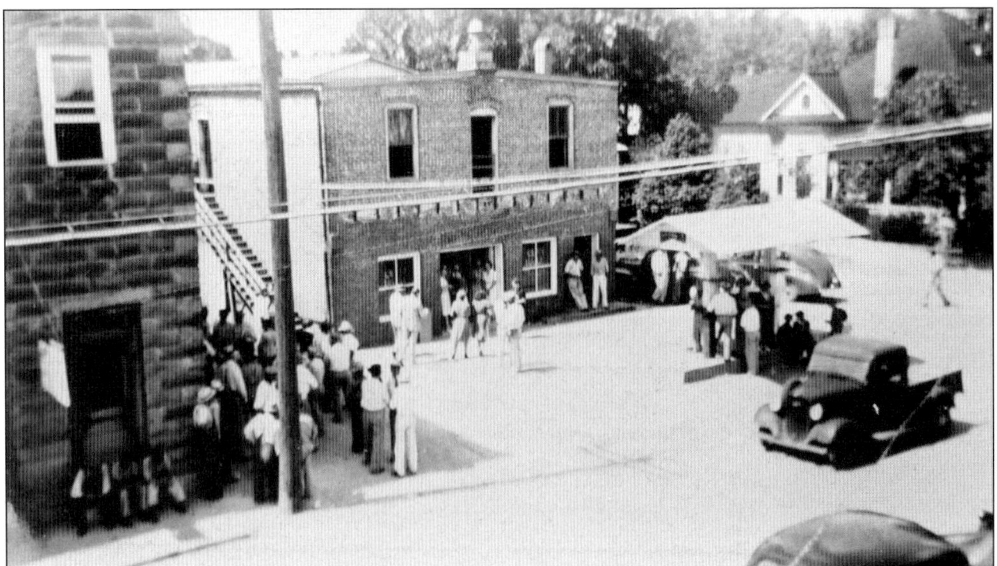

Glennville's first city hall, shown here on Election Day 1942, was built in 1903 and housed the fire station on the first floor and city hall on the second. It stood on the west side of North Caswell Street, just north of Barnard Street, behind Central Pharmacy. This building served the city until the present city hall was completed in 1969. The old city hall site is presently a parking lot. (Courtesy of Reggie Collins.)

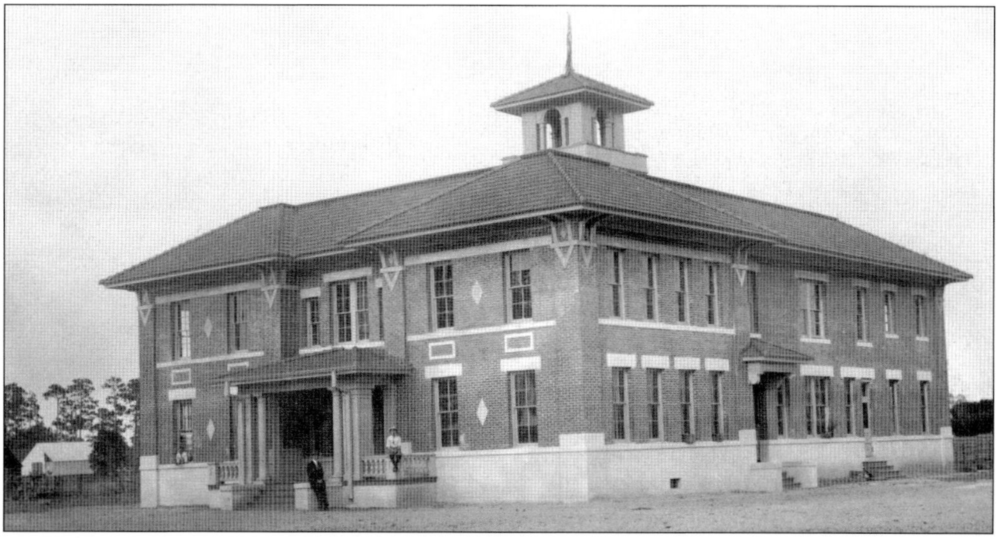

After the old Tattnall Institute burned in 1910, it was replaced by a larger brick building in 1911. This school, pictured in 1913, would serve as Glennville High School and later Glennville Middle School until 1993. It later housed Glennville's campus of Southeastern Technical College and is now home to the offices of Onshore Outsourcing as well as the Glennville-Tattnall Museum. (Courtesy of Brent Walker.)

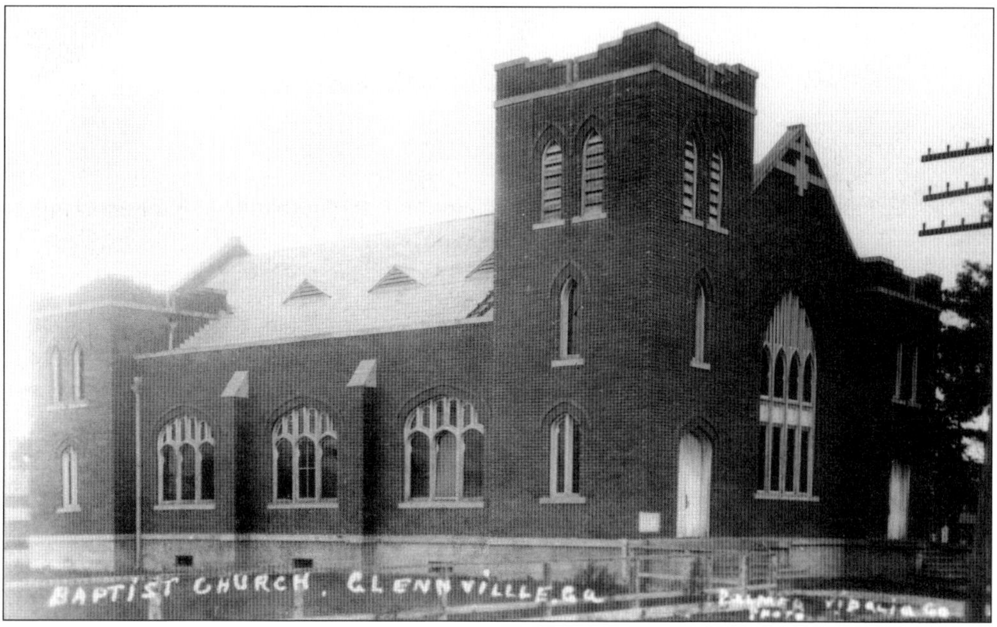

In 1914, Glennville First Baptist Church constructed this fine brick sanctuary to replace the old wooden church, which had been used since 1881. The new building also included separate rooms for Sunday school classes. This sanctuary remains active today and is one of Glennville's most prominent landmarks. (GTM.)

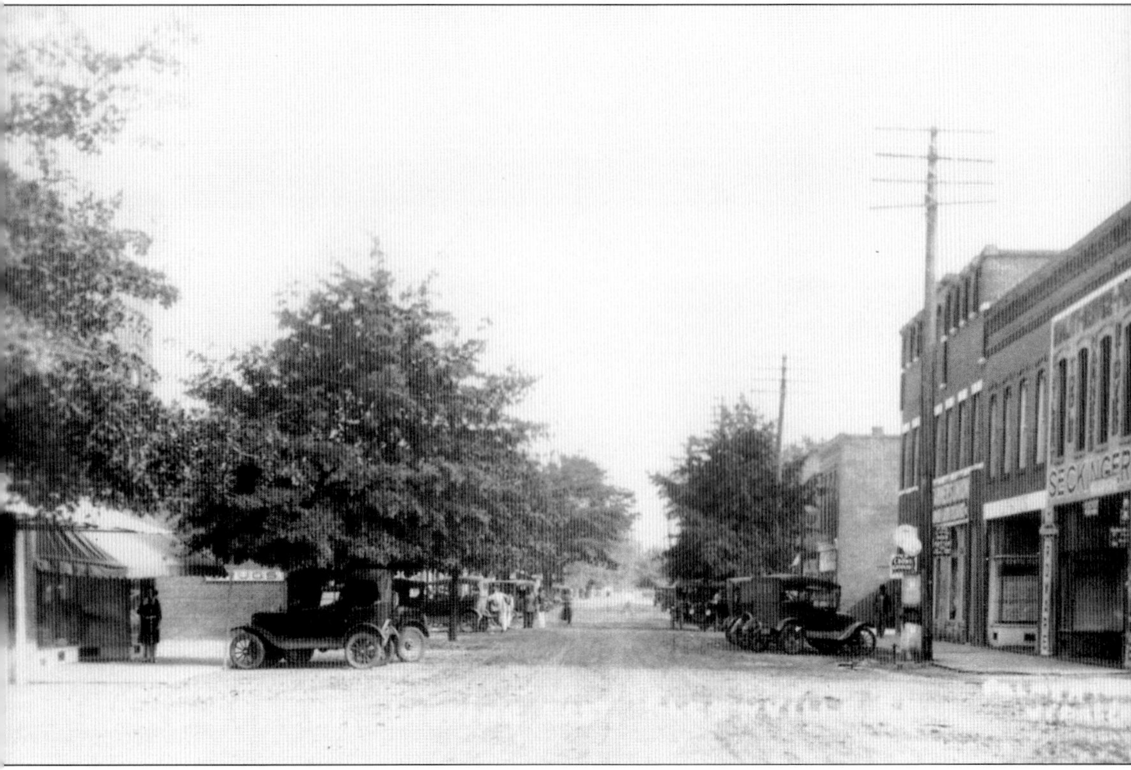

Glennville of 1915 would have been unrecognizable to the original settlers of Philadelphia Crossroads. By the time this photograph was taken, the south side of Barnard Street sported a row of fine two-story buildings, dominated by the People's Bank building––built by D.M. Bradley in 1907––which also for a time housed the dental office of Dr. W.O. Strickland upstairs. The People's Bank building was later home to Central Pharmacy and Greenberg Furniture Company, as seen on the cover. This building is today occupied by King's of Glennville. The building to the right was erected in 1907, also by D.M. Bradley, and was for a time home to Lipsitz Department Store on the left side and Seckinger Hardware on the right. (Perkins.)

Three

TRANSPORTATION

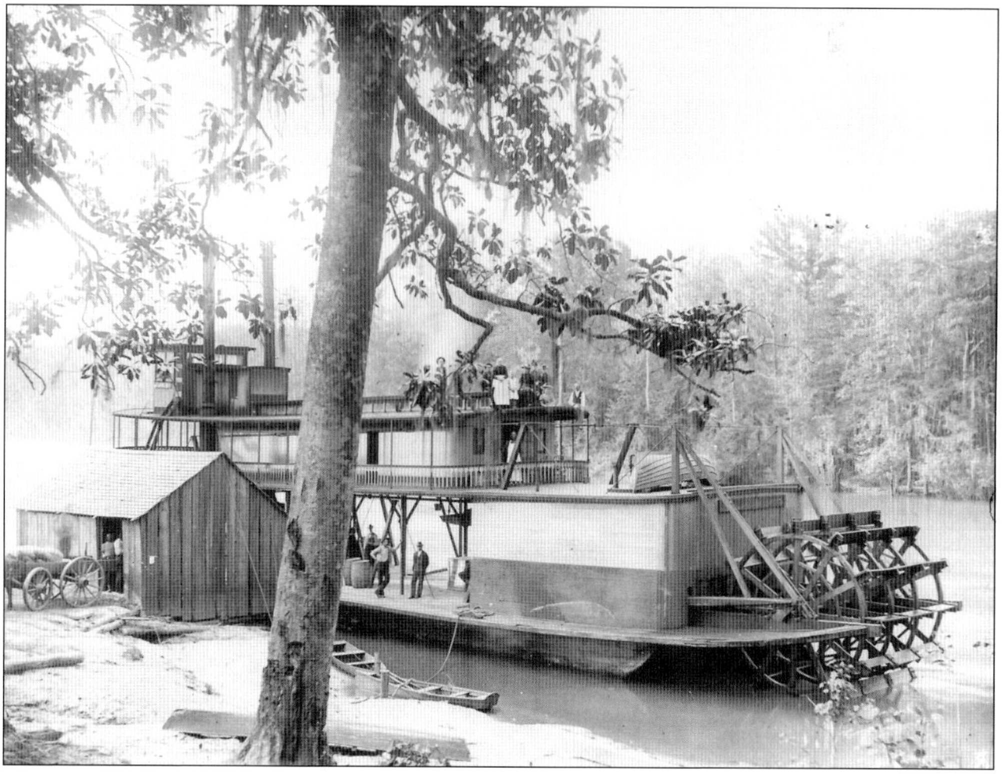

Before the railroad boom, when roads were less than hospitable, steamboats facilitated travel into Georgia's interior, with the first steamboat reaching Milledgeville from Darien by way of the Altamaha and Oconee Rivers in 1819. Most riverboats were narrow stern-wheelers, like the *John L. Day* pictured here on the Ocmulgee River. Wider side-wheelers were common on the coast, operating between Savannah, Darien, and Brunswick. (GTM.)

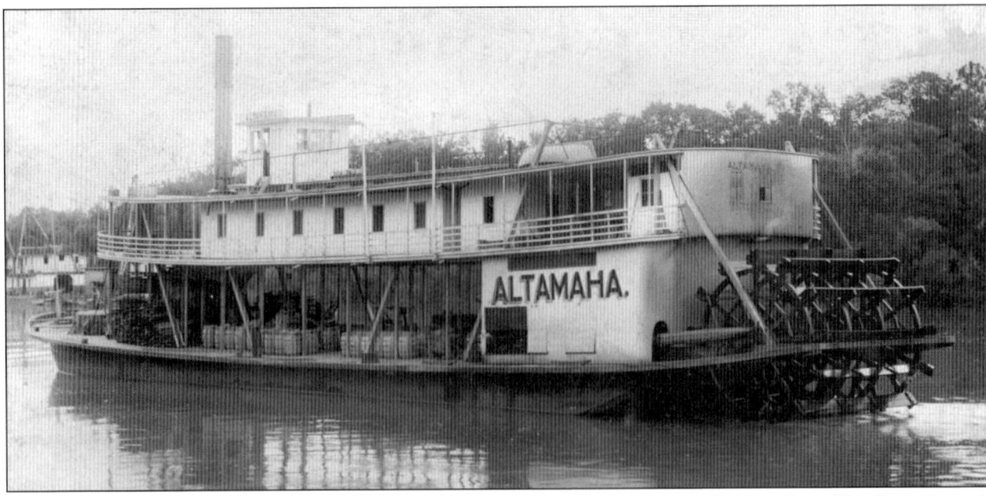

The *Altamaha* was the finest steamer ever to grace that river. It was designed and built at Beards Bluff in 1892 by Florence Breen of Jesup, who meticulously engineered the boat for traveling the treacherous waters of the Altamaha and Ocmulgee Rivers. It had a draft of 15 inches, which allowed it to travel at the rivers' lowest stages, making it far more successful than most other riverboats. (Courtesy of Dr. George Madray.)

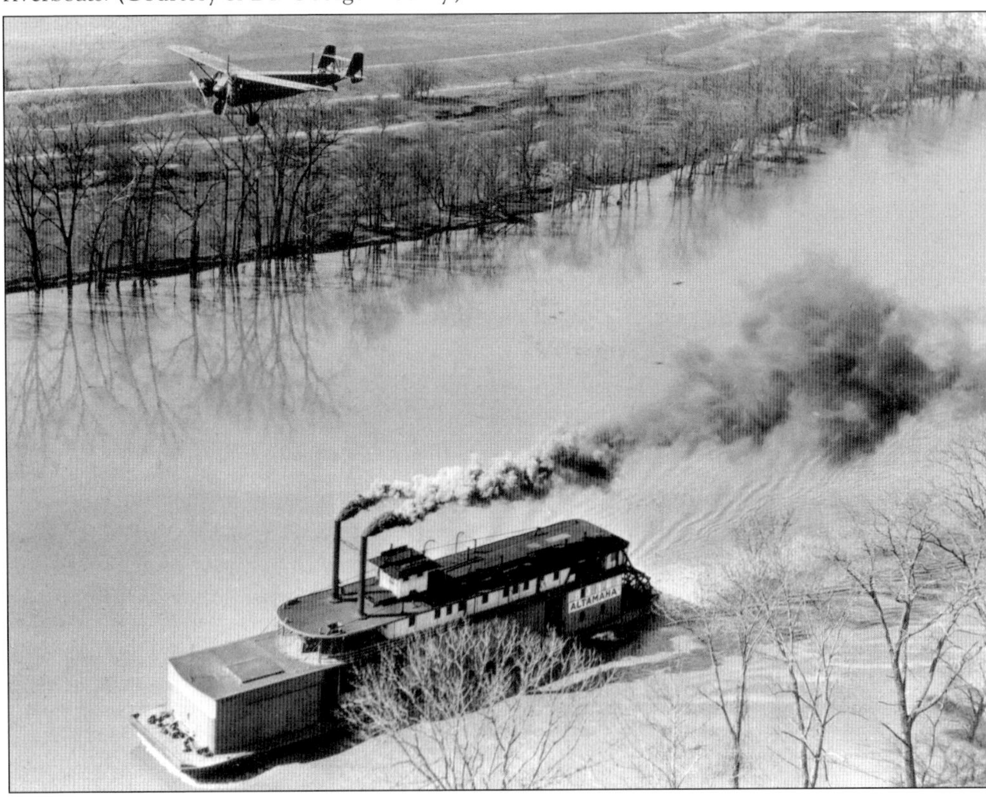

In 1921, the *Altamaha* was moved to the Savannah River and purchased by the City of Augusta in 1926 for use as a packet boat. This 1932 photograph captures the end of one era and the beginning of another, as a Curtiss Kingbird speeds at 100 miles per hour over the *Altamaha*, which, at full steam, could barely reach 10 miles per hour. (Courtesy of Dr. George Madray.)

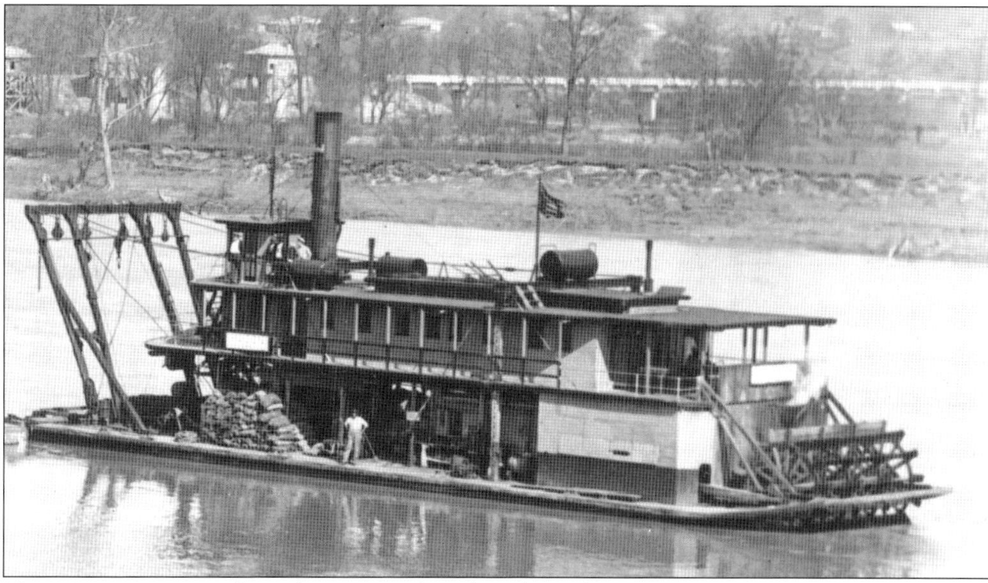

The *Macon* was a snag boat that operated on the Altamaha River and was run by Captain Clifton of Toombs County. A snag boat was equipped with forward cranes used to remove the many logs, or "snags," that made navigating the river so dangerous for wooden steamboats. Wrecks were common, and the ruined remains of steamboats can still be seen at points along the river. (Courtesy of Dr. George Madray.)

Register and Glennville Railway

TIME TABLE NO. 16.

Effective Sunday, June 6th, 1909.
Suspending all previous Time Tables

Daily Except Sunday					Sunday Only				
No.3	No.1		No.2	No.4	No.3	No.1		No.2	No.4
Read Down	Read Down	Stations	Read up	Read up	Read Down	Read Down	Stations	Read up	Read up
p.m.	a.m.		a.m.	p.m.	p.m.	a.m.		a.m.	p.m.
2:15	5:00	Lv Glennville Ar	10:50	8:00	2:55	5:00	Lv Glennville Ar	10:25	9:15
2:25	5:10	Lv Birdford Lv	10:40	7:50	3:05	5:10	Lv Birdford Lv	10:15	9:10
2:35	5:20	Lv Coe Lv	10:25	7:40	3:10	5:20	Lv Coe Lv	10:10	9:00
2:40	5:25	Lv Easterling Lv	10:20	7:35	3:15	5:25	Lv Easterling Lv	10:05	8:55
2:15	5:30	Lv Moody Lv	10:15	7:30	3:20	5:30	Lv Moody Lv	10:00	8:50
2:50	5:35	Lv Jennie Lv	10:10	7:25	3:35	5:35	Lv Jeanie Lv	9:55	8:45
3:00	5:45	Lv Dean Lv	10:00	7:15	3:45	5:45	Lv Dean Lv	9:45	8:35
3:15	6:00	Ar Winburn Lv	9:45	6:55	4:00	6:00	Ar Winburn Lv	9:30	6:55
3:35	6:20	Lv Winburn Ar	9:20	6:35	4:15	6:15	Lv Winburn Ar	9:15	6:35
3:40	6:30	Ar Claxton Lv	9:10	7:00	4:25	6:25	Ar Claxton Lv	9:05	8:20
3:45	6:30	Lv Claxton Ar	9:10	7:00	4:25	6:25	Lv Claxton Ar	9:o5	7:00
4:00	6:45	Ar Hagan Lv	8:50	6:25	4:35	6:35	Ar Hagan Lv	8:50	6:25
4:10	6:55	Lv Hagan Ar	8:40	6:10	4:35	6:35	Lv Hagan Ar	8:40	6:15
4:20	6:55	Lv Brookland Ar	8:30	6:00	4:45	6:45	Lv Brookland Ar	8:30	6:05
4:25	7:00	Lv Undine Ar	8:25	5:55	4:50	6:50	Lv Undine Ar	8:25	6:00
4:40	7:15	Lv Adabelle Ar	8:10	5:40	5:05	7:05	Lv Adabelle Ar	8:10	5:45
4:50	7:25	Lv Dink Ar	7:55	5:30	5:15	7:15	Lv Dink Ar	8:00	5:35
5:00	7:35	Ar Register Lv	7:45	5:20	5:25	7:25	Ar Register Lv	7:50	5:25

Train No. connects at Register with Central of Georgia for Statesboro, Dover, Savannah, Millen, Macon and Augusta.

Train No.2 connects at Hagan with Seaboard for Collins, Vidalia, Helena and points west.

Train No. 3 except Sunday connects at Register with Central of Georgia for Stillmore, Brewton and Dublin.

Train No. 4 connects with Seaboard Airline at Hagan for Savannah and points East, and for Collins, Vidalia, Helena, and points west

M.R. Perkins Gen. Supt R. A. Scott, Gen. Pass. Agt.

The first railroad to reach Glennville was the Register & Glennville, which began as a tram line of the Perkins Lumber Company in Hagan. In 1901, the line was extended north to Register and south to Glennville, making stops between Hagan and Glennville at Winburn, Dean's Crossing, Jennie Station, Moody's Crossing, Easterling, Coe, and Birdford, as shown on this 1909 timetable. (GTM.)

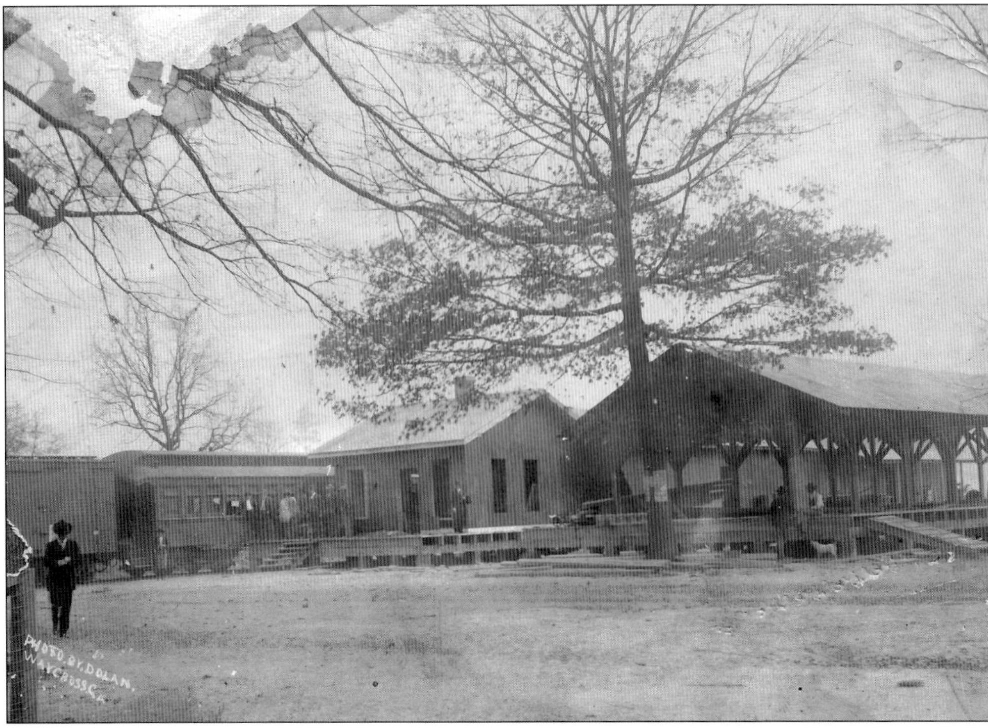

The Register & Glennville Railroad depot, pictured here in 1906, was constructed around 1901–1902 on the south side of Barnard Street, adjacent to the Hughes Hotel. The railroad was dismantled around 1917, and the old right-of-way became Railroad Street. (Perkins.)

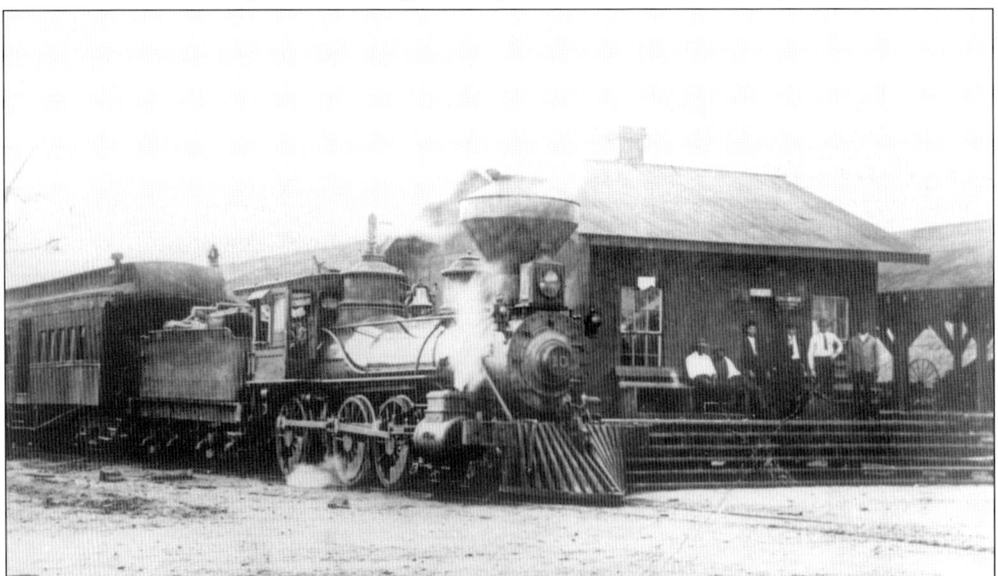

This iconic 1906 photograph shows the Register & Glennville locomotive at the depot. The tracks continued south, just past the depot, to the railroad shop and homes for rail hands before dead-ending. The depot was expanded in 1910 and in 1923 was converted into a filling station, later known as the Glennwanis Service Station, by James Kirkland. (Perkins.)

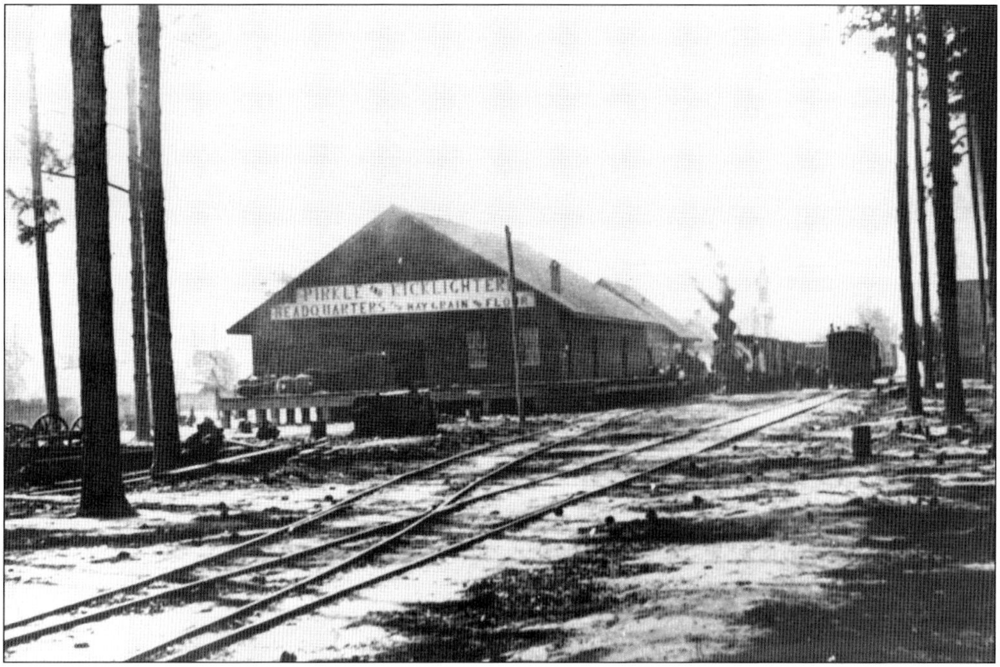

The line that would become the Georgia Coast & Piedmont Railroad first reached Glennville in 1905 and was constructed by D.M. Bradley. The depot stood on the east side of South Main Street, just south of Barnard Street. In this 1906 photograph, taken from near the intersection of Main and Barnard Streets, the steeple of the Free Will Baptist Church is barely visible behind the locomotive. (Perkins.)

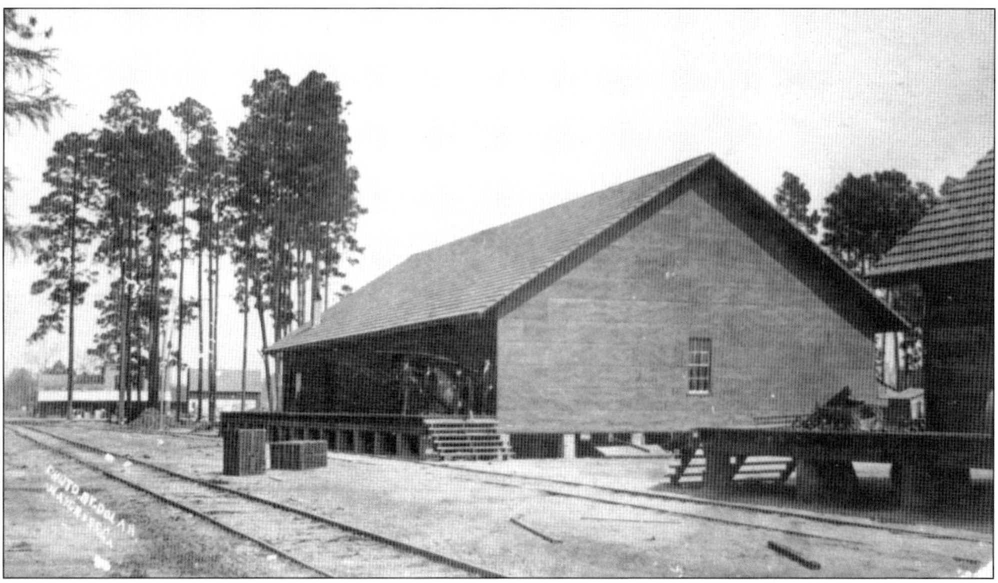

In another view of the Georgia Coast & Piedmont depot, the Barnard Street storefronts can be seen in the distance. The south-facing end of the building housed the depot, while the north end was home to Pirkle and Kicklighter Headquarters for Hay, Grain and Flour. This building was subsequently used when the Georgia Coast & Piedmont became the Collins & Glennville Railroad. (Perkins.)

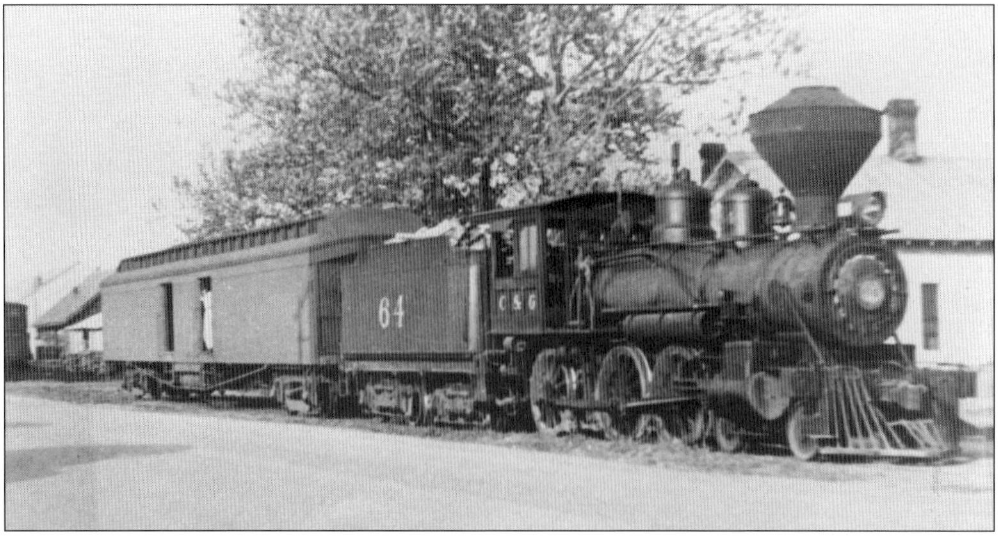

When D.M. Bradley repurchased the remnants of the Georgia Coast & Piedmont in 1921, he dismantled all but the segments between Collins, Reidsville, Mendes, and Glennville, renaming the line Collins & Glennville Railroad. Included in his purchase was a Baldwin locomotive, No. 64, pictured here in front of the later location of First Citizens Bank, facing north toward the depot, which can be seen in the distance. (GTM.)

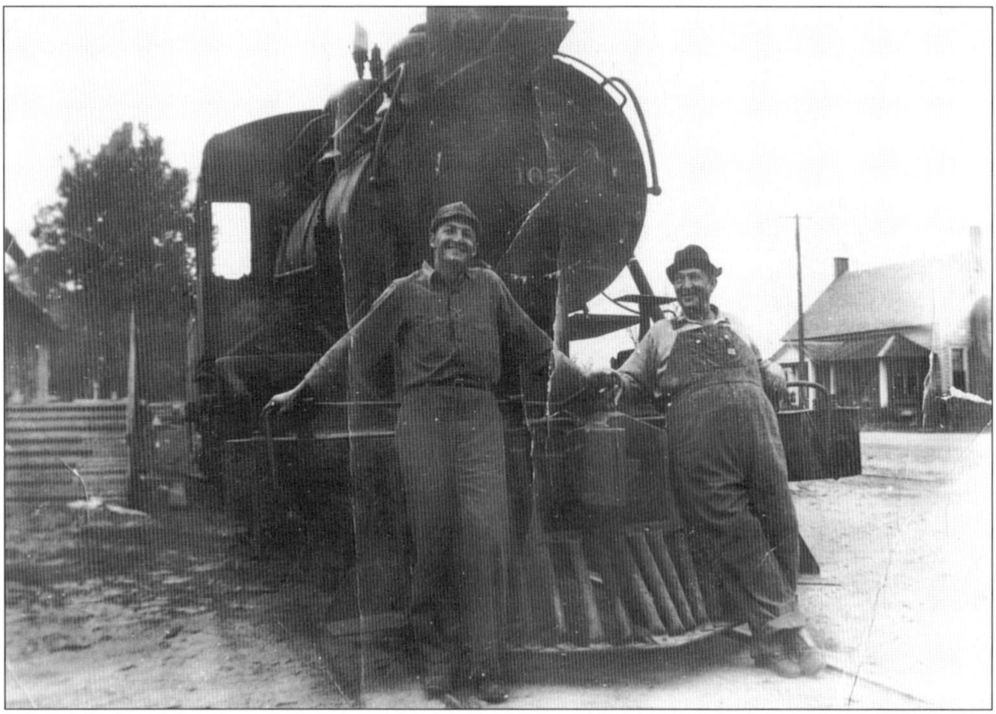

The greatest assets to the Collins & Glennville Railroad were its two engineers, father and son Percy J. Maund (right) and Mercer Maund (left). Here, the two pose on the cowcatcher of Engine 105, which the Bradleys purchased from the defunct Savannah & Southern (Tuten) Railway. The Maunds performed all maintenance on the railroad equipment and were known for their many technological innovations. (Courtesy of Asa Maund.)

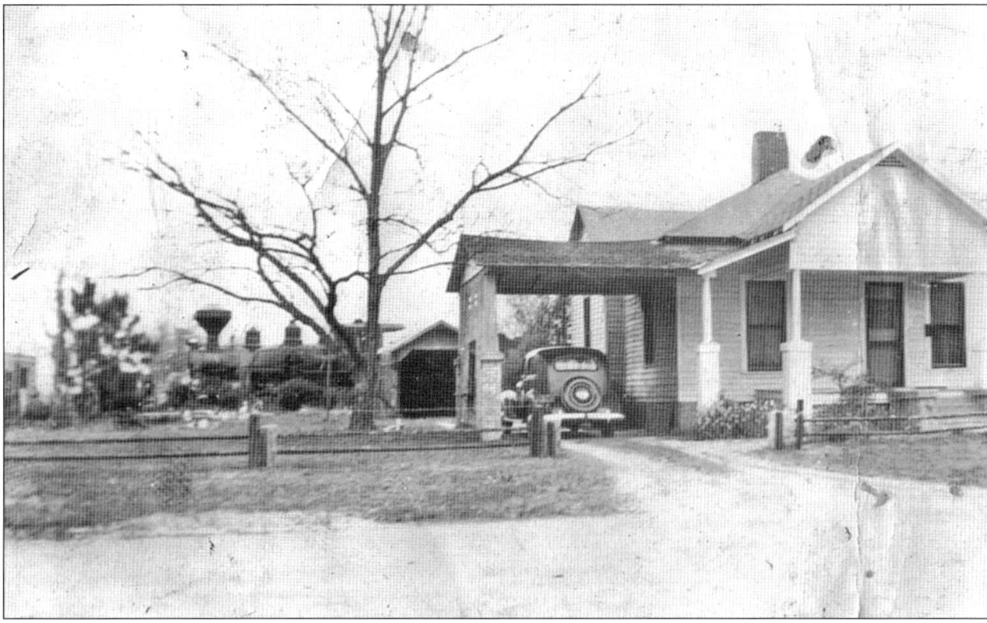

The "roundhouse" of the Collins & Glennville was the backyard of Percy Maund's home on East Mann Street between North Main and North Caswell Streets. A spur track ran into the yard from the main line on Main Street. In the evenings, Maund would park the locomotive, as seen here, and connect a pipe from the engine's boiler to his house to provide his family with heat and hot water. (Courtesy of Asa Maund.)

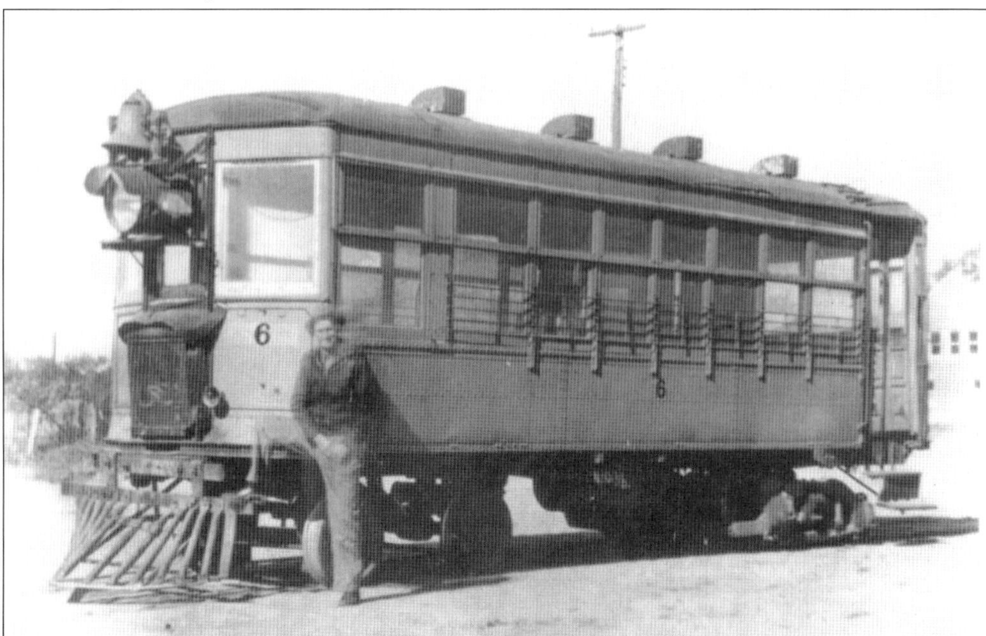

Percy Maund's greatest legacy was the "Jetney." When it was no longer profitable to run a passenger train between Glennville and Collins, Maund secured a used streetcar from Savannah or Augusta and installed a Chevrolet truck motor. The Jetney was operated by Willie Thompson (pictured) and earned the Collins & Glennville a reputation for innovation across the Southeast. (GTM.)

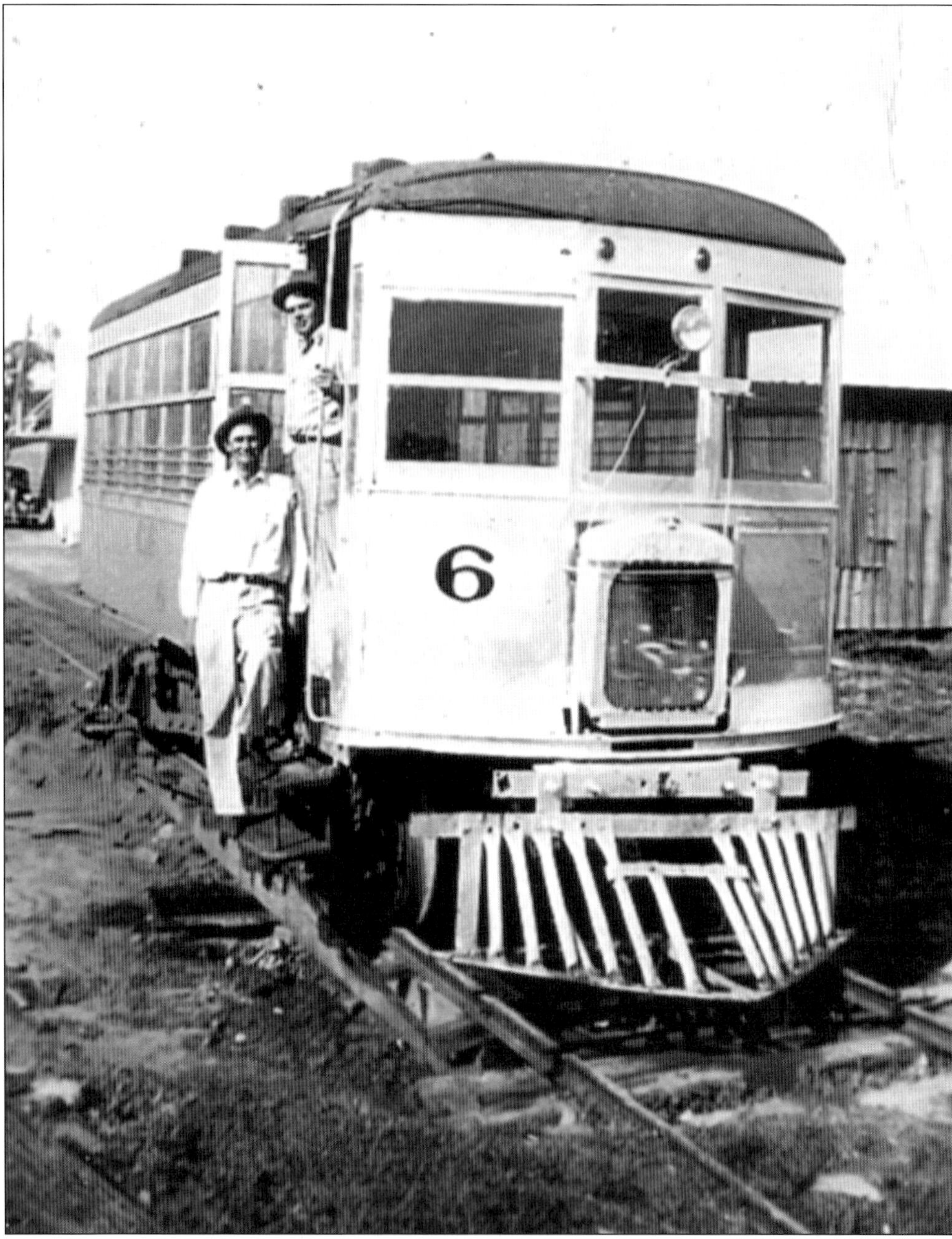

Chief motorcar operator Willie Thompson (left) and conductor C.W. Kicklighter Jr. (right) pose with the Jetney near the depot on the "armstrong" turntable, which was used to rotate the motorcar in place. The Jetney hauled passengers and mail between Glennville, Mendes, Reidsville, and Collins for many years before the Collins & Glennville was dismantled in 1941. The railroad owned a total of three such streetcars. One was used as a makeshift workshop at the Maund residence. The other, known as the "Yellow Dog," was used in conjunction with the Jetney. (Courtesy of the Glennville Bank.)

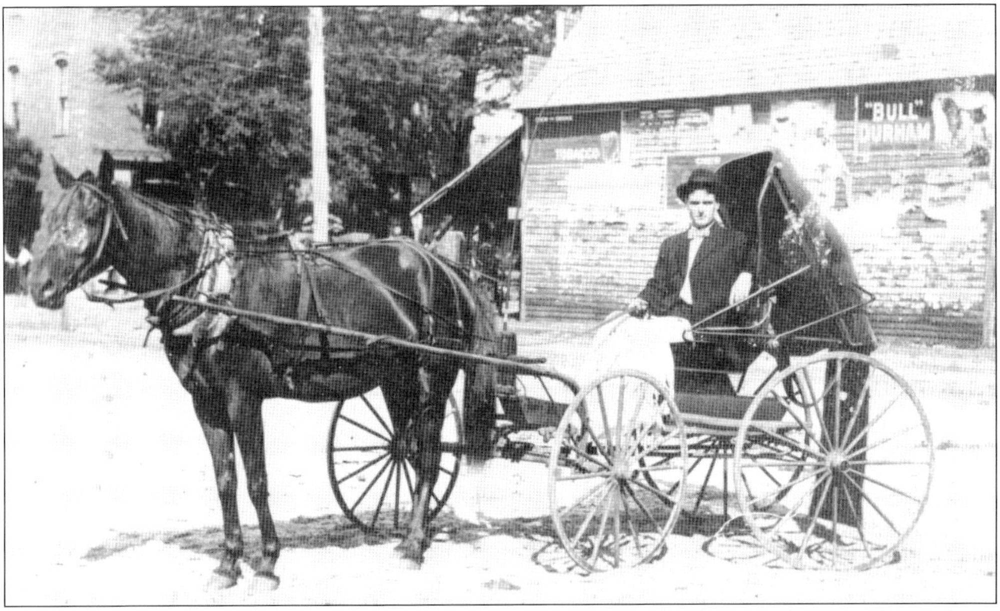

S.E. Kirkland was the son of Cuyler and Sarah Smiley Kirkland of Smiley, in Liberty (now Long) County, and the father of Nell Kirkland Avant. He is pictured here at the intersection of Caswell and Barnard Streets. The wooden Cordie Faircloth store, formerly owned by Glenn Thompson, can be seen in the background, as well as the Glennville Bank at left. (Courtesy of Nell Kirkland Avant.)

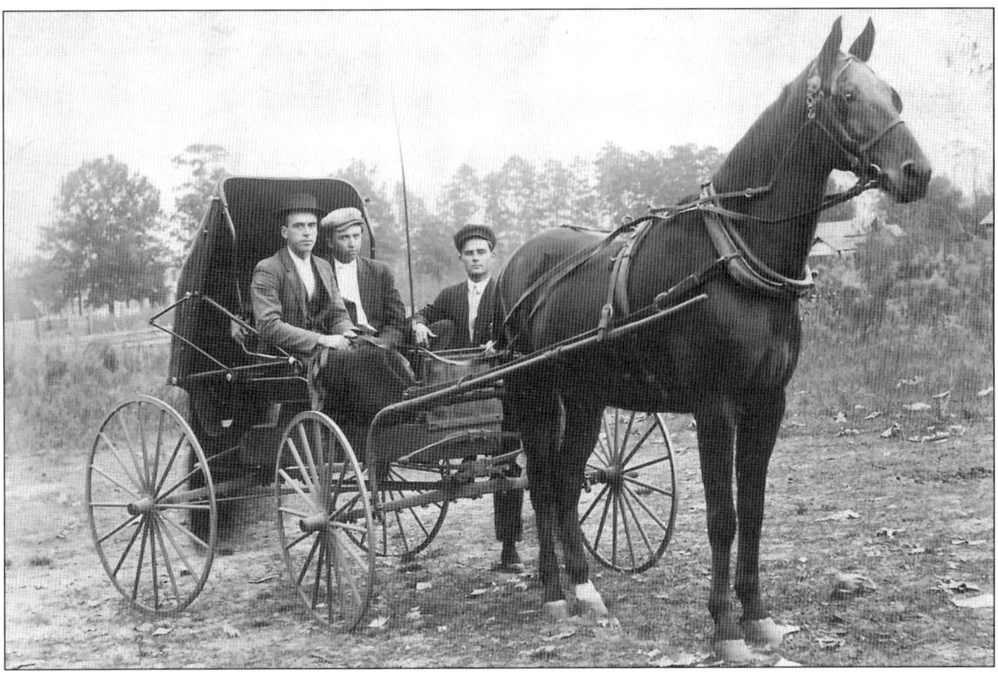

From left to right are Clarence Sands, Slater Tootle, and Holmes Sands on the eve of World War I, shortly before Holmes would be drafted. Clarence and Holmes were the sons of Allen Jones Sands and Georgia Jenkins Sands. They were first cousins to Slater, who was the son of Dr. G.W. Tootle and Lennie Jenkins Tootle. (Courtesy of Brent Walker.)

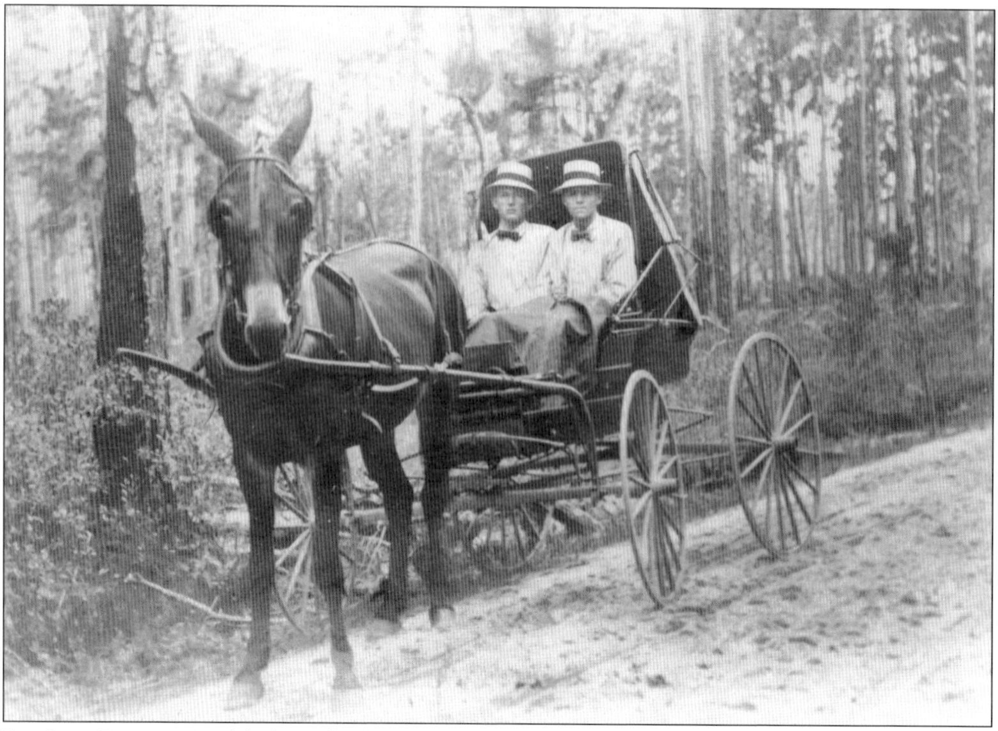

Brothers Prentice Kicklighter (left) and Lee Kicklighter take their mule and buggy for a ride around 1920. They were the sons of Hampton and Mary Jane Kicklighter. (GTM.)

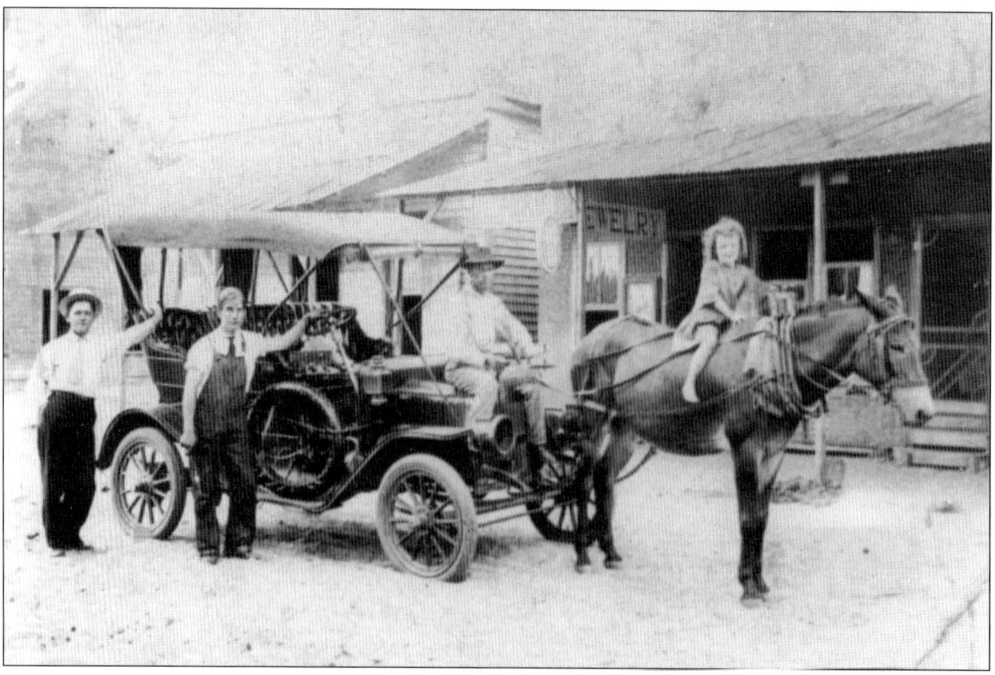

In this 1910 photograph, a mule pulls the car of Dr. G.W. Tootle. From left to right are Horace Surrency, Fred Oliveros, Lamar Strickland, and Rose Easterling on the mule. (GTM.)

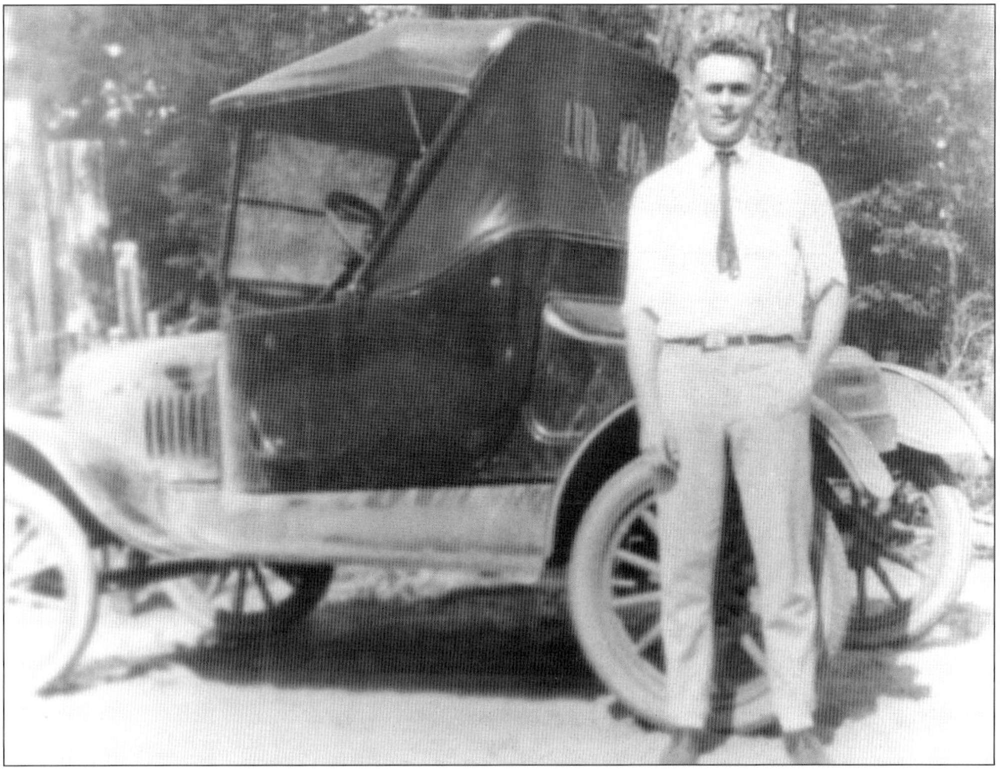

Prentice Kicklighter poses next to his convertible around 1917. (GTM.)

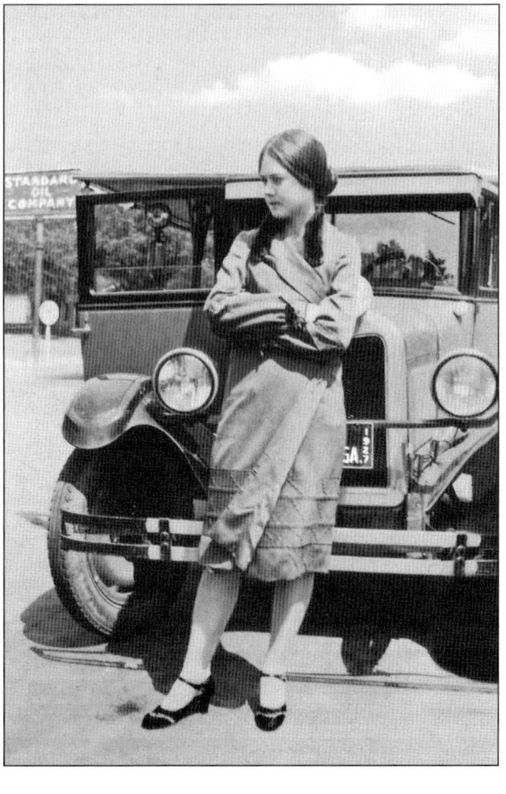

Gladys Spivey Dasher, pictured here in 1927, was the daughter of Virgil and Lula Bland Spivey of the Jones settlement between Glennville and Reidsville. She married Glennville farmer Dan J. Dasher. (Courtesy of Linda Dasher Brannen.)

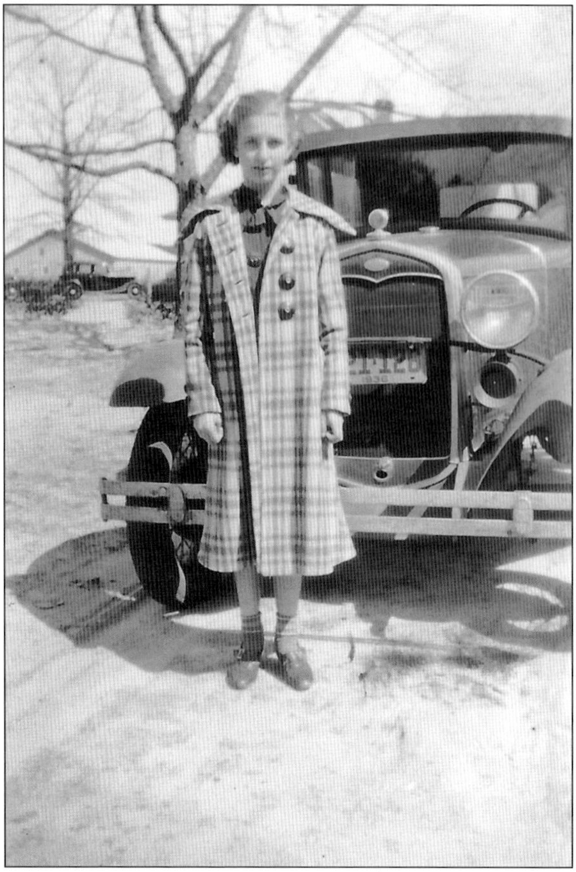

Rebecca Mulligan, daughter of Edward F. "Ned" Mulligan Sr. and Laura Rogers Mulligan, stands in front of the family's Ford Model A touring car in 1936. (Courtesy of Rebecca Mulligan.)

The first automobile bridge to span the Altamaha River, Lane's Bridge was constructed in the early 1920s through the efforts of C.W. Kicklighter Sr. and Mills B. Lane Sr., for whom the bridge was named. The photograph below shows the bridge and tollhouse, on the Appling County side of the river, shortly after completion. This bridge was rebuilt numerous times before construction of a concrete bridge began in 1946. (Courtesy of Betty Trapnell Burns.)

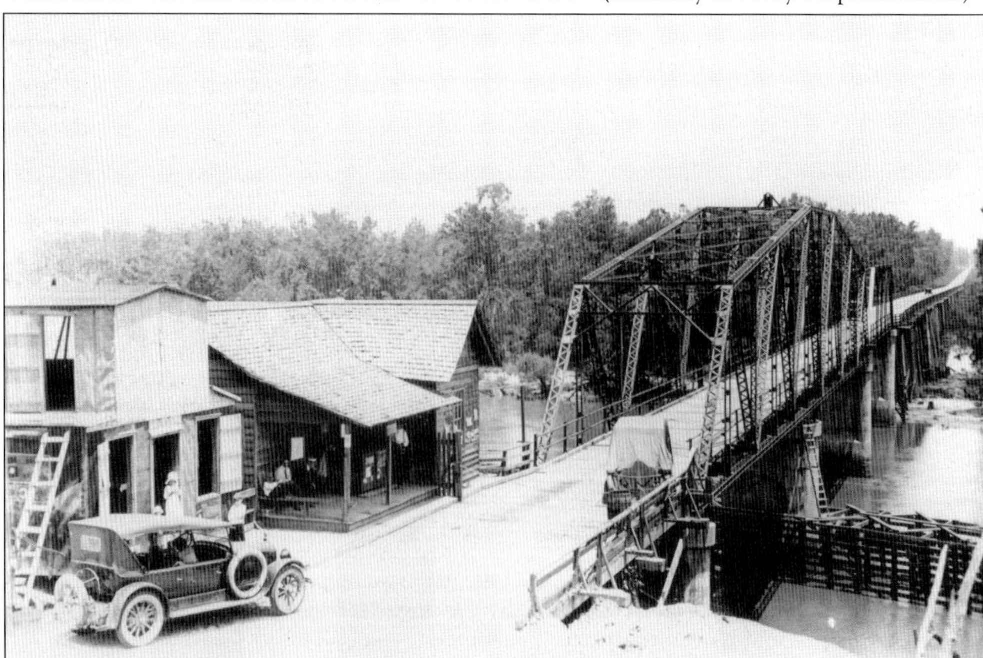

Four

LOCAL BUSINESSES

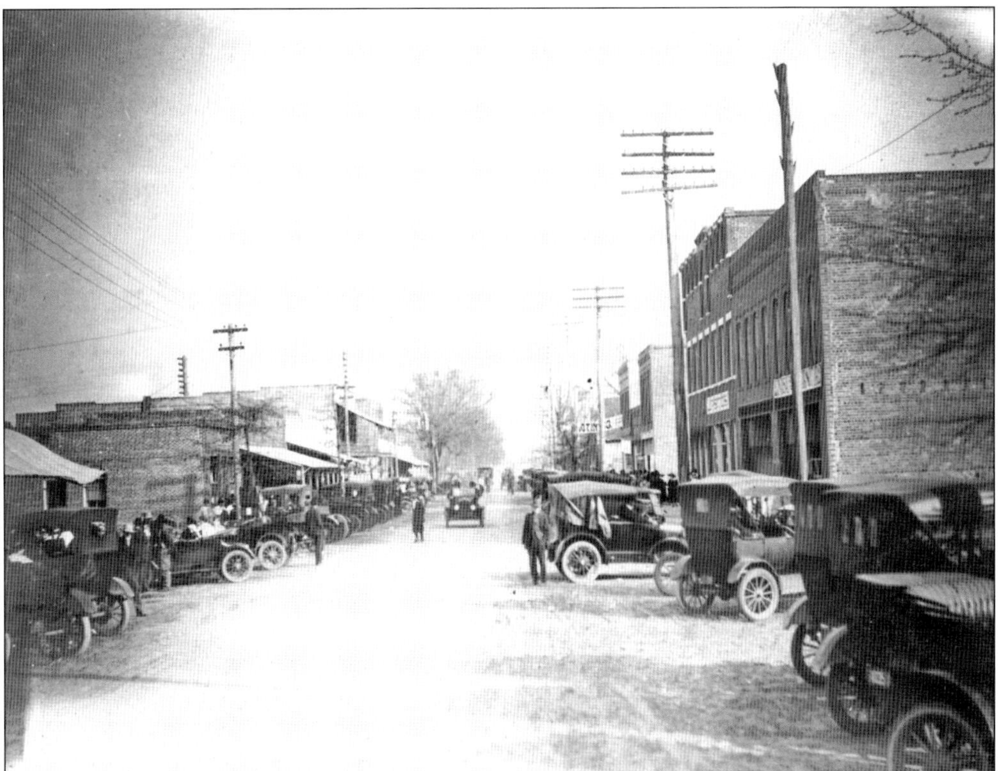

By the time this photograph was taken in 1926, Glennville was experiencing the Roaring Twenties at its best. Downtown Barnard Street, shown here facing east from Main Street (Highway 301), was fully developed and had taken on the appearance that it still mostly bears today. There was a two-story covered porch on the Margurite Hotel in the distance at left. (Perkins.)

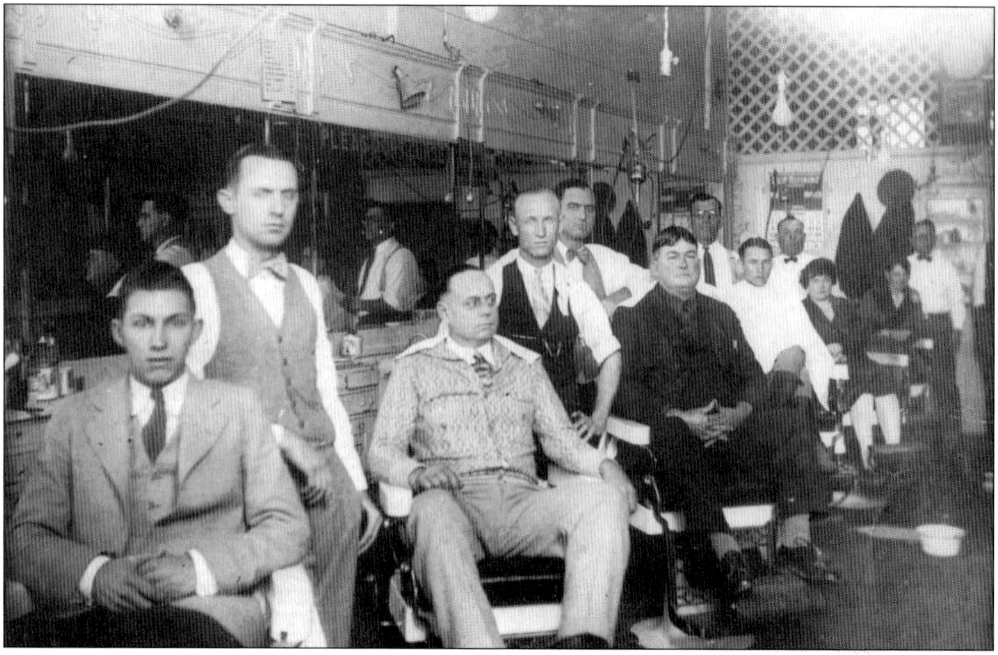

The City Barber Shop, pictured in 1925, was on the south side of Barnard Street across from the Glennville Bank. From left to right are Justin Byrd, Carlton Kicklighter, Iverson Branch, Lucius Woodcock, Smith Eason, Lum Nobles, Manning Johnson, unidentified, John Dasher, Dorothy Kirkland, Jettie Beasley, and owner Andrew T. Mixon. (Courtesy of Bobby Kicklighter.)

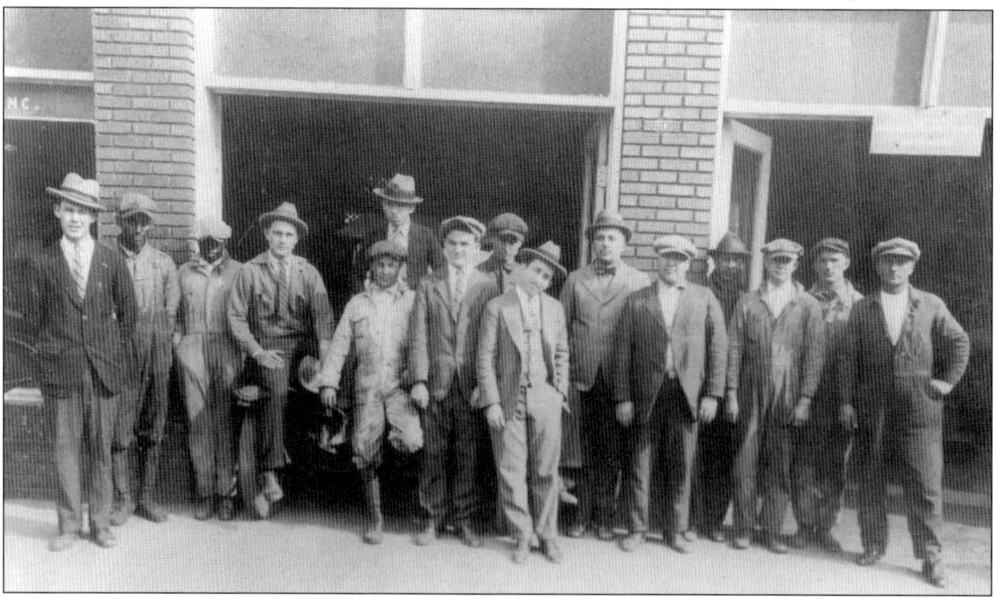

Nelson-Kicklighter Motors, pictured in 1924, was co-owned by C.W. Kicklighter Sr. and brothers Lee Roy Nelson and Hinton Nelson. At one time, the dealership stood at the northwest corner of Barnard and Railroad Streets. From left to right are Bruce Kennedy, A.D. Butler, Eli Thomas, T.E. Kirkland, Roy Banks, Hinton Nelson (standing in background on a car), Ward Waters, Lem Hare, Roy Nelson, Bo Rustin, Olin C. Floyd, Charlie Warren, Bill Beasley, Foster Durrence, and Bub Weitman. (Courtesy of Bobby Nelson.)

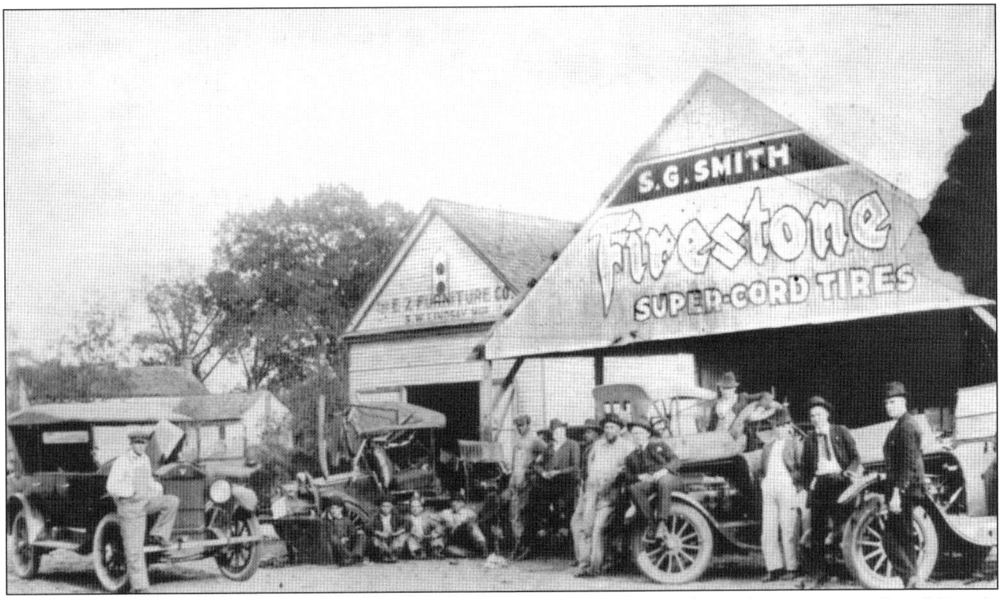

S.G. Smith's Firestone tire shop, pictured here in the 1920s, stood on the eastern side of South Caswell Street, across from the Methodist church. (GTM.)

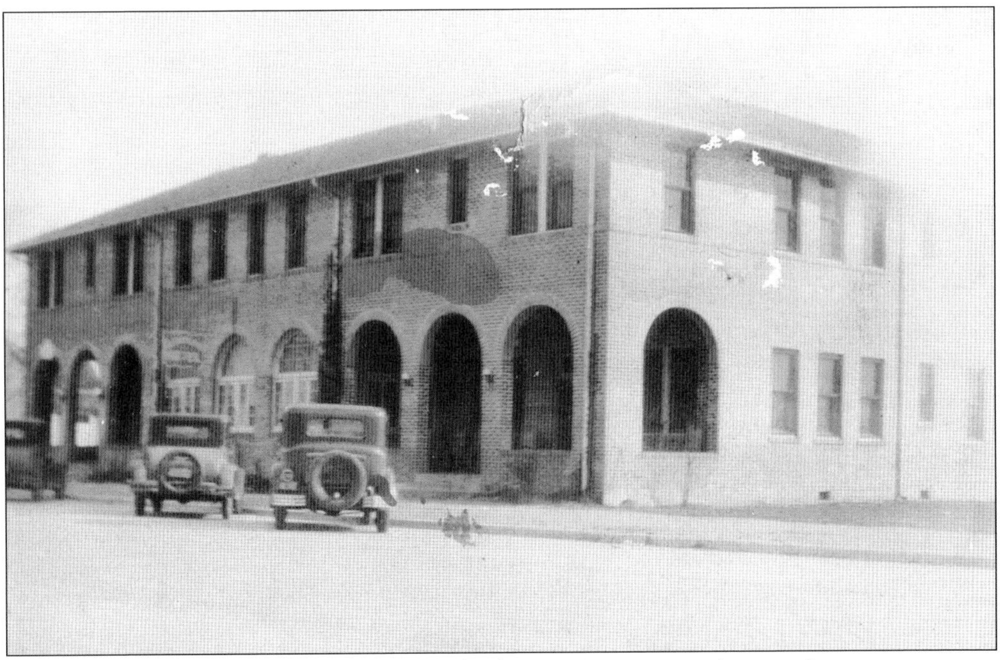
The Glennwanis Hotel, pictured here in the late 1920s, remains the grandest structure ever constructed on Barnard Street. Following the destruction of the Hughes Hotel by fire in 1920, the Glennwanis Hotel was constructed on-site in 1926 at a cost of $31,500. With no paved streets in Glennville at the time, the hotel featured state-of-the-art technology including electric lights, steam heat, and running hot and cold water in all guest rooms. The name Glennwanis was selected as a combination of the town's name and the Kiwanis Club, which was instrumental in the hotel's construction. (Courtesy of the Glennville Bank.)

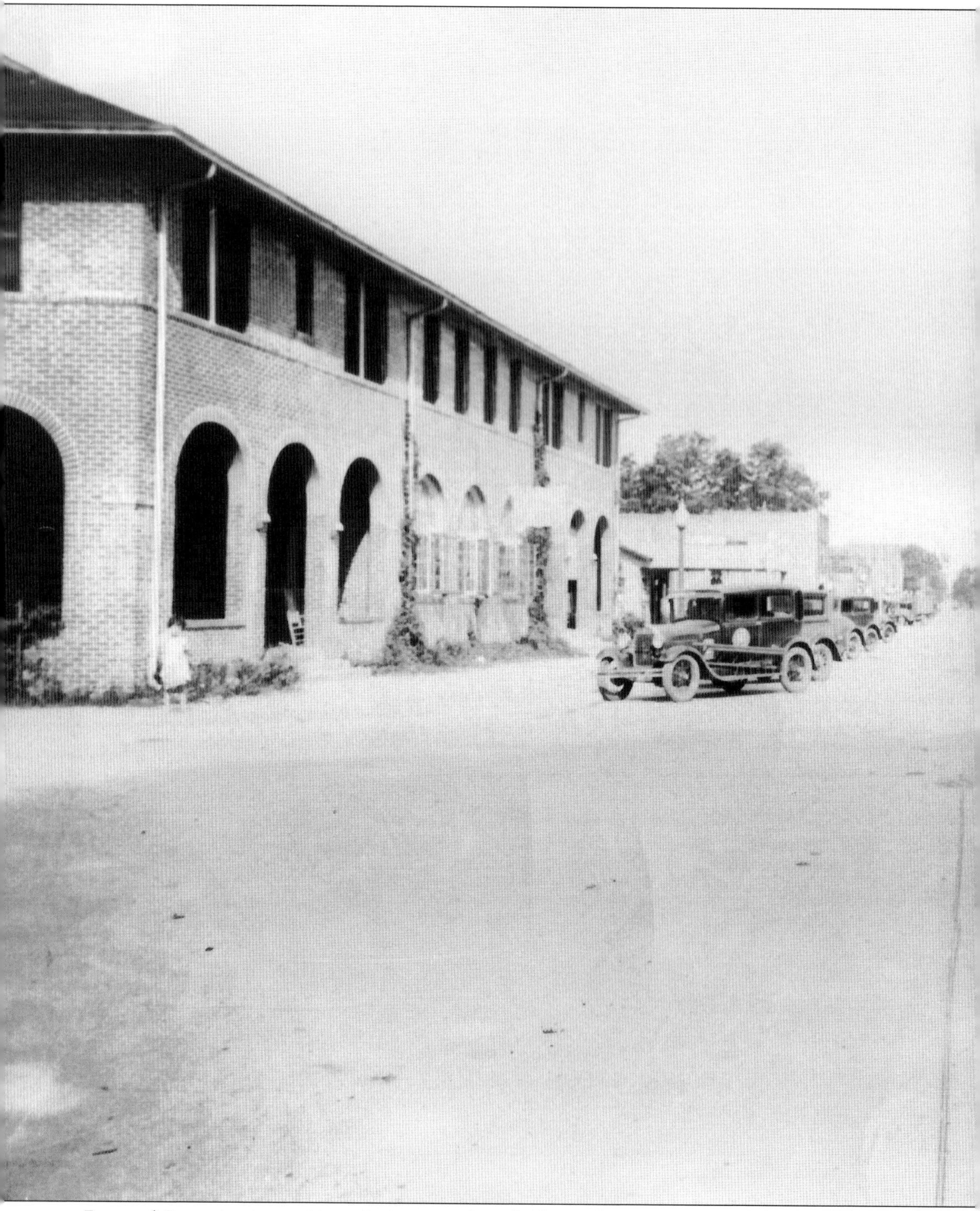

Barnard Street is pictured here facing west from Tillman Street in 1929 on the eve of the Great Depression. The Glennwanis Hotel, at left, was built by the Glennville Hotel Company, which was organized for that purpose after the Hughes Hotel's demise. Its directors were Dr. S.O. Edwards, president; S.J. Kicklighter, vice president; C.L. Cowart, attorney, secretary, and treasurer; Dr. J.M. Hughes Sr.; C.W. Kicklighter Sr.; Roy Nelson; J.B. Seckinger; W. Arnie Strickland; and Lint

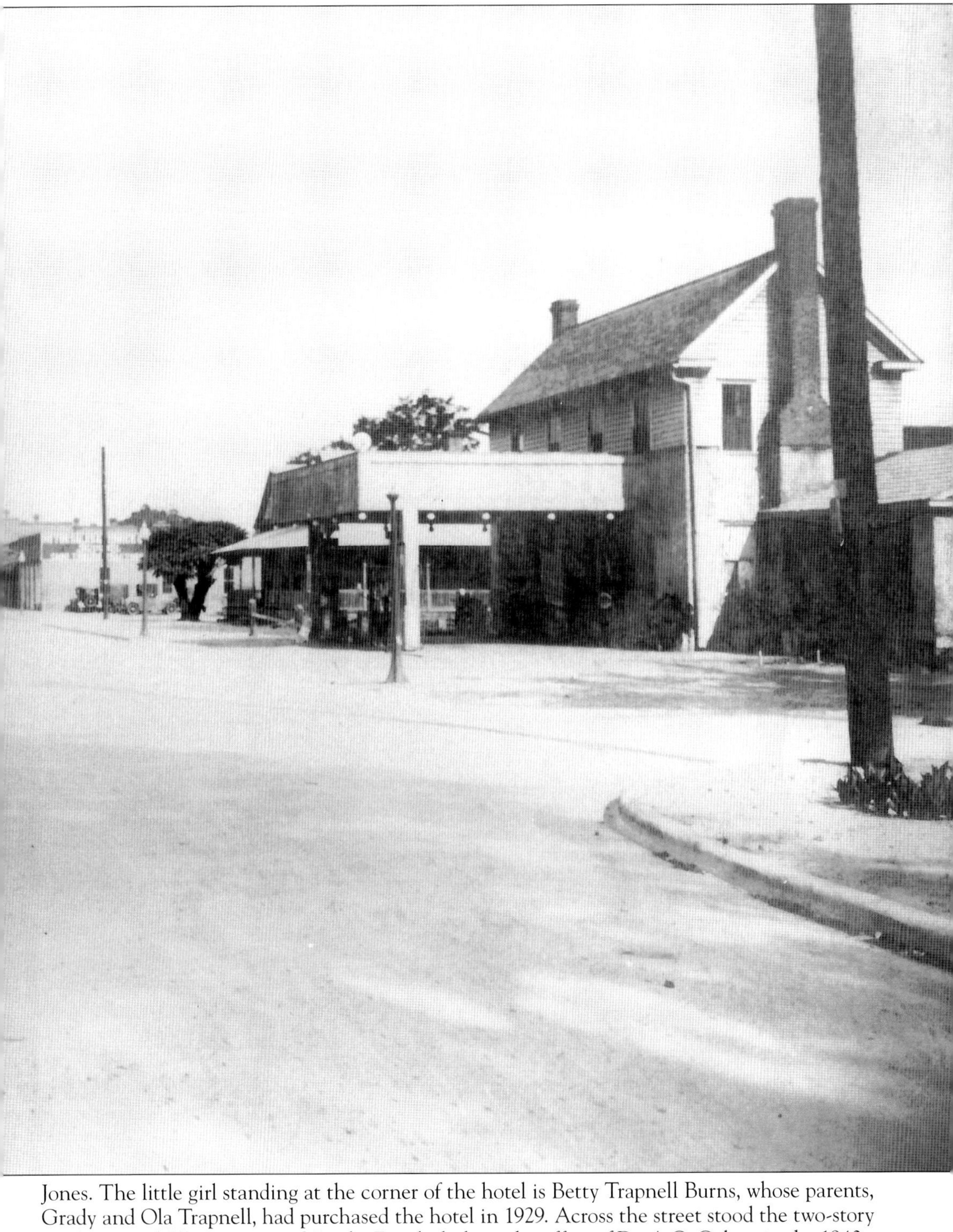

Jones. The little girl standing at the corner of the hotel is Betty Trapnell Burns, whose parents, Grady and Ola Trapnell, had purchased the hotel in 1929. Across the street stood the two-story residence and filling station of Cordie Faircloth, later the office of Dr. A.C. Colson in the 1940s. (Courtesy of Betty Trapnell Burns.)

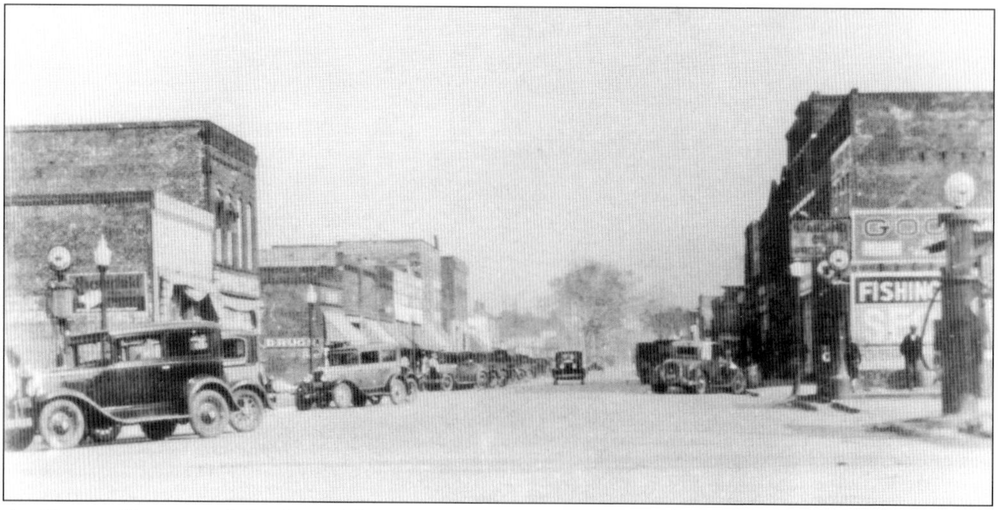

As Glennville entered the Great Depression, downtown Barnard Street—pictured here in 1931 facing east from Main Street—was a thriving center of commerce. The Depression claimed many local businesses, including the People's Bank; however, the completion of Highway 301 around 1940 and the introduction of a successful tomato industry in the mid-1930s gave Glennville much-needed assistance and moderated the effects of the Depression. (Courtesy of Betty Trapnell Burns.)

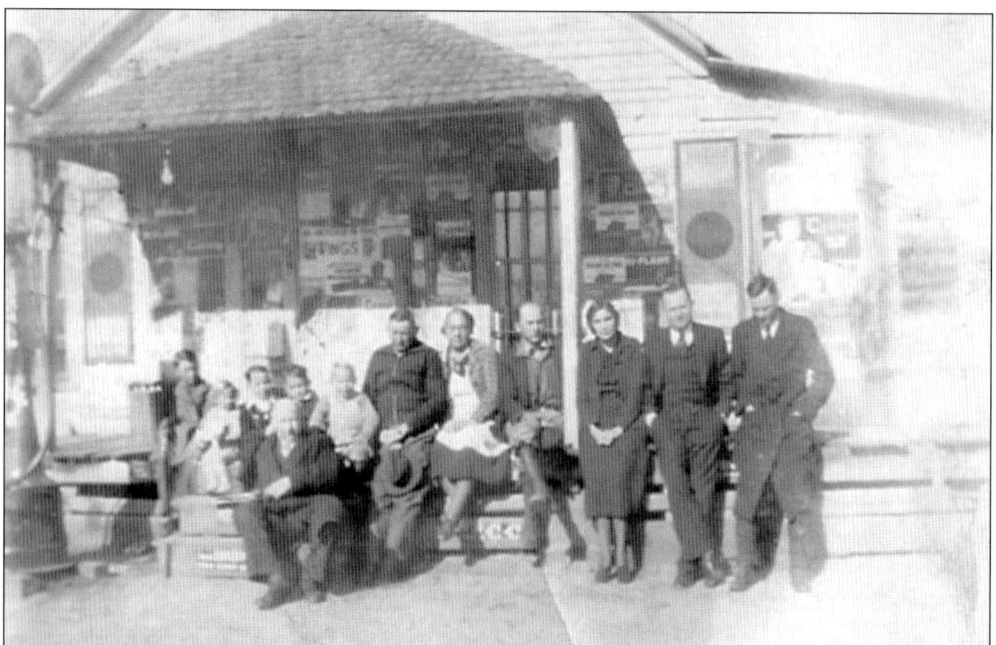

Beards Creek Store, pictured here in 1937, was owned by Asbery and Retta Kicklighter and stood across from their home on East Hencart Road, a few miles northeast of town near Beards Creek Church. (Courtesy of Bobby Kicklighter.)

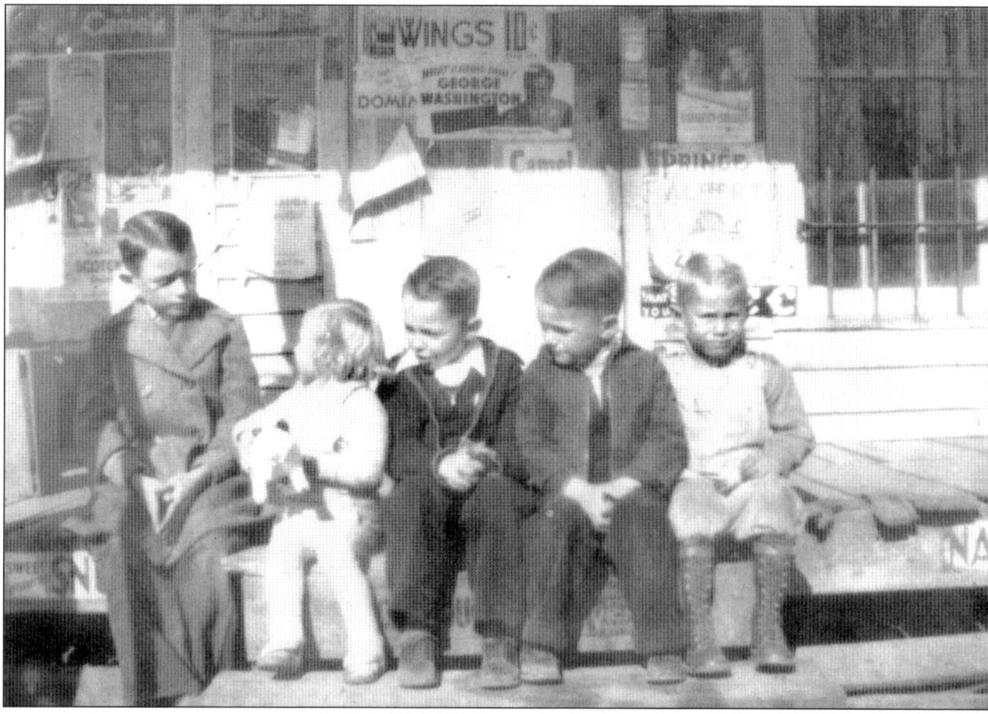

From left to right are Robert Collins, Shirley Smith, Jerry Kicklighter, Bobby Kicklighter, and Neil Smith on the porch of Beards Creek Store in 1937. The old wooden store stood vacant on the side of Hencart Road for many decades. (Courtesy of Bobby Kicklighter.)

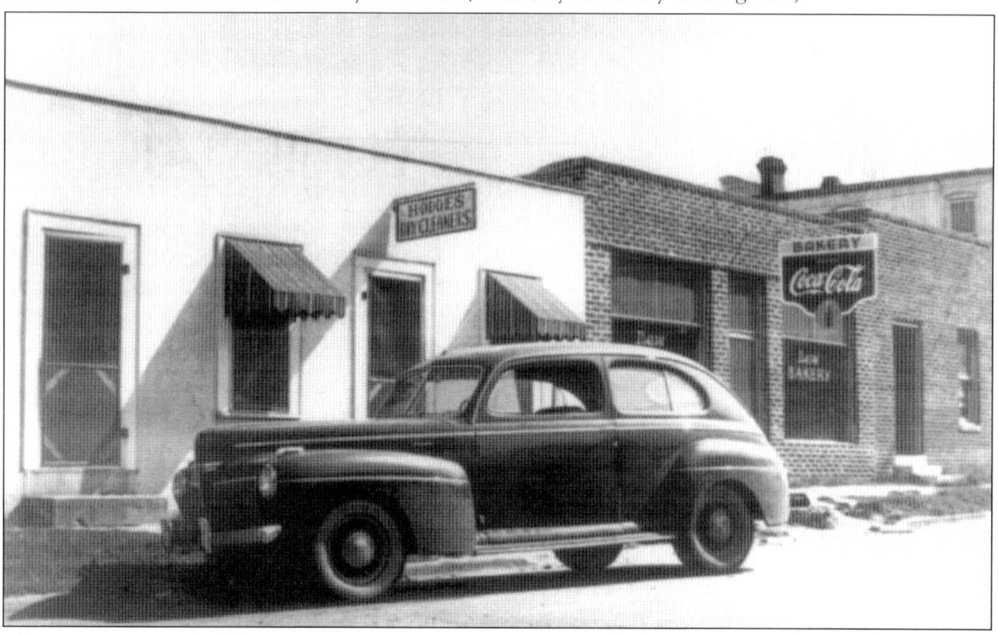

This row of store buildings stood on the east side of North Caswell Street, directly behind the original Glennville Bank, on the site where the present bank building now stands. From left to right are Gene Hodges's "pressing club" (dry cleaner), W.H. Bazemore's bakery, and Bruce D. Dubberly Sr.'s law office. (GTM.)

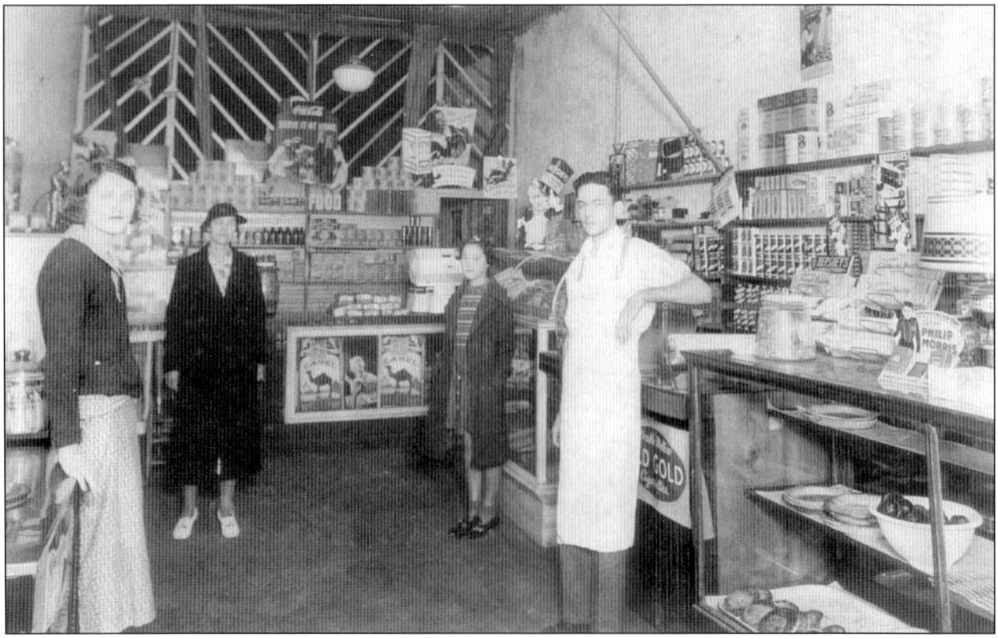

The interior of Bazemore Bakery is shown in this 1937 photograph. From left to right are Sladie Bacon Bazemore, Hattie Tootle, Lois Tootle, and W.H. Bazemore. Bazemore was known throughout Tattnall County for his culinary skills, and his bakery produced everything from bread and cakes to doughnuts. (GTM.)

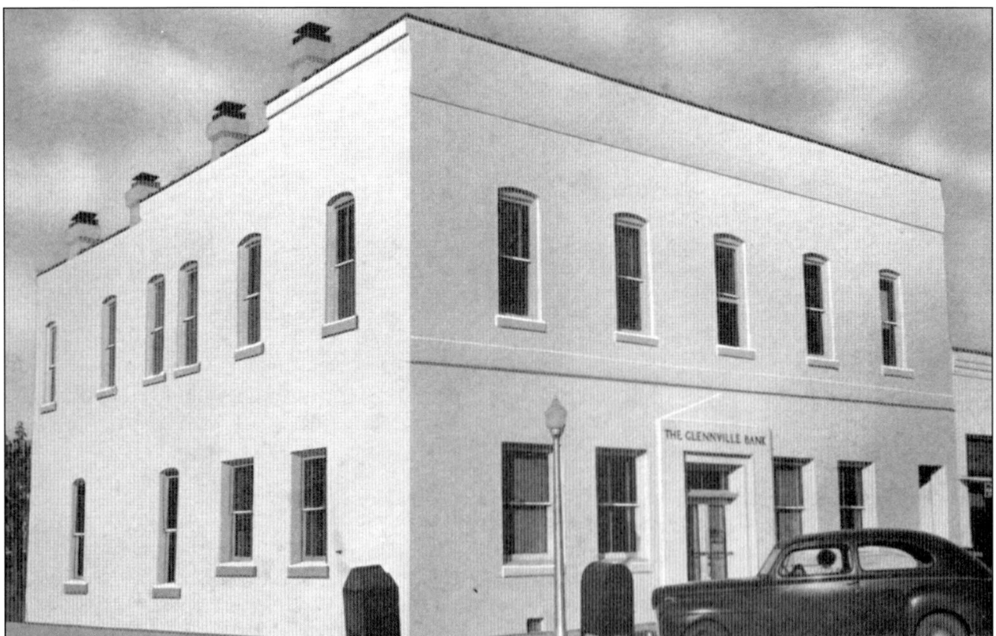

Glennville was far more fortunate than many South Georgia communities during the Great Depression, as town after town watched businesses and banks close their doors. Although Glennville was not immune, the Glennville Bank—pictured in 1940 as the Depression was drawing to a close—managed to survive through careful management. (Courtesy of the Glennville Bank.)

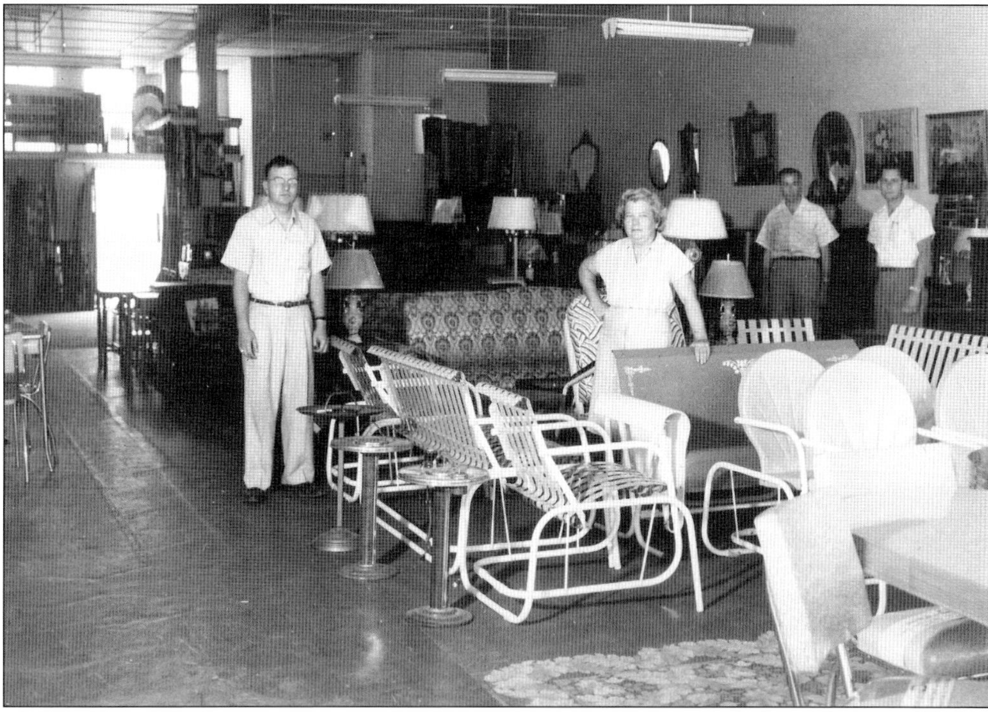

Pictured above around 1946–1947 is the showroom of the H.E. Danner Furniture Company, located on Barnard Street next to the Glennville Bank. From left to right are Hampton Edgar Danner Jr., Bertha Danner (his mother), Oran Waters, and Alvo V. Durrence. Directly behind the furniture store and bank stood the furniture warehouse, pictured below. From left to right are Bennie Campbell, Oran Waters, Hampton Edgar Danner Jr., Bertha Danner, and Alvo V. Durrence. The white building in the distance to the left was city hall. (Both, courtesy of Paulette Durrence Weaver.)

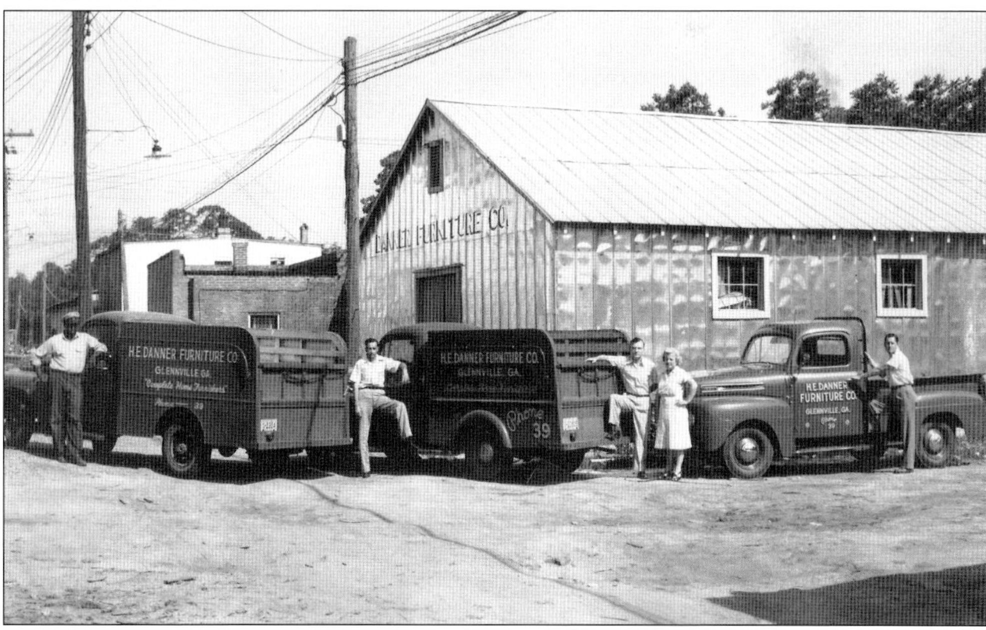

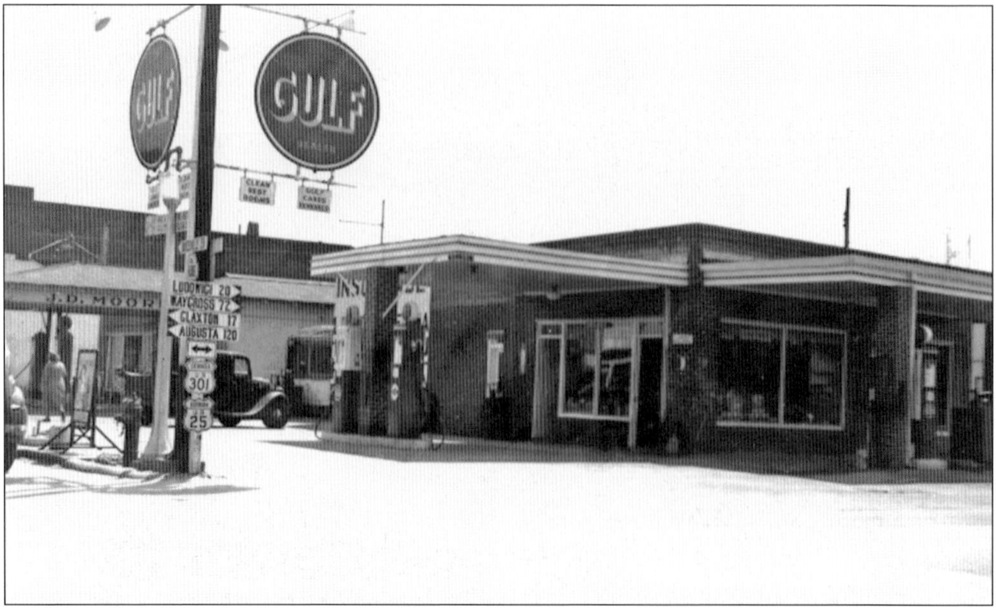

Standing on the southeast corner of Barnard and Main Streets (Highway 301) was the Barrow Brothers' Everready Gulf Station, pictured in 1950. With the completion of Highway 301 around 1940, Glennville began to witness a steady stream of tourists traveling north and south along the East Coast. As the Interstate 95 of its day, Highway 301 was the lifeblood of Glennville for several decades. (GTM.)

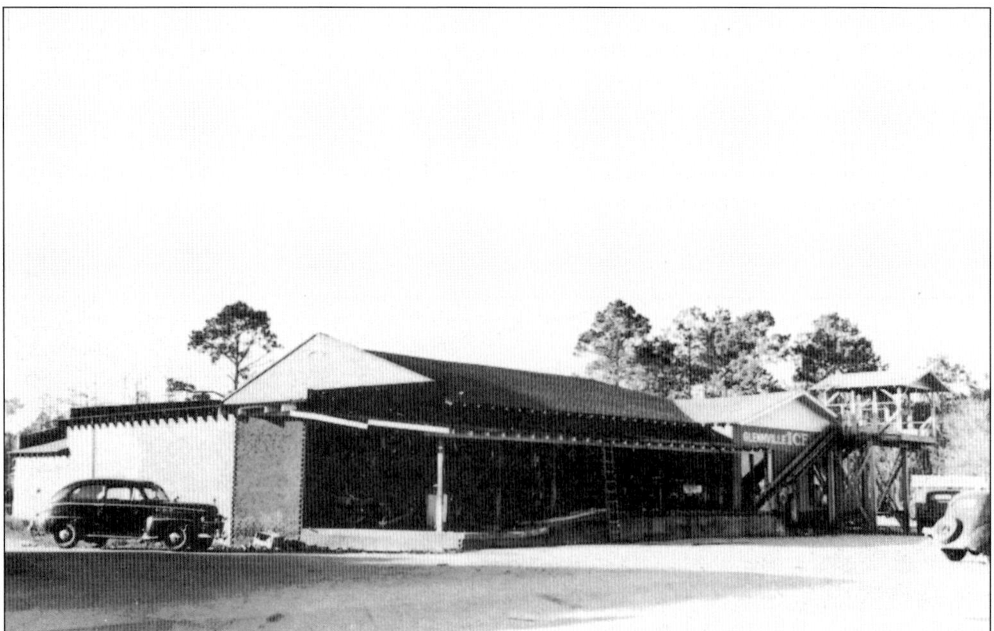

The Glennville Ice Company, pictured here in 1950, was owned by W.G. McCurdy, who had first arrived in Glennville as manager of the ice plant in 1931. The plant closed in 1970 and was demolished in 1972 to make way for the present Glennville Bank branch office on Highway 301 North. (Courtesy of the Glennville Public Library.)

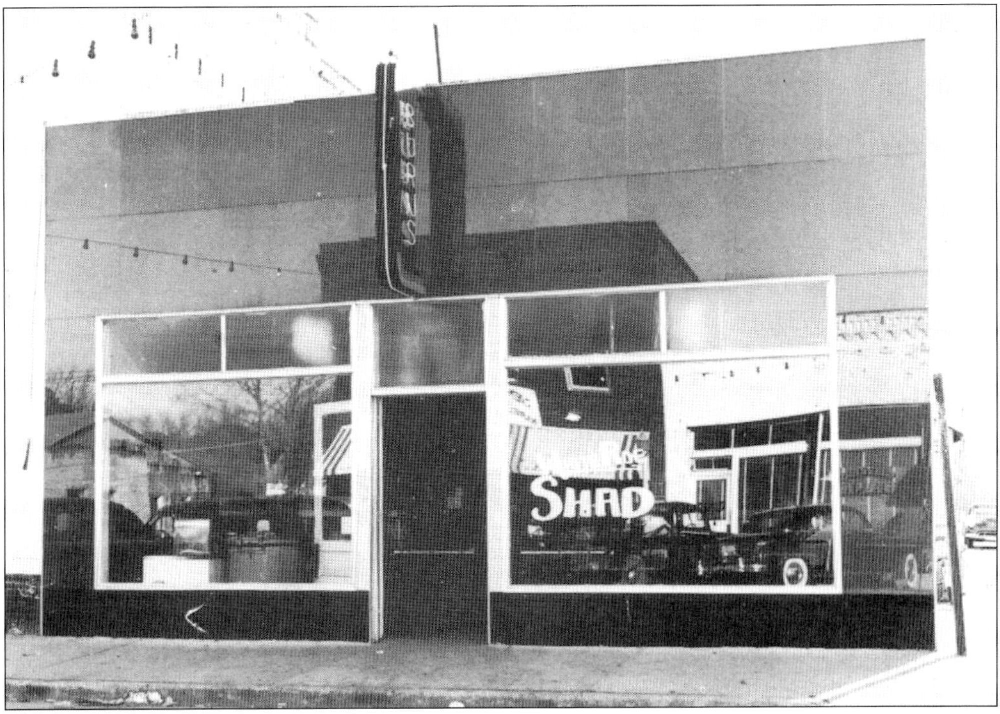

Burns Groceteria, later known as Burns Red & White and Burns Food Palace, was owned and operated by Curtis and Betty Burns. The building pictured above in 1950 was the original location on the south side of Barnard Street and is now home to Tattnall Insurance. Burns later moved to a building directly across from First Baptist Church, pictured below in 1962. The Red & White business was later purchased by Terry Waters and moved to a larger building in Glennville Plaza on Highway 301 South, where Waters Bi-Rite, Piggly Wiggly, and BiLo would later be located. (Both, courtesy of the Glennville Public Library.)

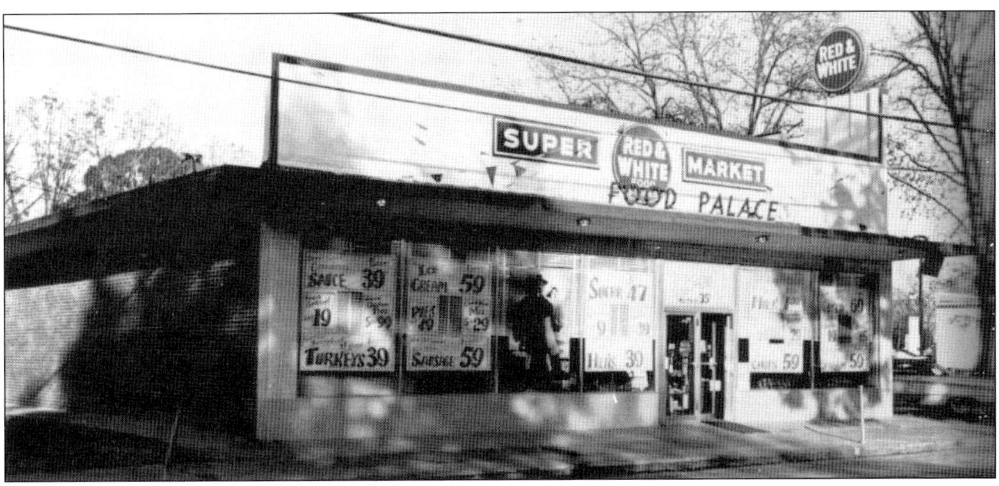

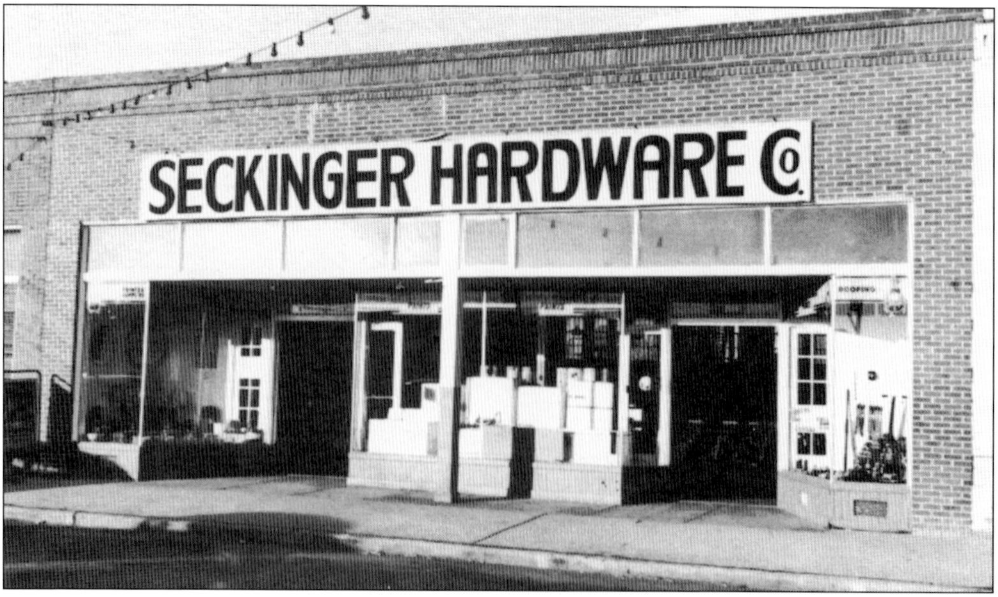

Seckinger Hardware, pictured above in 1950, was owned by J.B. Seckinger and stood on the north side of Barnard Street between Highway 301 and Gross Street. The building is shown below in 1959 after the front was remodeled to give it the flat appearance that it still bears today. The business was later purchased by Gene Lewis and Richard Dasher, the latter of whom eventually bought Lewis's share as well. (Both, courtesy of the Glennville Public Library.)

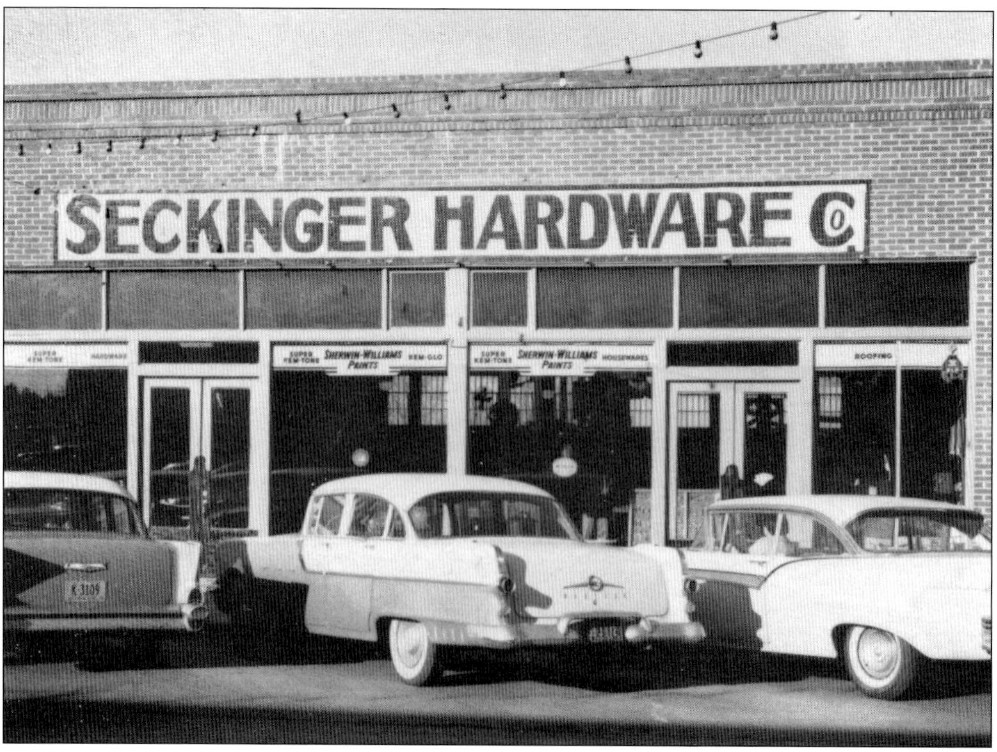

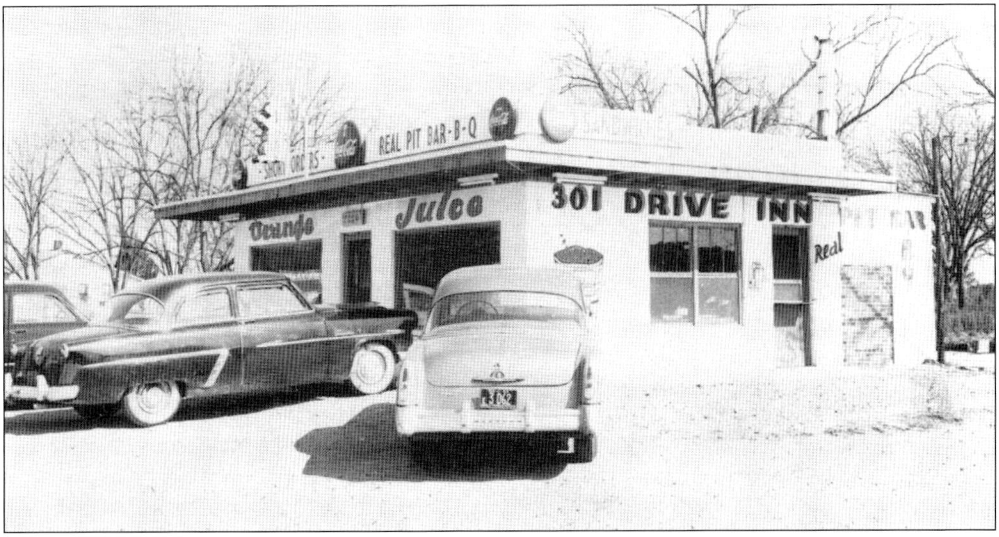

Reese's 301 Drive Inn, located on Highway 301 South, was a favorite restaurant and hangout for teenagers and adults alike from its inception in 1953 through the 1980s. Owned by R. Reese DeLoach, who also served as manager of the adjacent state farmers' market, 301 Drive Inn was famous for its hamburgers and barbecue. The above photograph, from 1955, shows the original restaurant before the drive-in was added onto the front, as shown below. (Above, courtesy of the Glennville Public Library; below, GTM.)

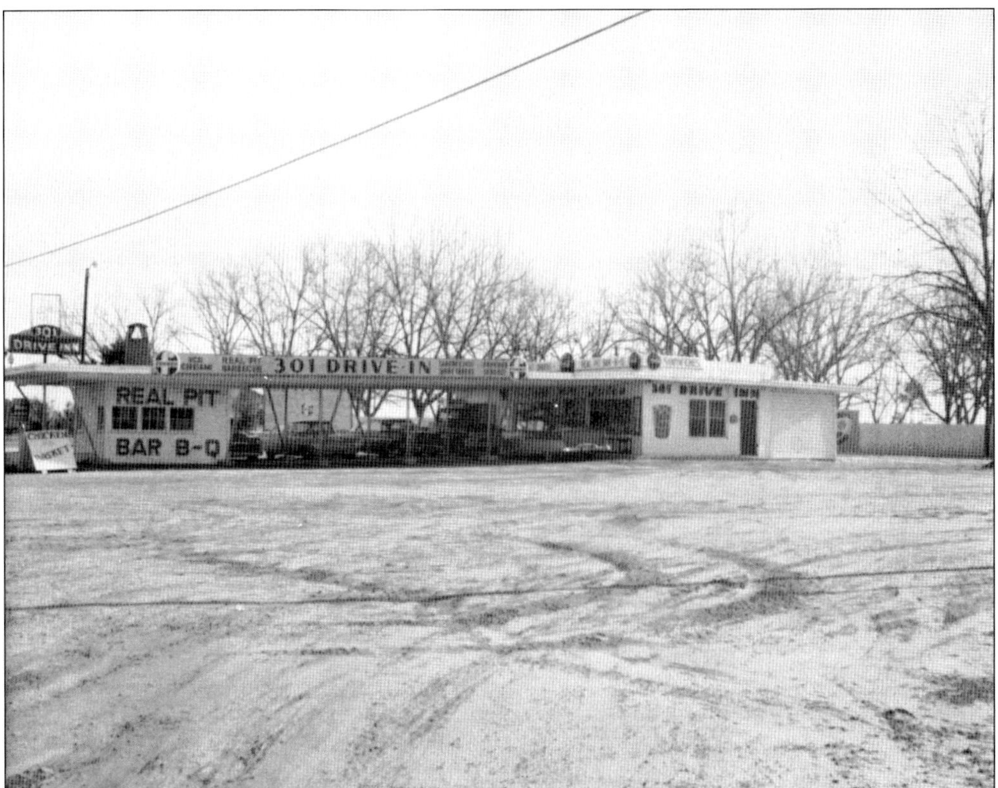

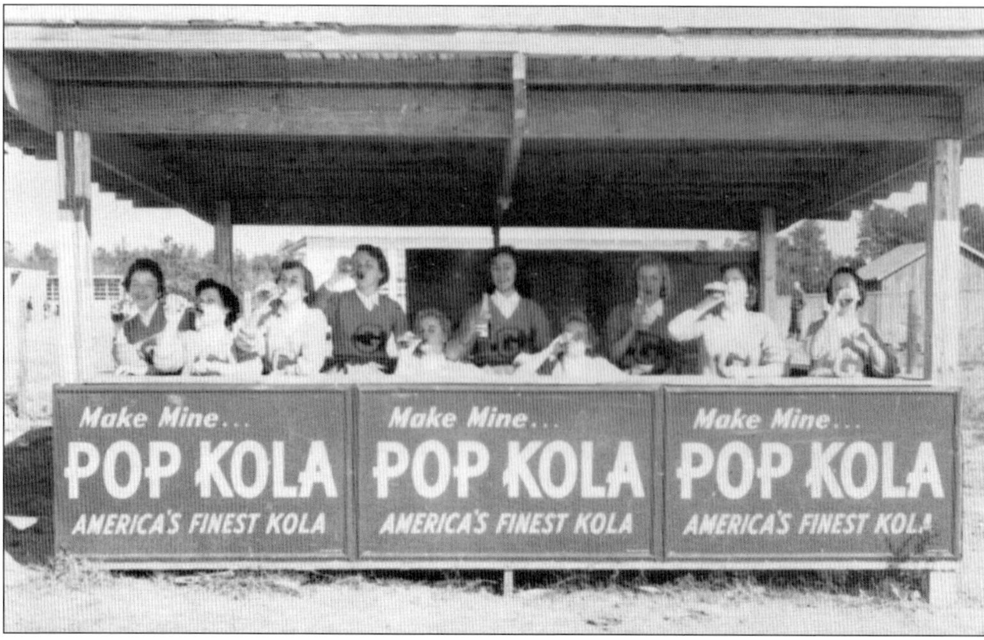

Williams Bottling Company, located a block west of Highway 301 South, produced two favorite local soft drinks, Pop Kola and Kist. Pictured here are the concession stands at Glennville High School in 1956. (Courtesy of the Glennville Public Library.)

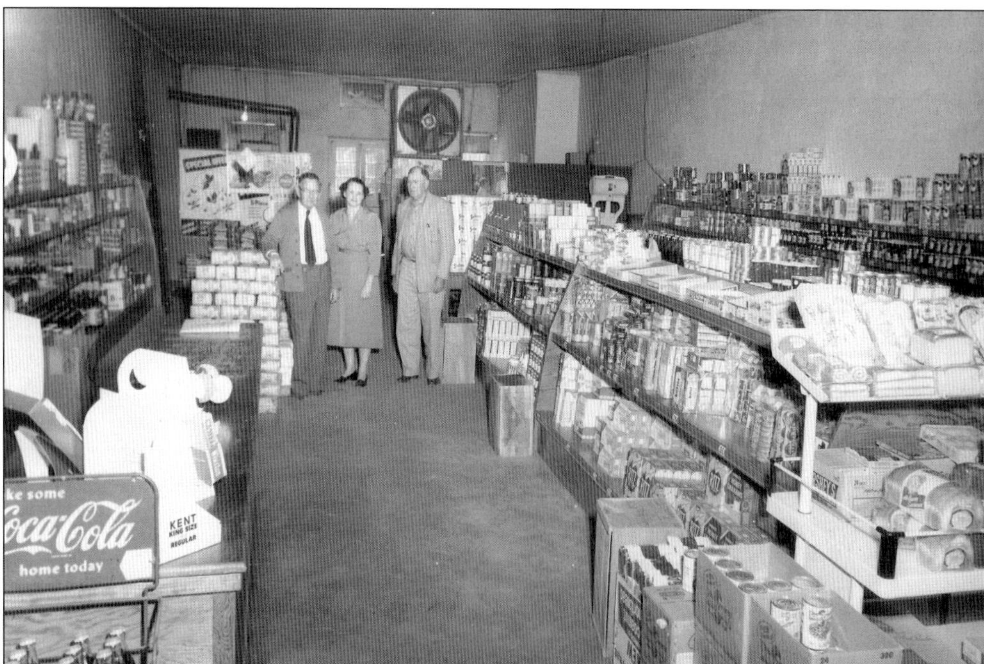

Pictured in the mid-1950s is the Suwannee Store, managed by Holmes Sands. The store was located on the east side of Highway 301, just south of Barnard Street. From left to right are Holmes Sands, Annie Merle Lewis, and Sam Tabor, a friend of Sands's from Atlanta who enjoyed relaxing and fishing in Glennville so much that he moved here. (Courtesy of Brent Walker.)

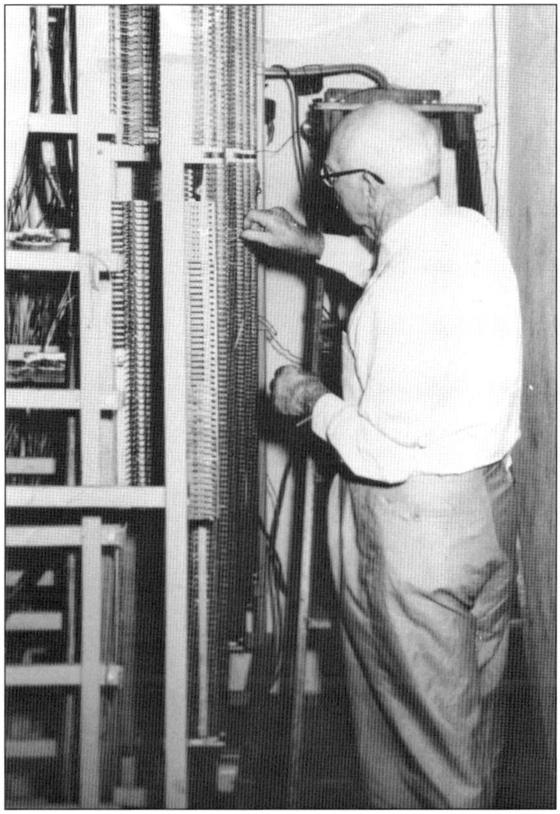

Glennville's first telephones arrived in 1912 with the founding of Sikes Telephone Company by Clarance R. Sikes. C.R. Sikes began installing telephone lines in town and then moved to rural areas. He is pictured at right in 1956 during the changeover to the dial system. Pictured below during the 1956 changeover are, from left to right, Kathryn Persons Sikes, Watson Winn, unidentified telephone engineer, Aubrey E. Sikes Sr., Harvey Persons Jr., and J.M. "Joe Boy" Hughes Jr. (Both, GTM.)

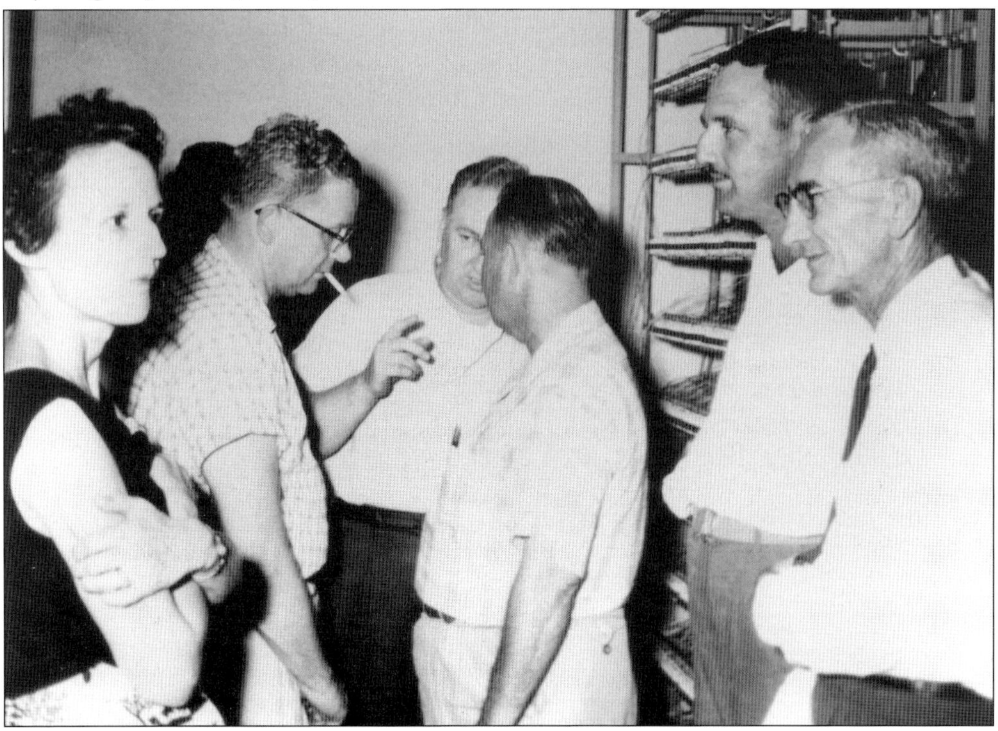

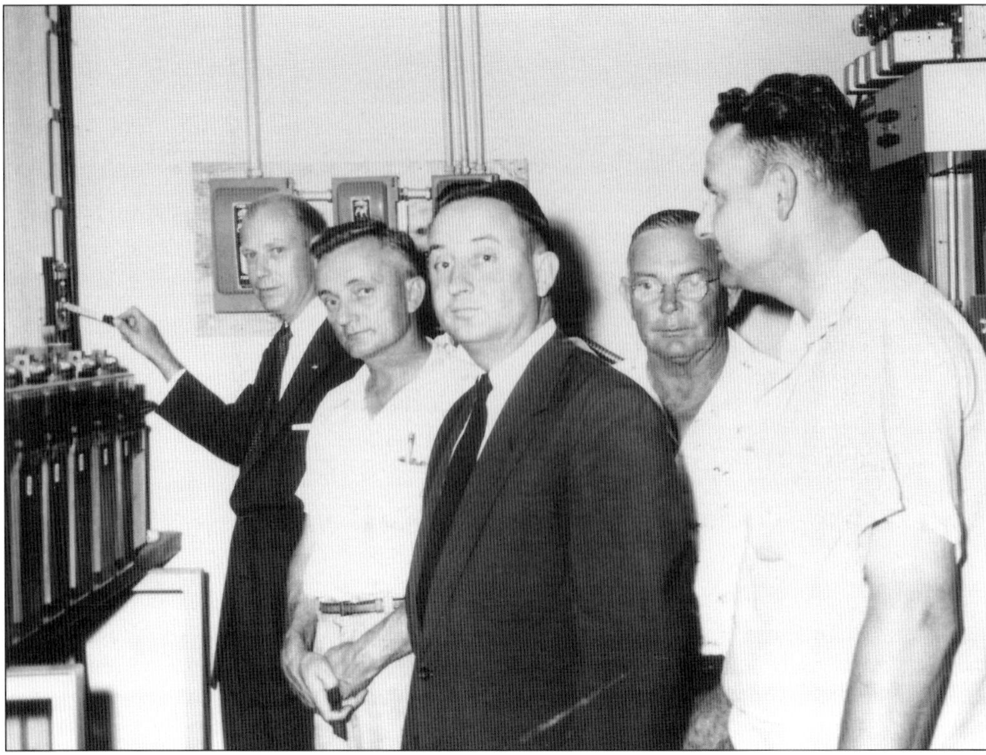

Pictured above during the 1956 changeover to the dial system are, from left to right, Mayor Jean D. Kicklighter, Lyman Burkhalter, Rev. E.G. Hutchins, John E. "Babe" Brewton, and an unidentified telephone engineer. Pictured below in 1963 is the exterior of Sikes Telephone Company on Gross Street. The telephone company had once been located on the second floor of a nearby Barnard Street building. (Above, GTM; below, courtesy of the Glennville Public Library.)

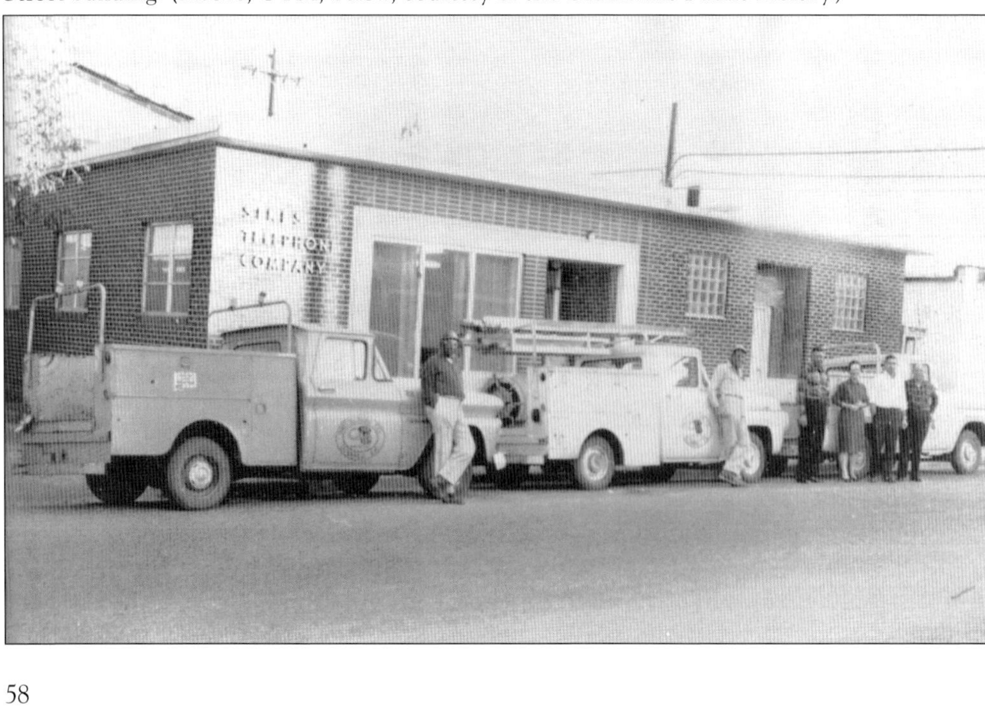

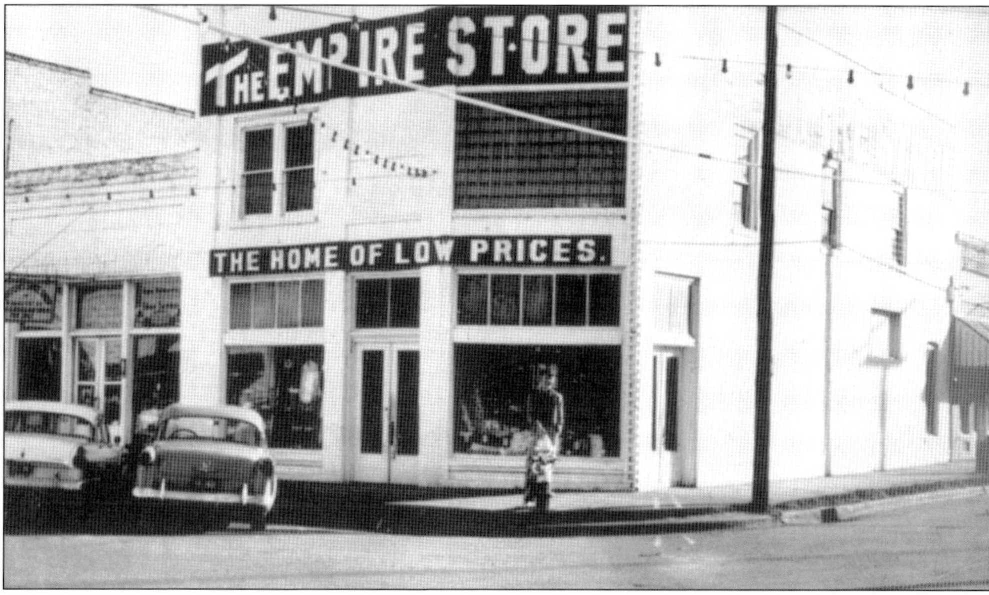

The Empire Store, pictured here in the 1950s, was a prominent business located on the southeast corner of Barnard and Caswell Streets that sold a variety of household items. The Empire Store was founded around 1930 by a Russian Jewish immigrant, Jacob Arenson. After Arenson's death, the store was managed for many years by his daughters, Ray and Jane. (GTM.)

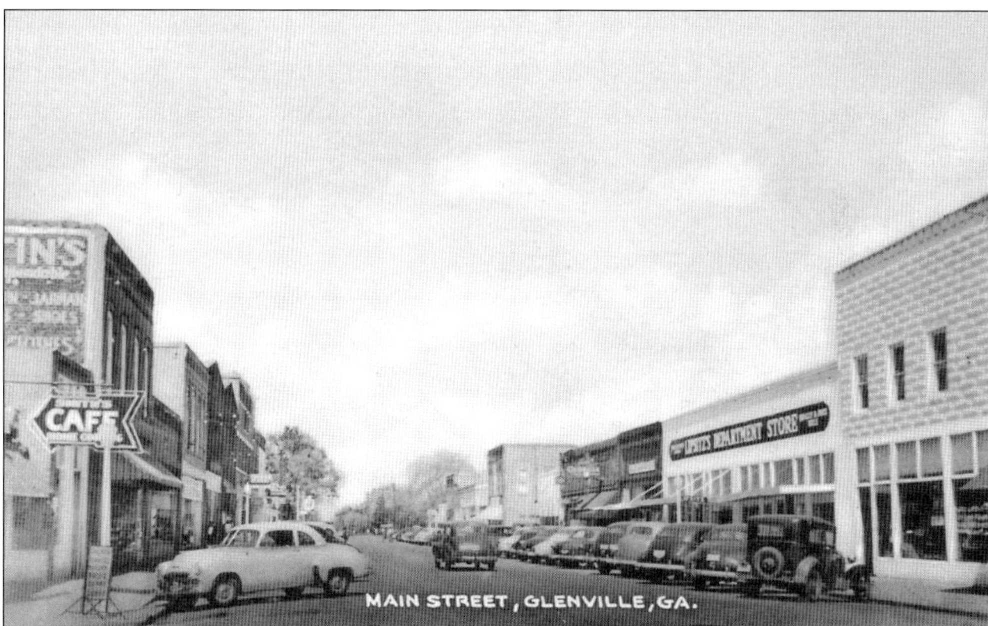

This 1950s postcard, incorrectly labeled as "Main Street," shows a bustling Barnard Street facing west from Caswell Street. Notice Smith's Café on the left corner, adjacent to Slotin's Dry Goods (now home to the *Glennville Sentinel*). Lipsitz Department Store is across the street. (Courtesy of Brent Walker.)

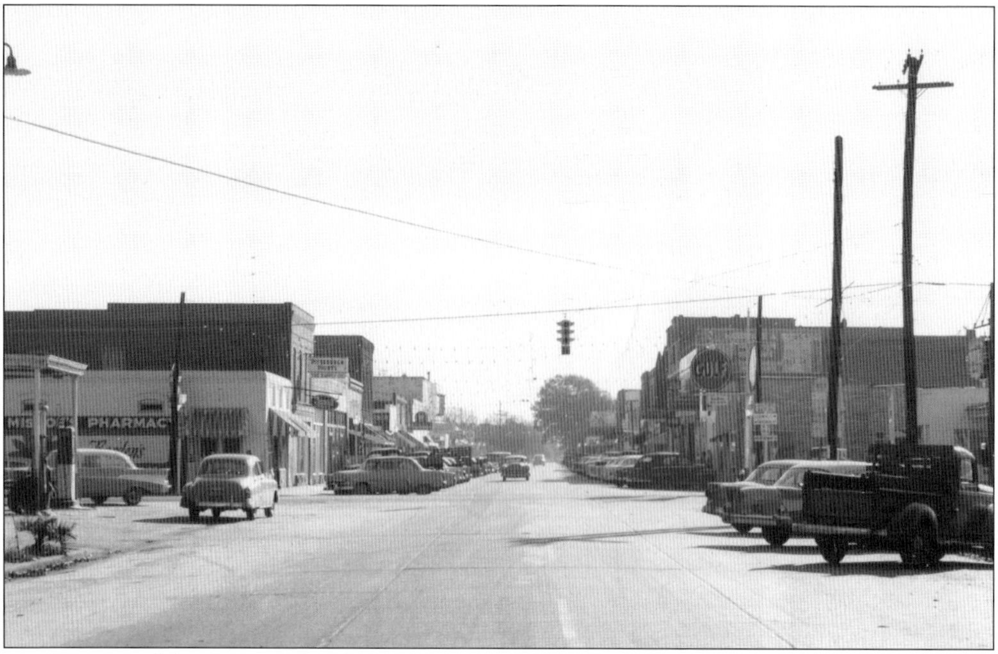

By the time of this 1957 view of Barnard Street facing east from the vicinity of First Baptist Church, downtown Barnard boasted a number of pharmacies, grocery stores, dry goods and department stores, hardware and furniture stores, banks, a hotel, and a theater. (Courtesy of the City of Glennville.)

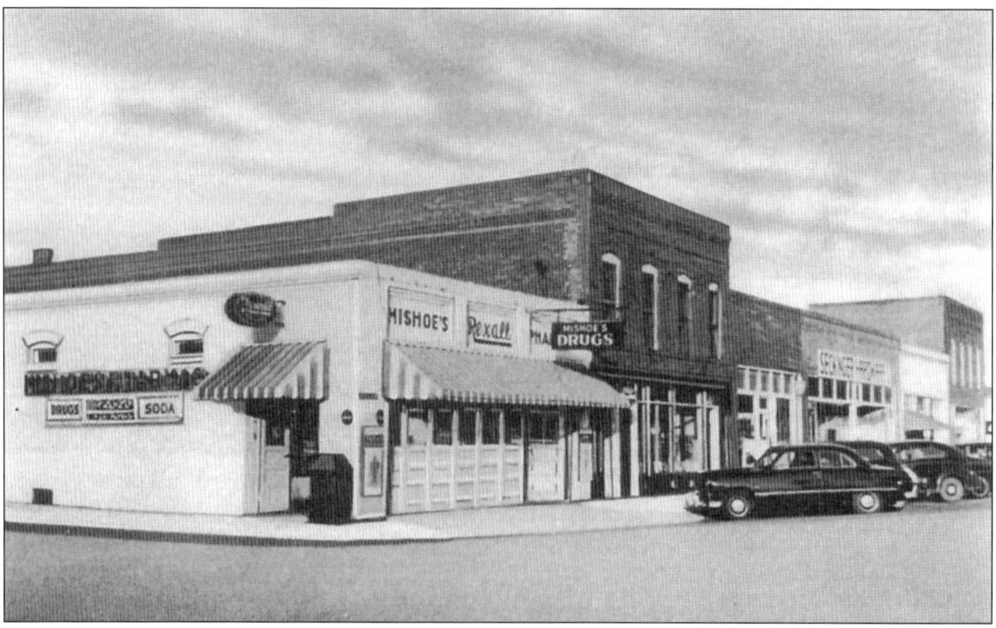

This 1950s postcard shows the north side of Barnard Street from the intersection at Highway 301. The two-story building next to Mishoe's Pharmacy housed the Supply Company on the first floor and Sikes Telephone Company on the second. The single-story building between the Supply Company and Seckinger Hardware was once home to the post office. (Courtesy of Brent Walker.)

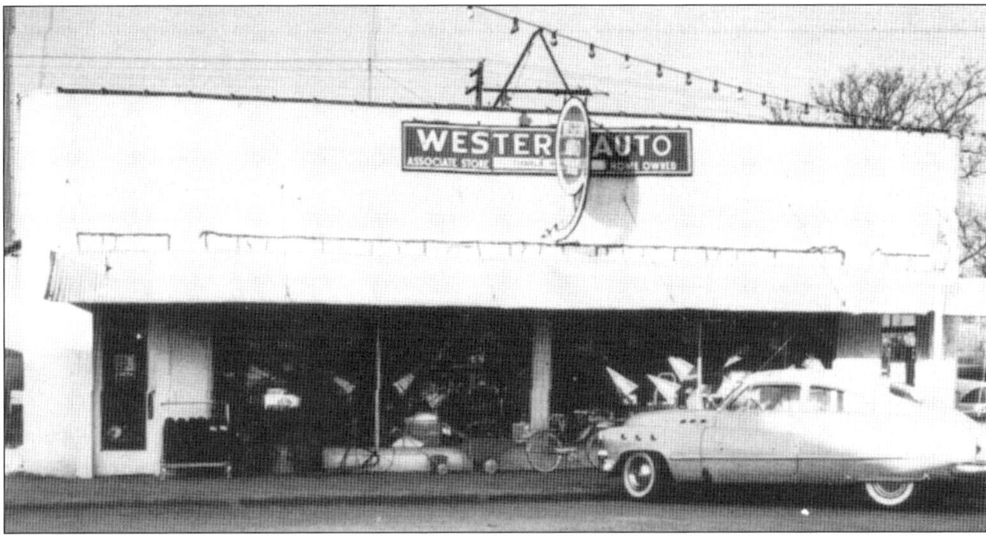

The building pictured here around 1957 was on the northwest corner of Barnard and Railroad Streets and housed Charlie Rowland's Western Auto and later James Faircloth's Cotton States insurance office. Western Auto was later located in the building just west of this one. The Faircloth building is no longer standing, and the site is now a parking lot. (Courtesy of the Glennville Public Library.)

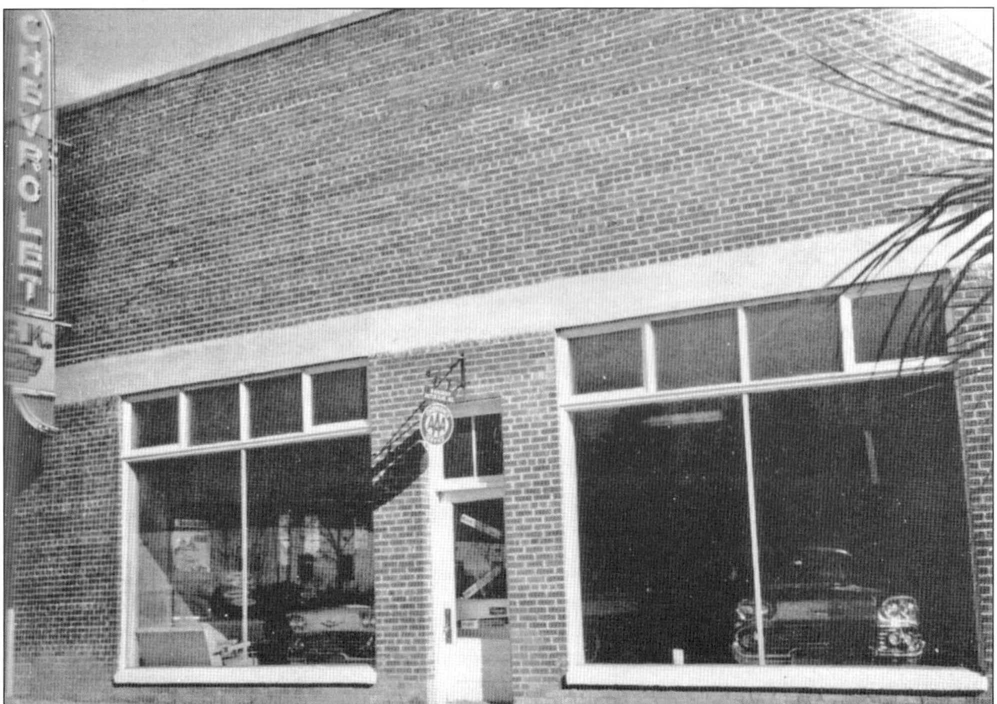

K&K Chevrolet, pictured here in 1958, was on the east side of Highway 301 North between Mann and China Streets, adjacent to the later location of Brent Walker Ford. K&K Chevrolet was originally owned by Jean Kicklighter and Louis Kennedy and later by Gene Pedrick. The business closed around 1980. (Courtesy of the Glennville Public Library.)

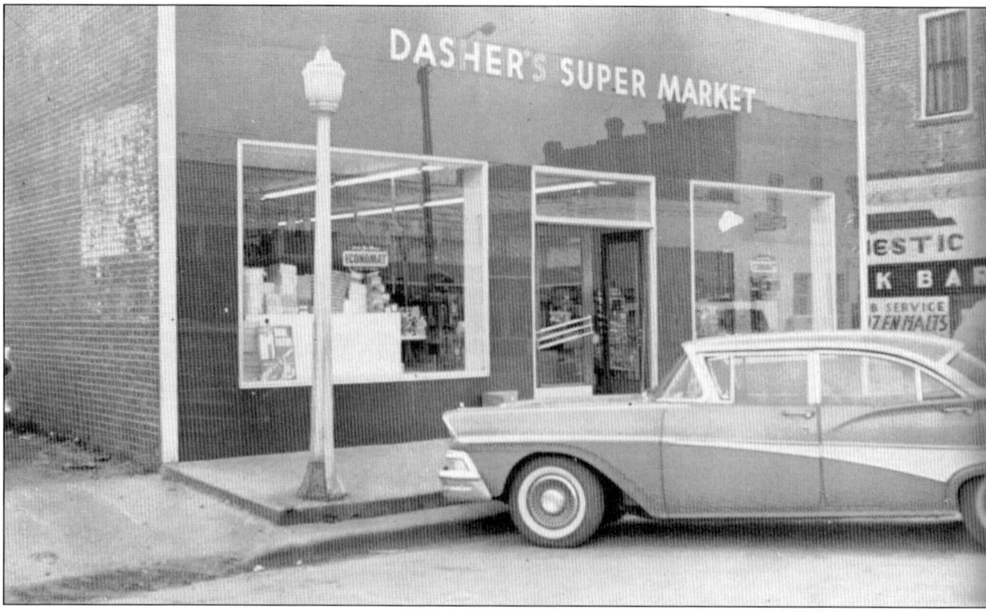

Dasher's Super Market, pictured above in 1959 and below in 1963, was on the south side of Barnard Street in the building now occupied by Strickland's Pharmacy. The popular grocery store was built in 1946 by owner Vernon W. Dasher Sr. Dasher also owned a farm supply store on South Caswell Street, the Red Steer restaurant on Highway 301 South, and an abattoir northwest of town on Loves Chapel Road. (Both, courtesy of the Glennville Public Library.)

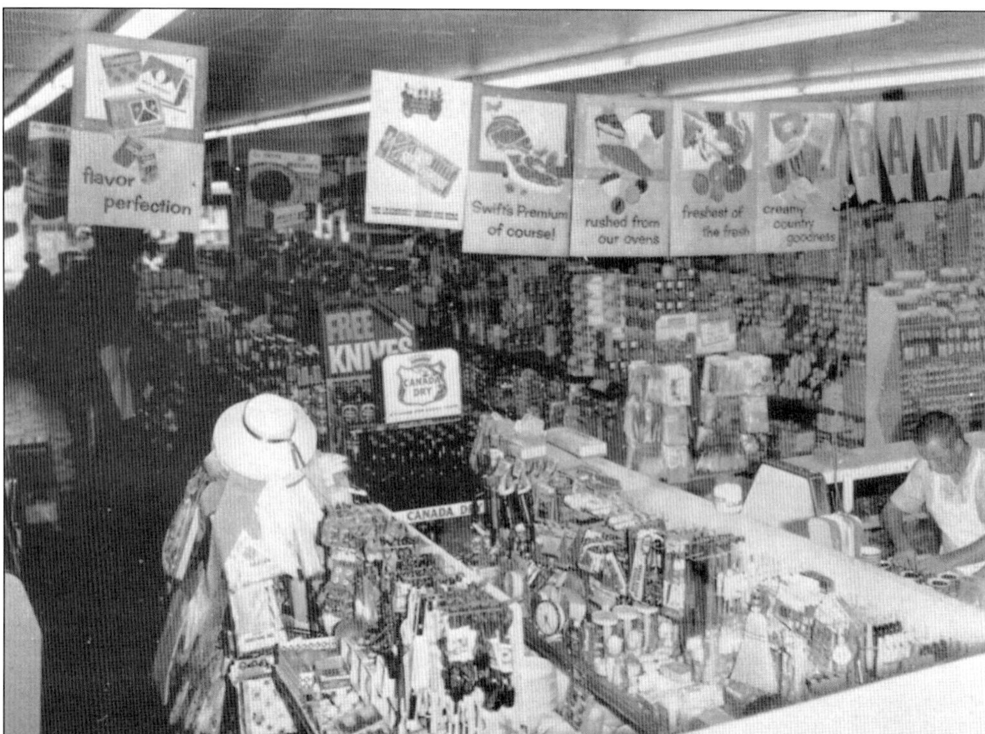

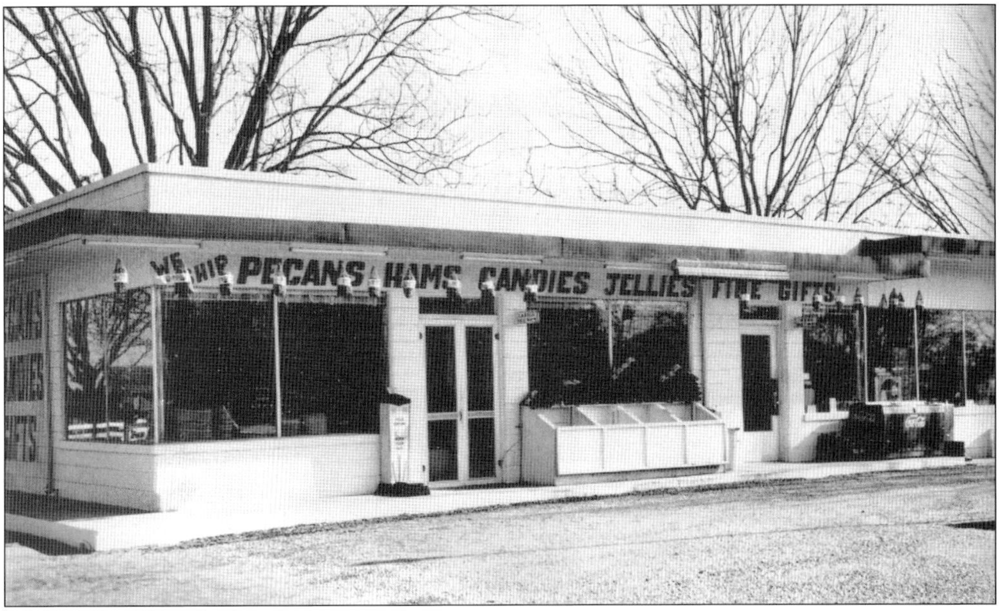

The Mascot Pecan Company, pictured above in 1958, was founded in 1952 by Mills Tarver and Hugh Oliver as a service station and gift shop to cater to tourists traveling Highway 301. Tourists were especially fond of shelled pecans, so the Mascot began shelling pecans by hand to sell. The business continued to expand as its pecans and candy became increasingly popular. (Courtesy of the Glennville Public Library.)

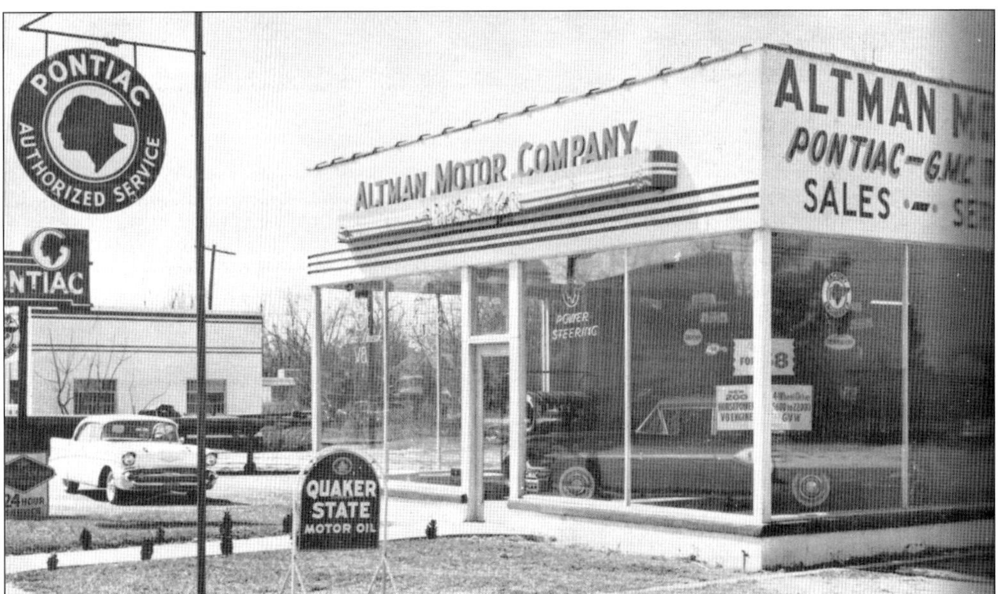

Altman Motor Company, pictured here in 1958, was owned by Frank Altman. The GMC and Pontiac dealership was later owned by David Burns and still later by Doug Oxford before closing around 1975. The building stands on Highway 301 North directly across from China Street and now houses Glennville Auto Parts. (Courtesy of the Glennville Public Library.)

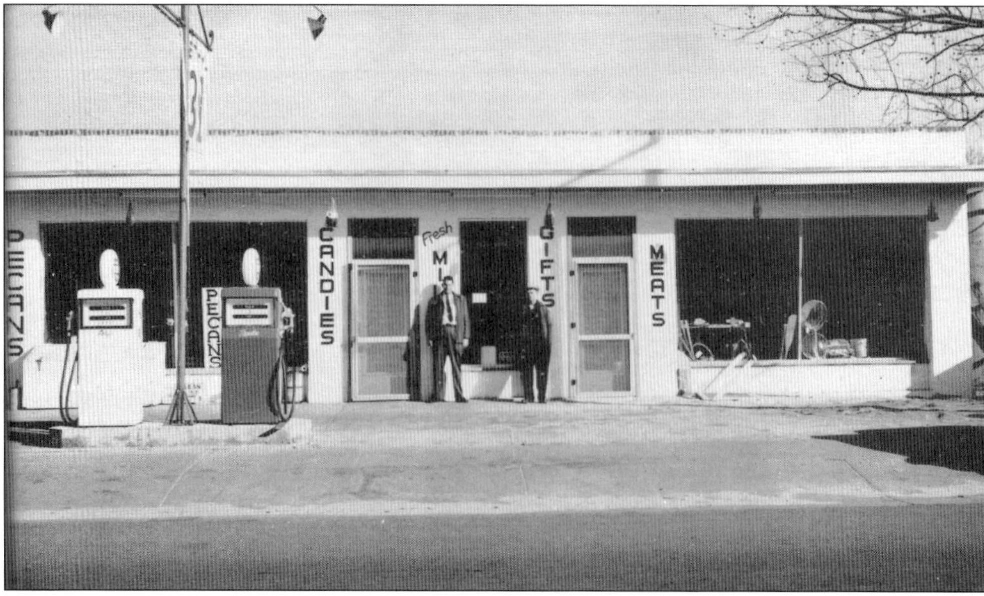

Woodcock Pecan Market and Grocery, pictured above in 1958 and below in 1960, was owned and operated by Slater and Tink Woodcock and stood on Highway 301 North near the old farmers' market near Hencart Road. (Above, courtesy of the Glennville Public Library; below, courtesy of the Glennville Bank.)

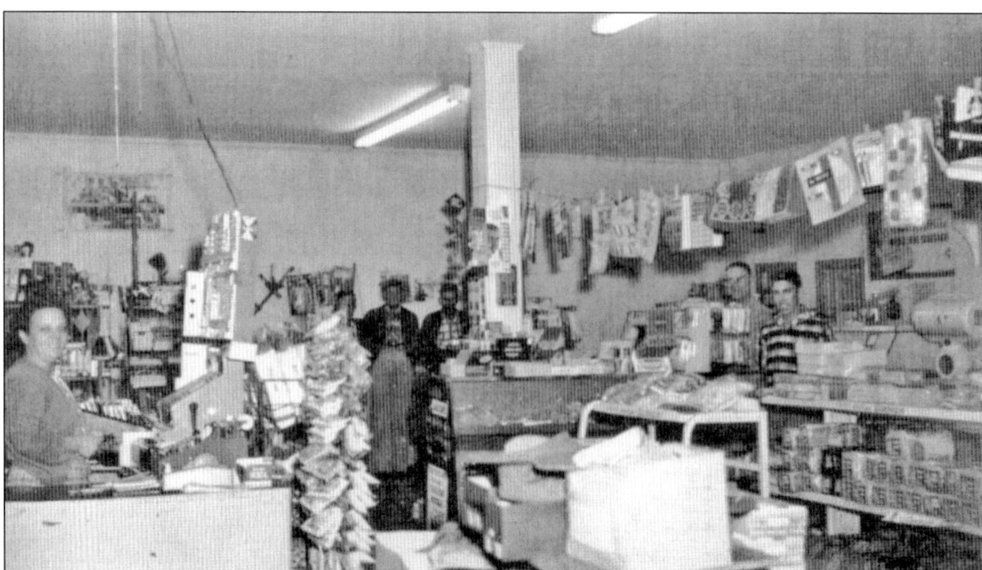

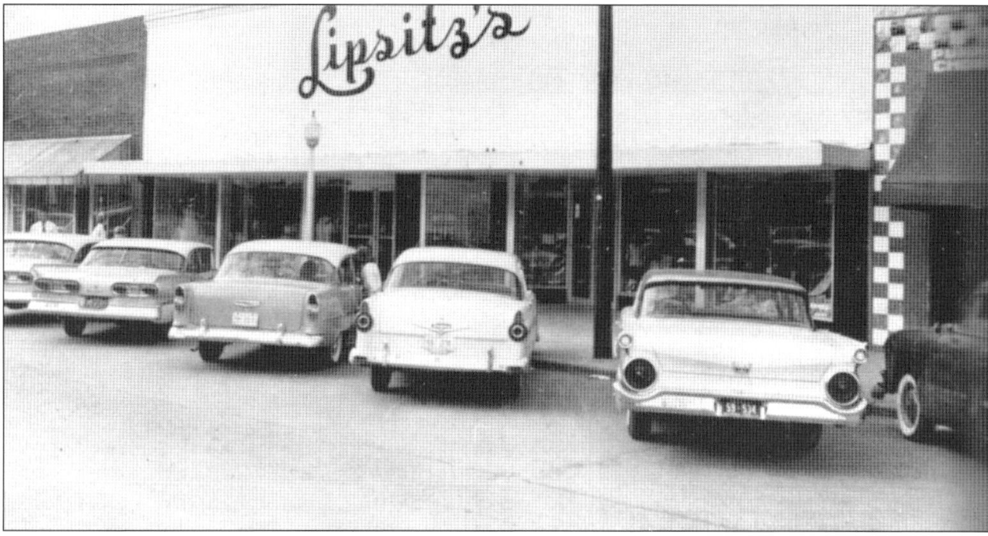

Lipsitz Department Store, shown here in 1959, was founded in 1897 by Russian Jewish immigrant Joseph Lipsitz. Following his death in 1919, his son Hyman (better known as "Hymie") operated the store, which was a mainstay of Glennville for many decades. In 1985, Lipsitz sold the business to Hugh Dorsey "H.D." Thompson Sr., who had already purchased part of the business years earlier. (Courtesy of the Glennville Public Library.)

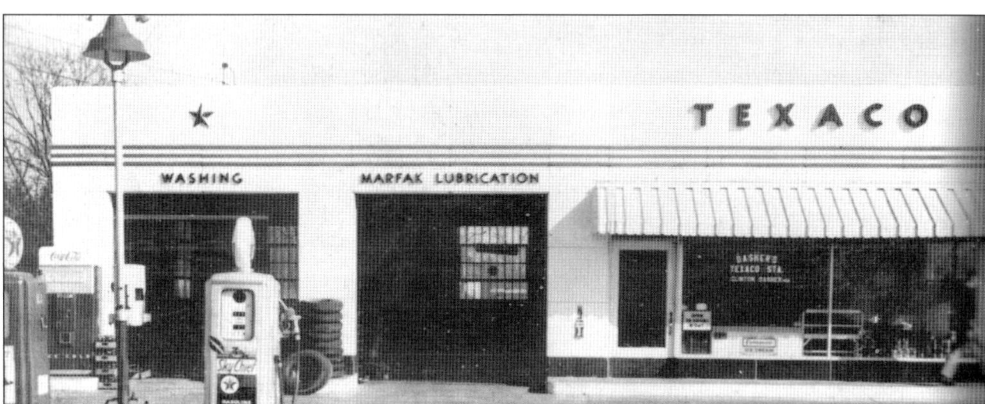

Dasher's Texaco Station, pictured here in 1958, was owned and operated by Mayor Joe Clinton Dasher Sr. The station still stands at the northeast corner of Charlton Street and Highway 301 South. (Courtesy of the Glennville Public Library.)

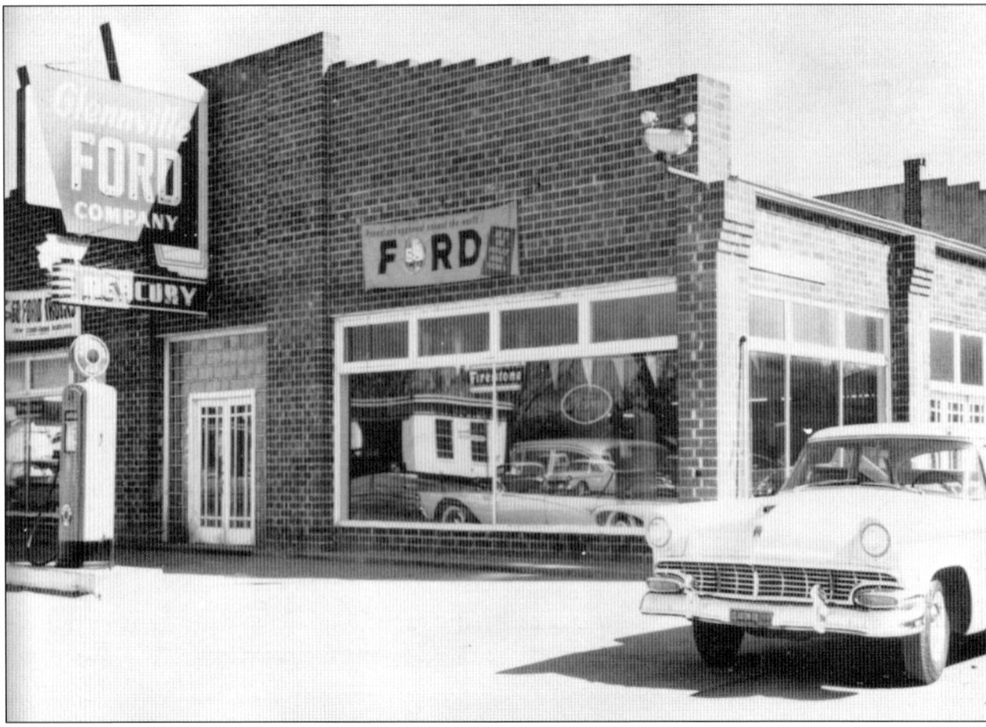

Glennville's Ford dealership, pictured above in 1958 and below in 1959, was built around 1946 by Erastus Waters as a Dodge and Plymouth dealership. It became a Ford dealership under the ownership of Clarence "Speed" Edenfield around 1951. Over the ensuing years, it was owned by Joe Wilkinson and later by Carl Butler and a Mr. Franklin, who operated the business as B&F Ford. In 1972, it was purchased by Eustis Waters, Wayne Durrence, and Brent Walker and operated as Brent Walker Ford-Mercury. Walker Ford remained in business until 2008. (Both, courtesy of the Glennville Public Library.)

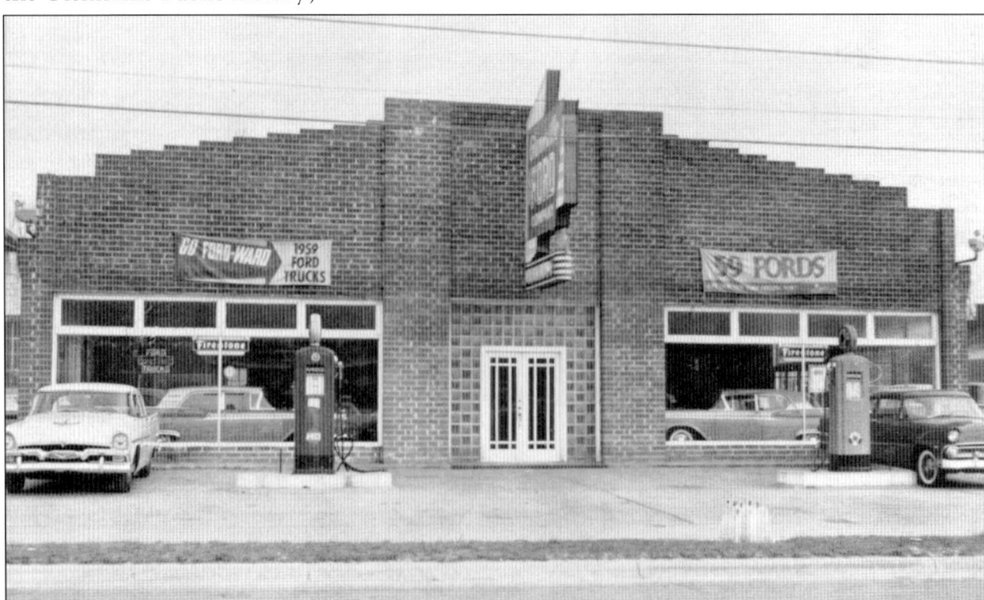

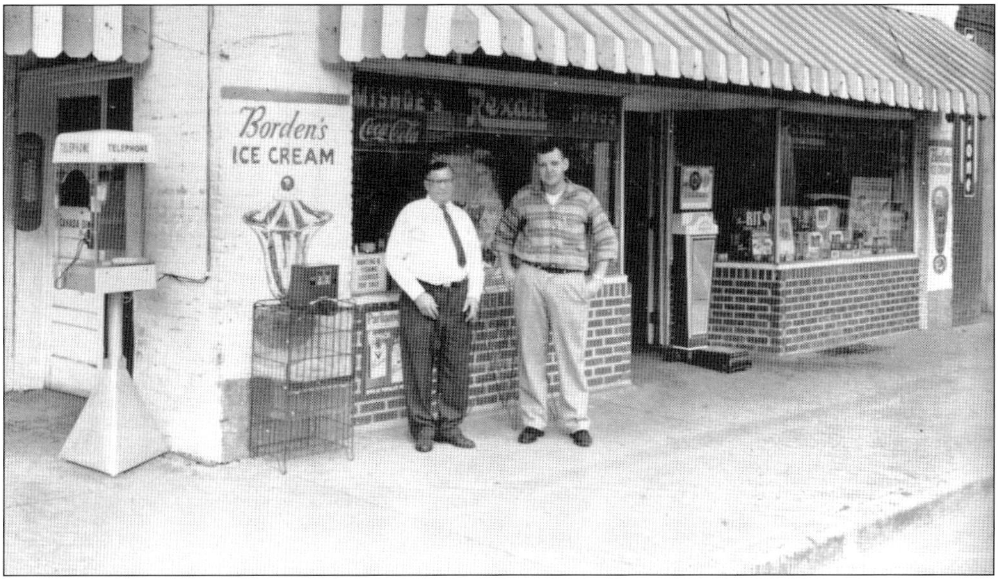

Pictured here in 1959 are Hal M. Mishoe (left) and John Ronald Durrence in front of Mishoe's Pharmacy, which stood at the northeast corner of Barnard and Main Streets. In addition to Rexall drugs, Mishoe's—like most drugstores—featured a soda fountain and sold ice cream. (Courtesy of the Glennville Public Library.)

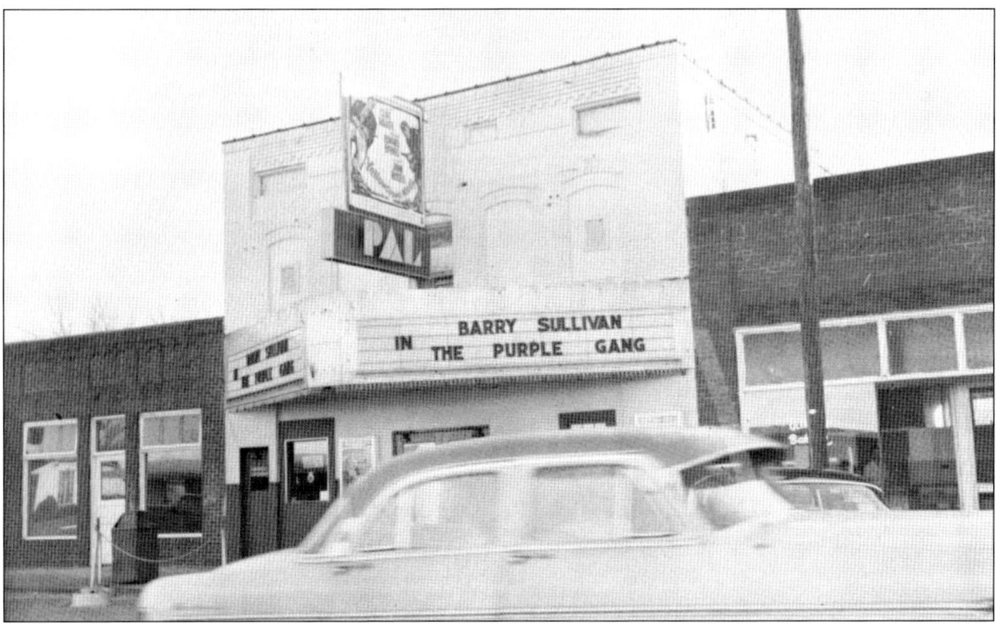

The Pal Theater, pictured around 1960, was built in 1926 by Hymie Lipsitz and Hinton Nelson and was one of Glennville's most popular venues, providing entertainment for many years before closing around 1970. Formerly known as the Glennville Theater, Princess Theater, and Rex Theater, it was located in the two-story building that still stands between the Glennwanis Service Station and Strickland's Pharmacy. (Courtesy of the Glennville Bank.)

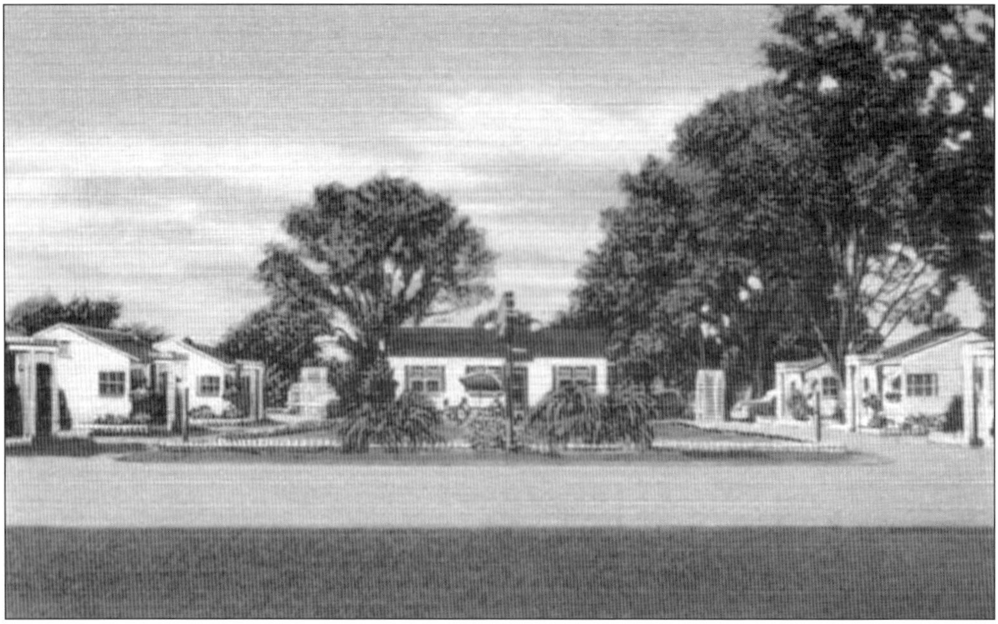

Glen Haven Motor Court, pictured above, was Glennville's first motel and was owned by Curtis and Betty Burns. It stood on the west side of Highway 301 just south of Mendell Avenue. The "cottages" were actually repurposed barracks moved from Fort Stewart just after World War II. Just south of the motor court was the Burns's Glen Haven Restaurant, pictured below. This restaurant was later purchased by Robert Rushing and Vernon Dasher Sr., who renamed it the Red Steer. Dasher eventually bought Rushing's share and managed the restaurant with his wife, Glorida. The Red Steer, which was recognizable by a large cow in front, was located at the present site of McDonald's. (Above, courtesy of Brent Walker; below, courtesy of the Glennville Bank.)

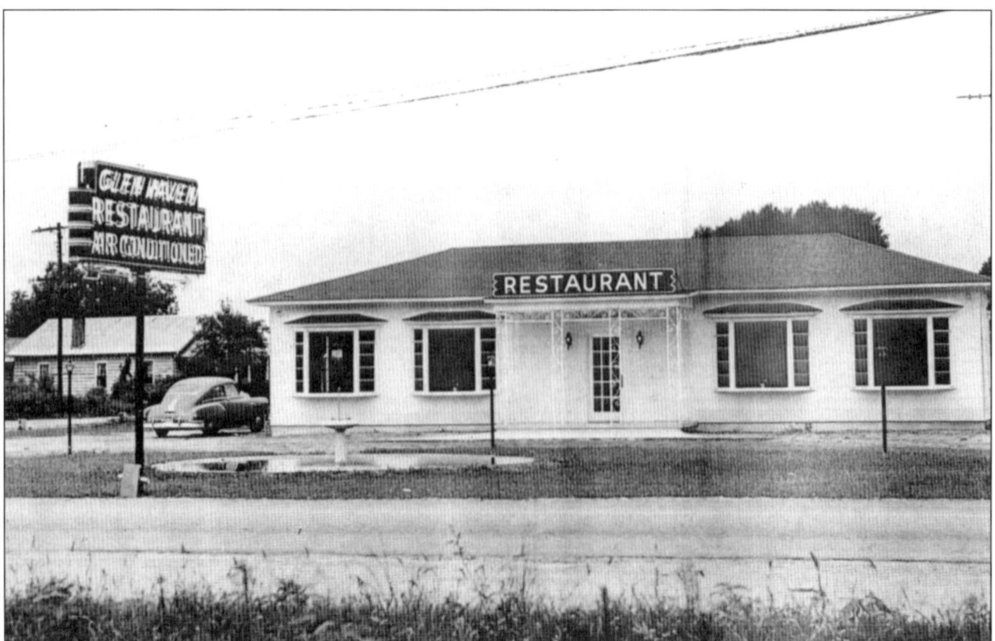

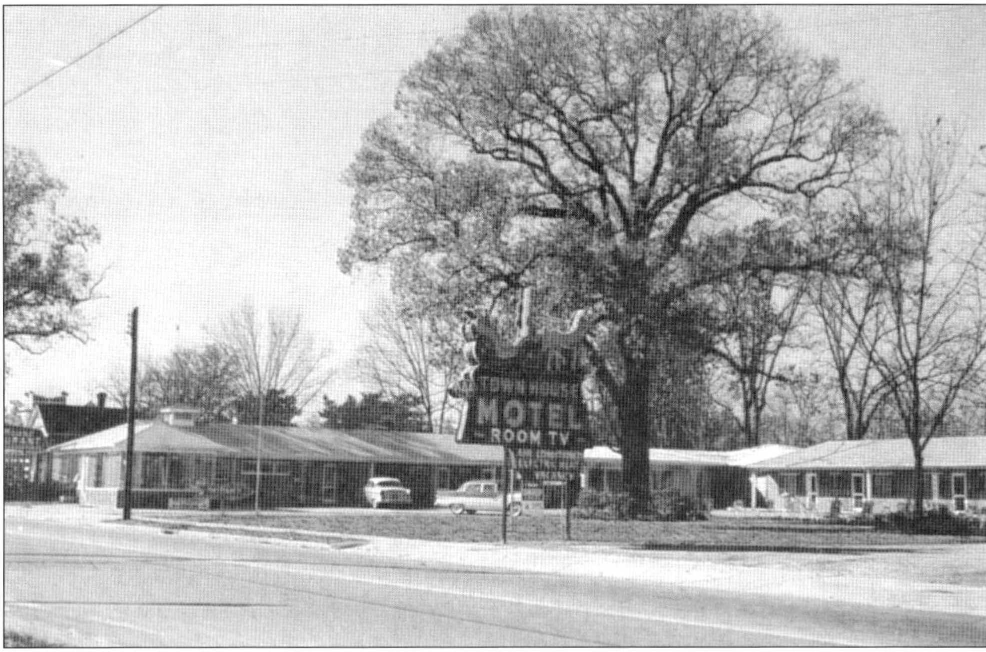

The Town House Motel, pictured in this 1958 postcard, stood on the west side of Highway 301 just north of Barnard Street next to Rimes Mortuary. Like many motels, the Town House featured a restaurant that was a popular gathering place for local men in the mornings to eat breakfast and discuss the news of the day. (Courtesy of Brent Walker.)

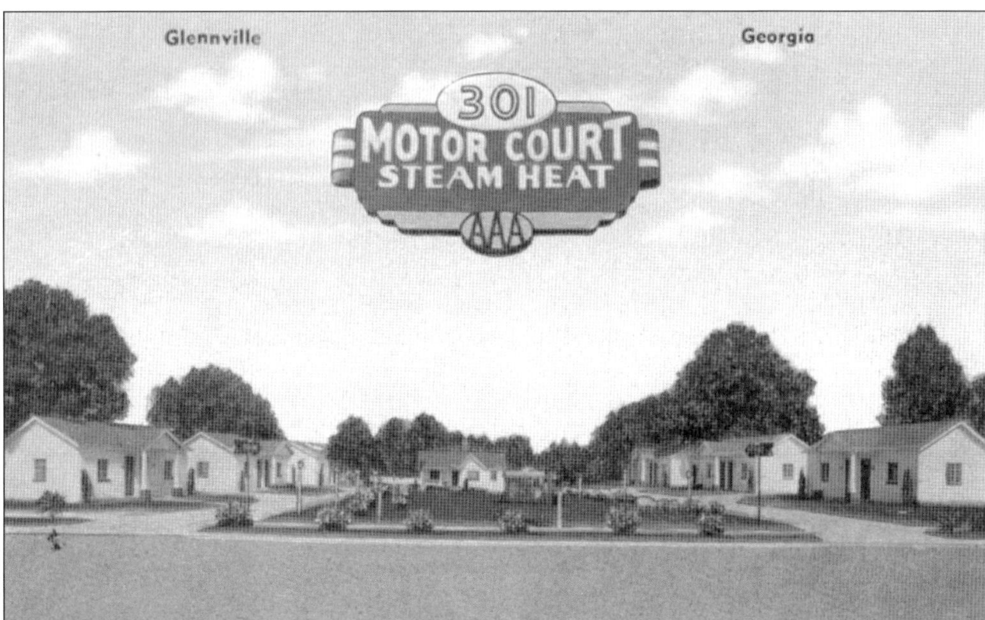

The 301 Motor Court stood on the west side of Highway 301 North across from Cedar Street. The site is now occupied by Mi Plaza Mexican restaurant. (Courtesy of Brent Walker.)

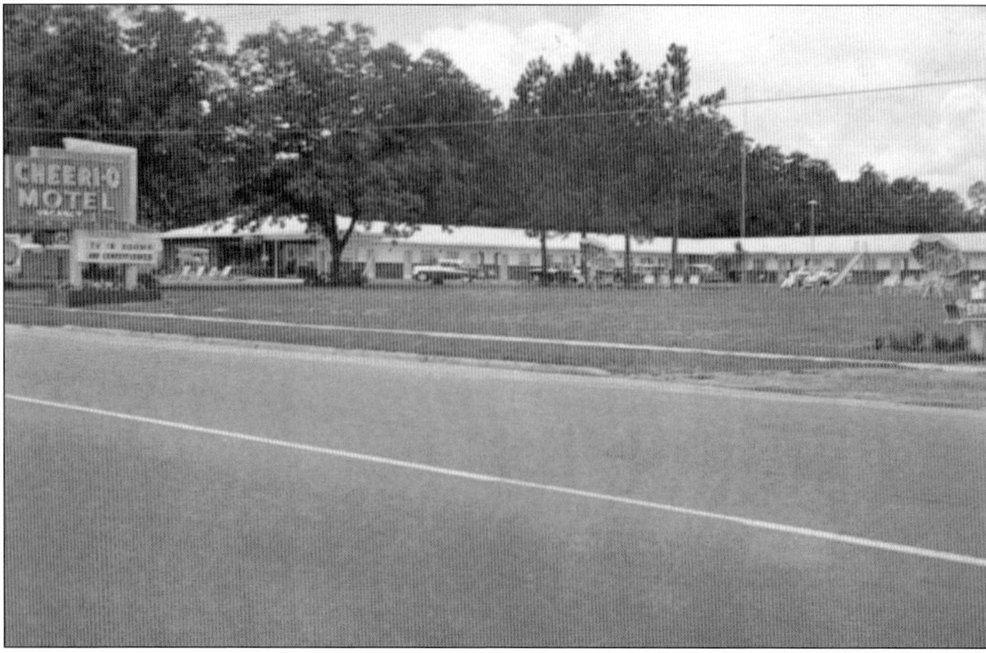

Of all the motels that once thrived in Glennville, only the Cheeri-O on Highway 301 South remains in business. (Courtesy of Brent Walker.)

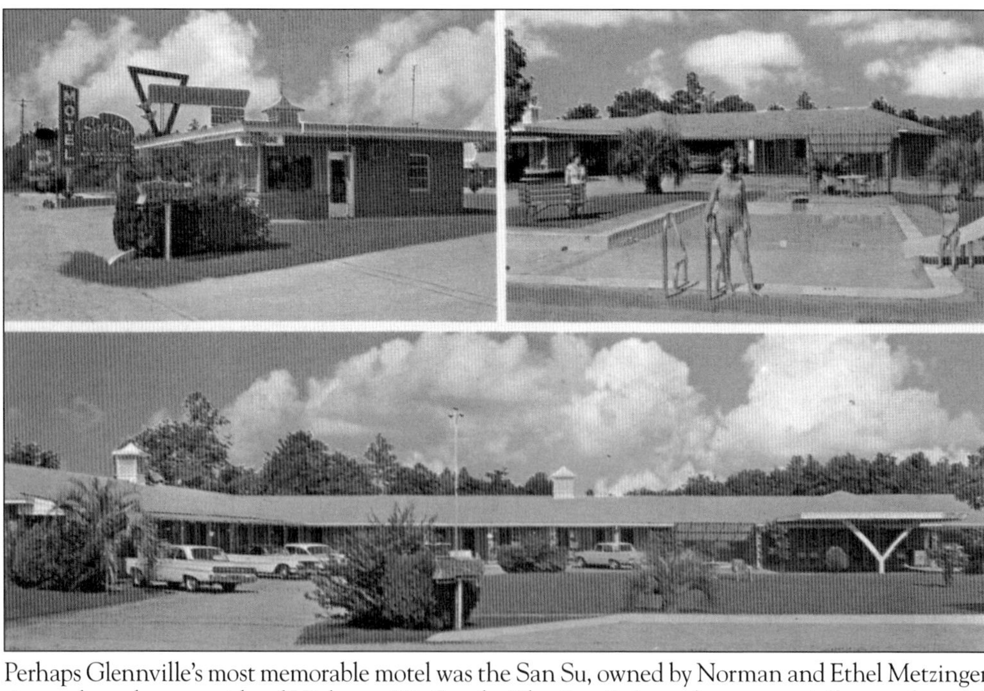

Perhaps Glennville's most memorable motel was the San Su, owned by Norman and Ethel Metzinger, situated on the west side of Highway 301 South. The San Su's pool was especially popular with local youth. In the 1970s, one could pay $1 per person to swim all day. The concrete slabs and palm trees of the San Su are still visible today. (Courtesy of Brent Walker.)

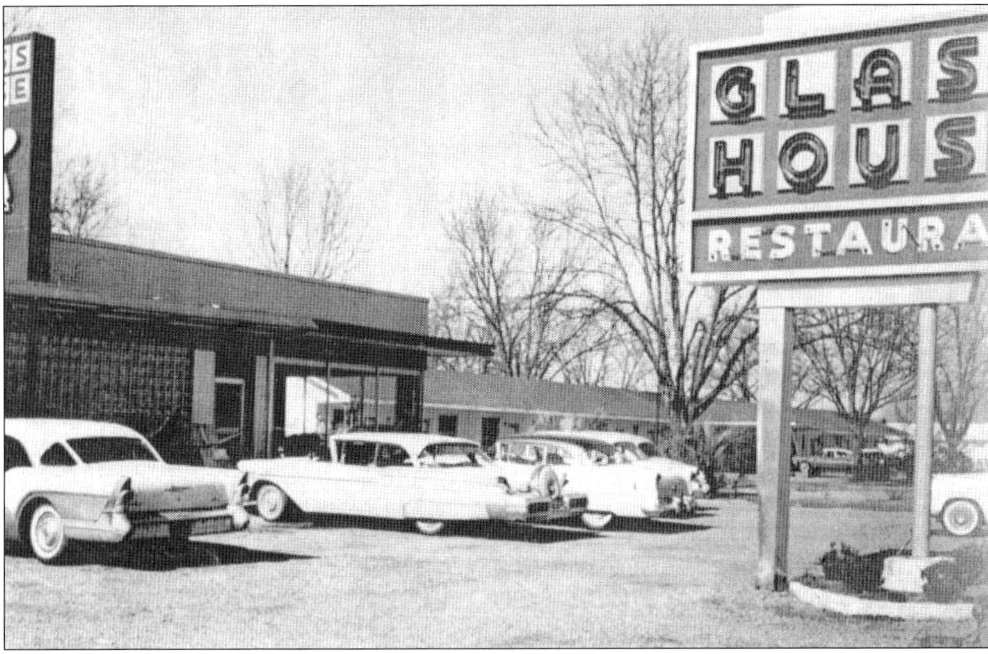

The Glass House Motor Lodge stood on the west side of Highway 301 South, across from the Mascot. Adjacent to the motel was the popular Glass House Restaurant, actually a franchise separate from the motel. Both the restaurant and motel are still standing, though the motel is abandoned and the restaurant is no longer open. (Courtesy of the Glennville Bank.)

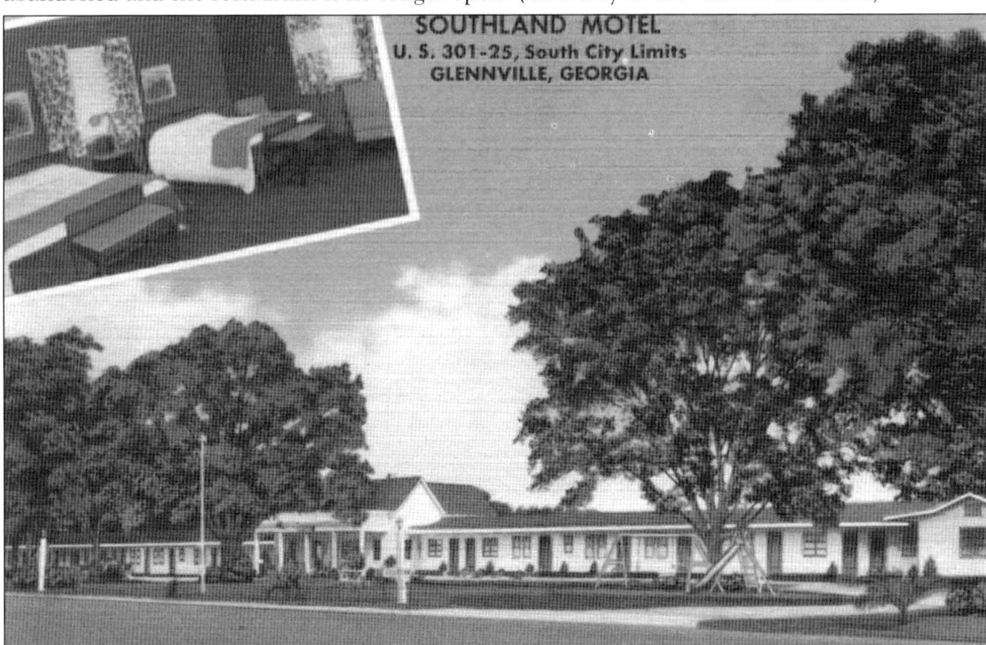

Built in 1948 as Glennville's second motel, A.G. Oliver's Southland Motel stood on the east side of Highway 301 South just north of the Mascot, where that business's parking lot is now located. During the Vietnam War, many Army officers from Fort Stewart called the Southland home. (Courtesy of Brent Walker.)

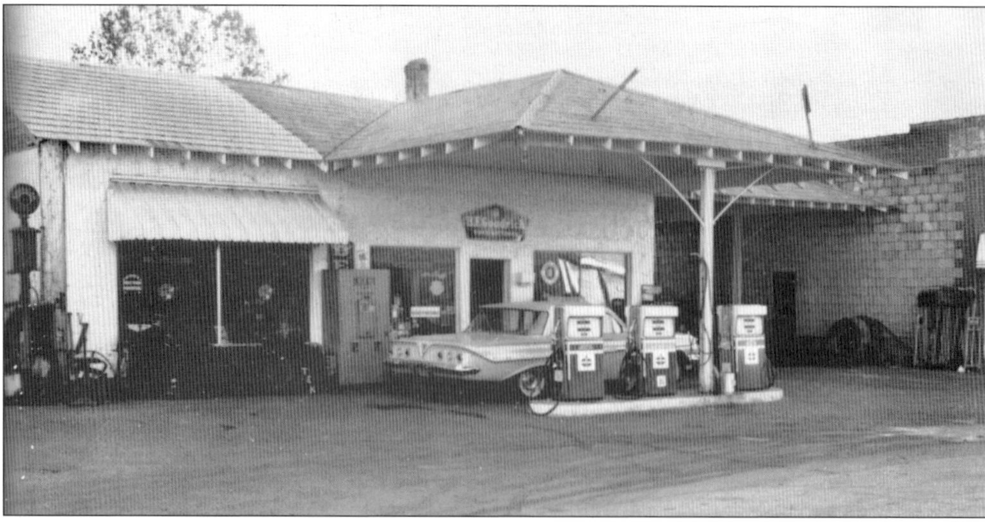

After the dismantling of the Register & Glennville Railroad, the depot was converted into a filling station in 1923. The popular Glennwanis Service Station, shown here in 1962, was operated for several decades by Tommie Kirkland. A machine selling locally-bottled Kist drinks is visible against the wall. (Courtesy of the Glennville Public Library.)

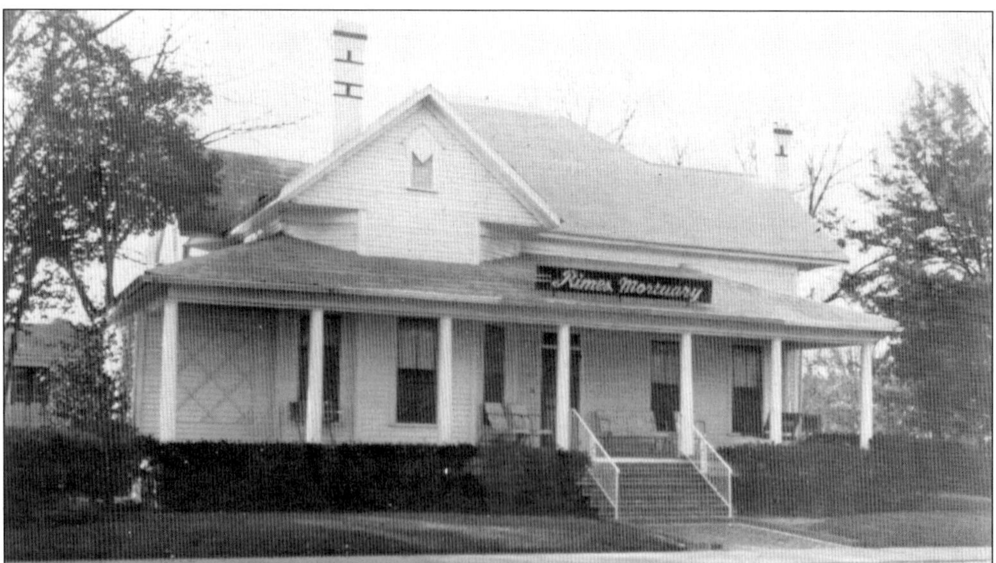

Jack A. Rimes Sr. and Lillian Rimes first went into business with Tanner-Poindexter Funeral Home in 1935 and purchased the business soon after. In 1947, Rimes Mortuary purchased the home pictured here in 1963. The house had been built around 1910 by Russell Clayton "Uncle Rat" Dubberly. Jack A. Rimes Jr. would continue his father's business, along with his wife, until 1993. (Courtesy of the Glennville Public Library.)

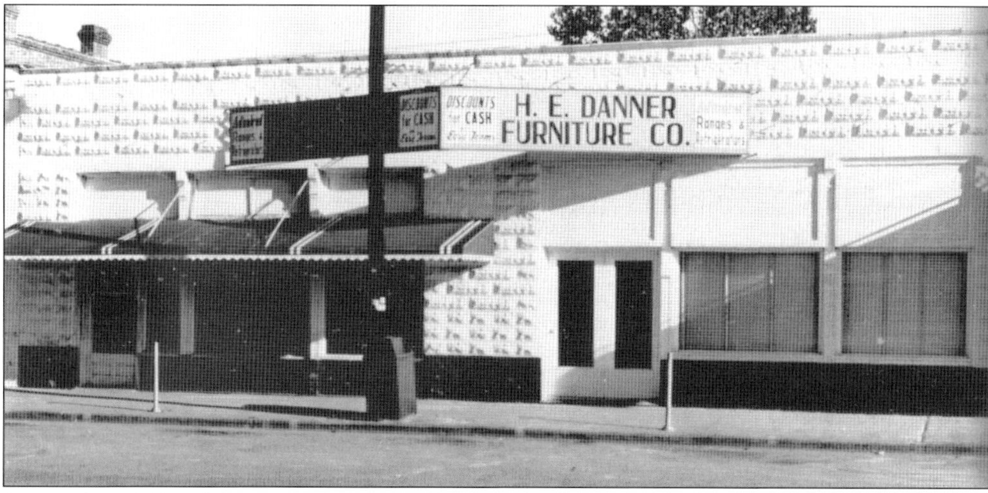

Pictured in 1963 is the H.E. Danner Furniture Company, owned by Edgar Danner Jr. This building was located on Barnard Street between the Glennville Bank and Charlie Rowland's Western Auto. The furniture company occupied this site until 1967, when it moved to a metal building (now the Supply Company) on Highway 301 South, where it remained until closing in 1981. (Courtesy of the Glennville Public Library.)

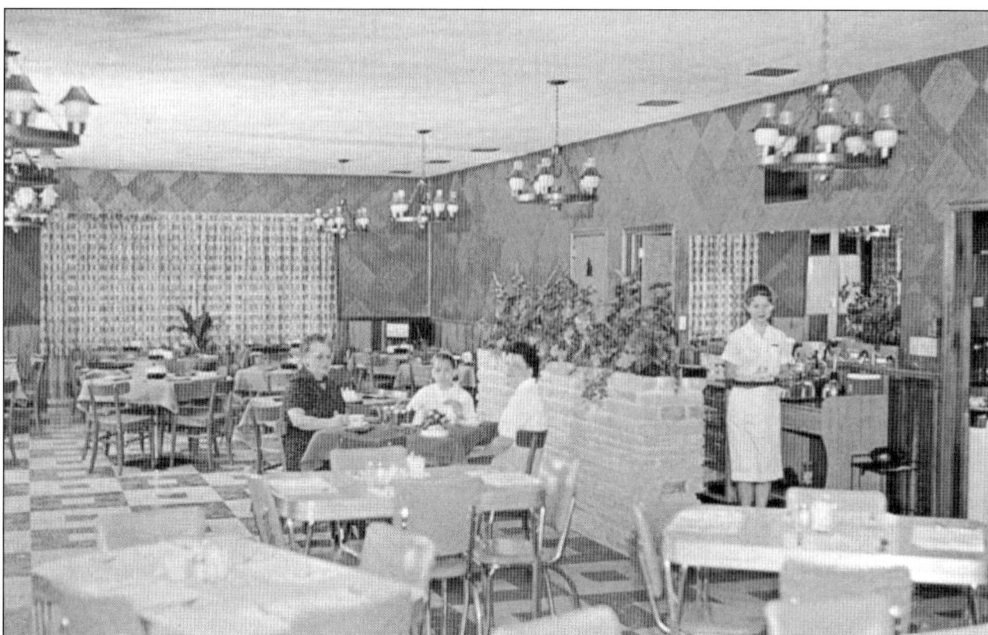

The Red Steer restaurant, pictured in this postcard from the early to mid-1960s, stood on Highway 301 South at the present site of McDonald's. Seated at the table are, from left to right, Nell Kirkland Avant, Jeanie Dasher, and Glorida Durrence Dasher. Glorida and Jeanie were the wife and daughter of the restaurant's owner, Vernon Dasher Sr. (Courtesy of Brent Walker.)

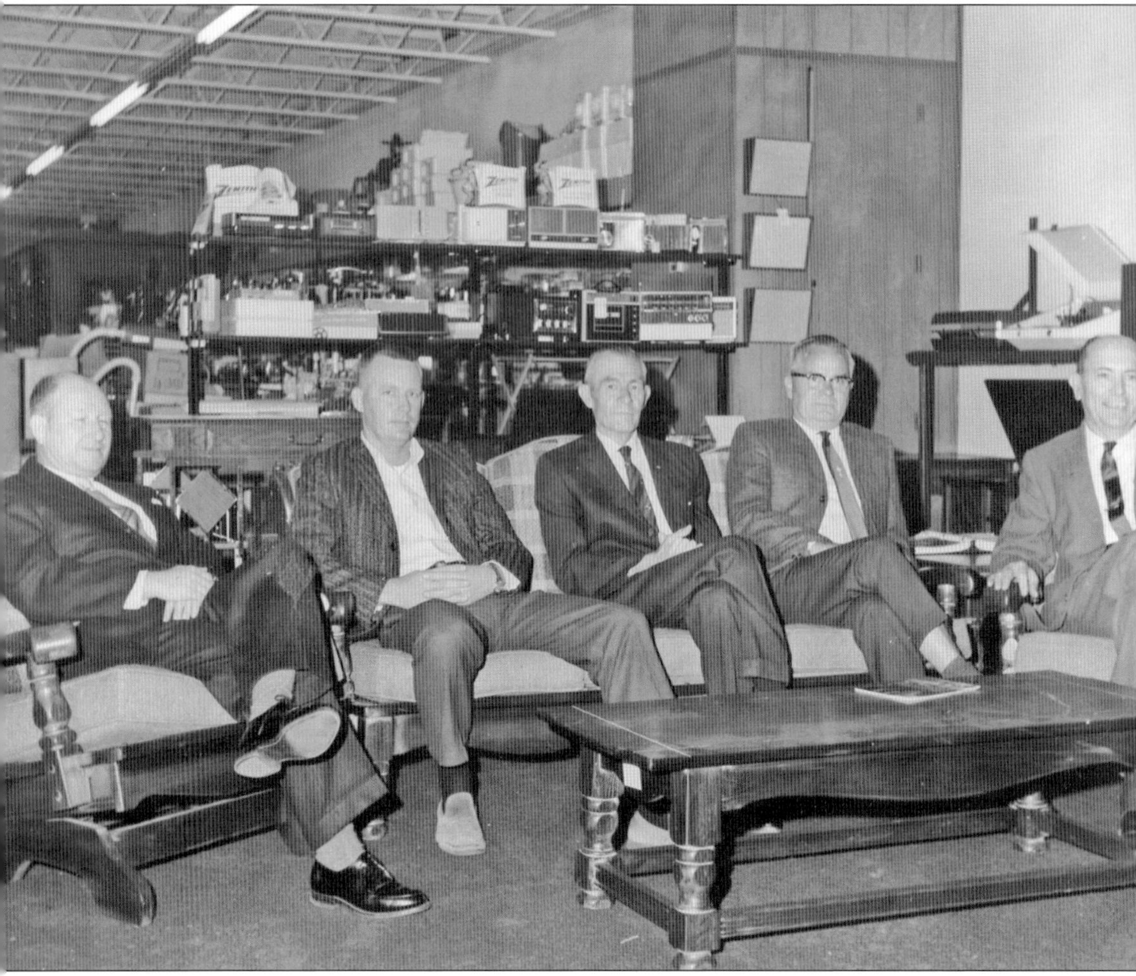

From left to right are city councilmen J.C. Woodcock, James "Jim" Tootle, James "Jimmy" Kemp, Waldo Kicklighter, and Mayor Charlie E. Rowland in Dream Home Furnishings—Rowland's prominent furniture store located in the large building on Barnard Street between Railroad and Tillman Streets. This building is now home to Gibson-McDonald. This photograph was taken in 1968 or 1969, soon after the store opened. Rowland (1916–2000) was a native of Buena Vista, Tennessee. Rowland and his wife, Susie, moved to Glennville in July 1952 after Rowland served in World War II. Rowland served as one of the town's most beloved and progressive mayors from 1970 to 1973, 1976 to 1977, and 1982 to 1987, and made many substantial contributions to the town's development during those times. (Courtesy of the City of Glennville.)

Five

INDUSTRY AND AGRICULTURE

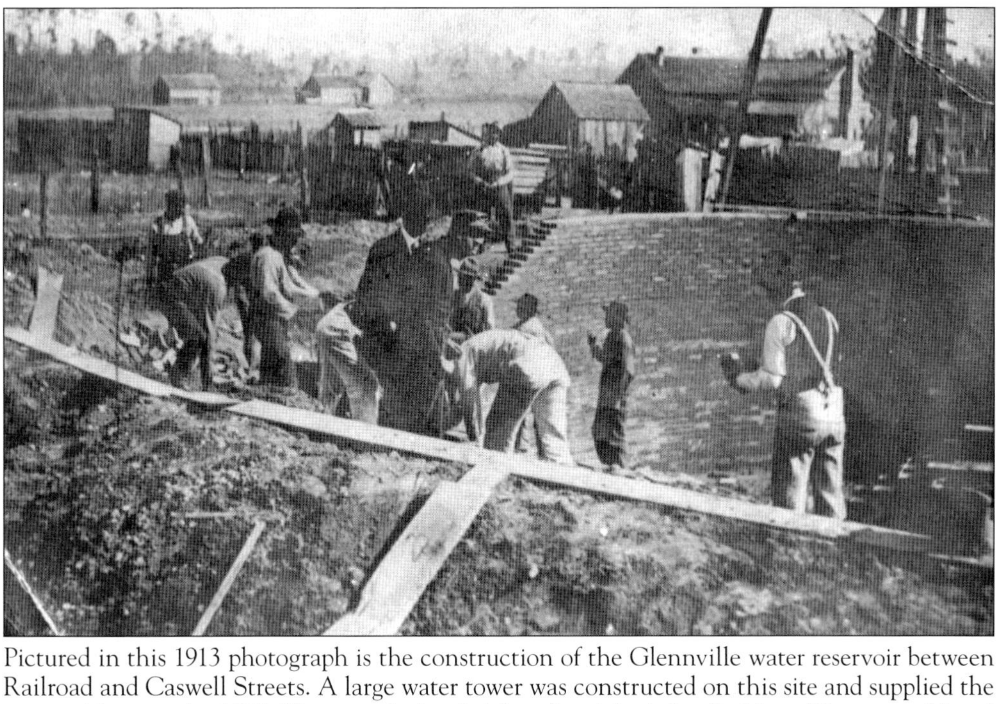

Pictured in this 1913 photograph is the construction of the Glennville water reservoir between Railroad and Caswell Streets. A large water tower was constructed on this site and supplied the town with water by 1915. The man laying brick at far right is Iva Perkins. (Courtesy of Jewel Perkins Woodcock.)

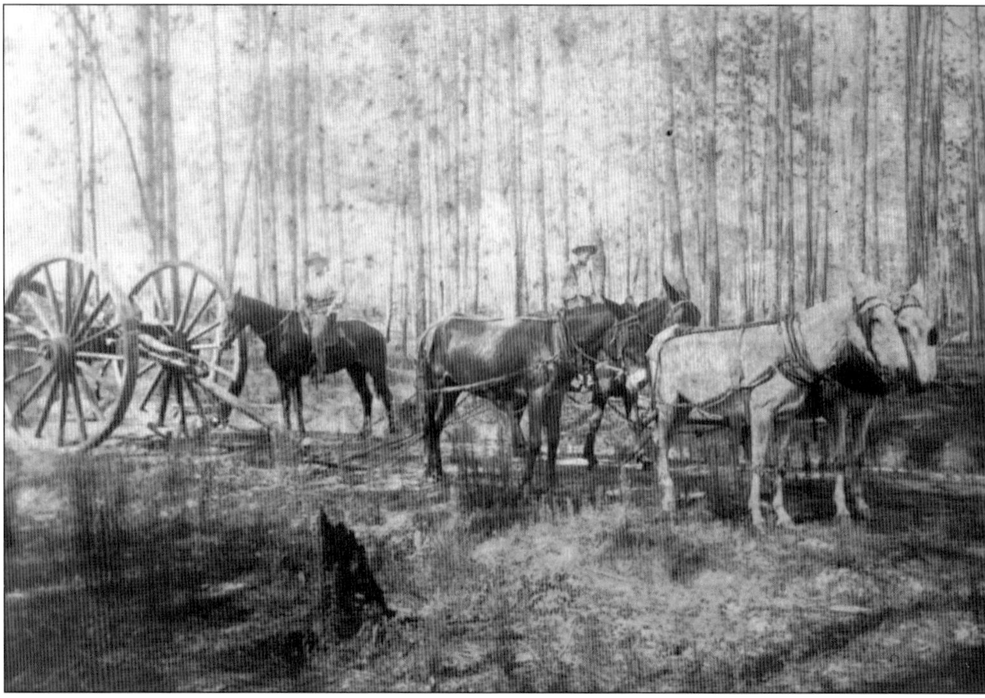

Since the earliest days of settlement in Tattnall County, timber has always been a mainstay of the local economy. After the Civil War, the Georgia timber industry began to grow exponentially. After the timber was cut, large logs were suspended beneath a skidder pulled by mules or oxen, as pictured here. (Perkins.)

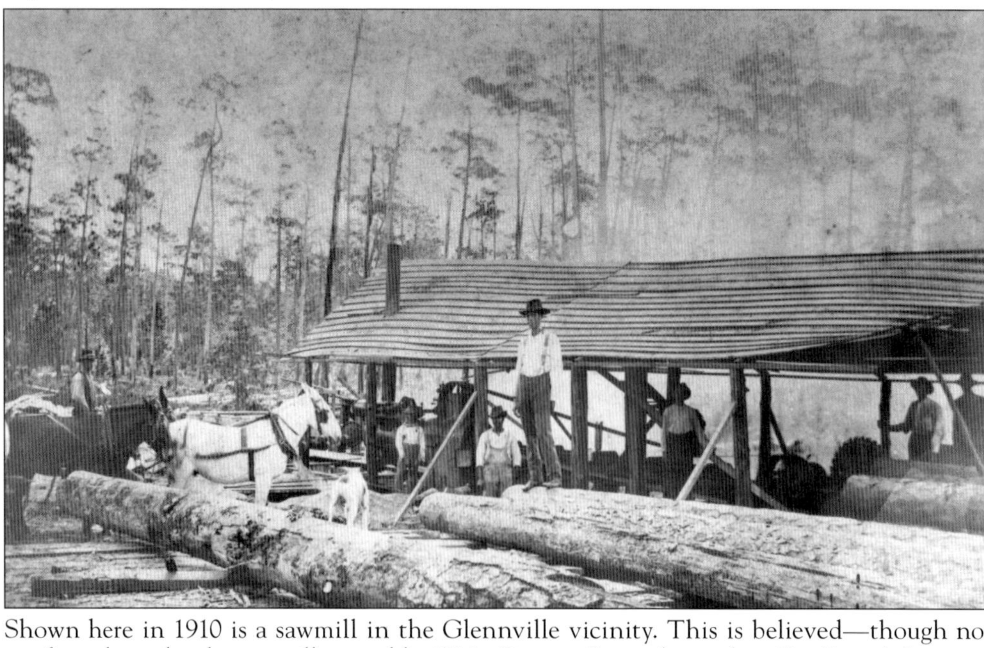

Shown here in 1910 is a sawmill in the Glennville vicinity. This is believed—though not confirmed—to be the sawmill owned by W.A. Canuet. It was located on Big Branch between China and Marietta Streets and was the scene of a horrific boiler explosion on February 22, 1929. The blast completely destroyed the mill and left several dead and seriously injured. (Perkins.)

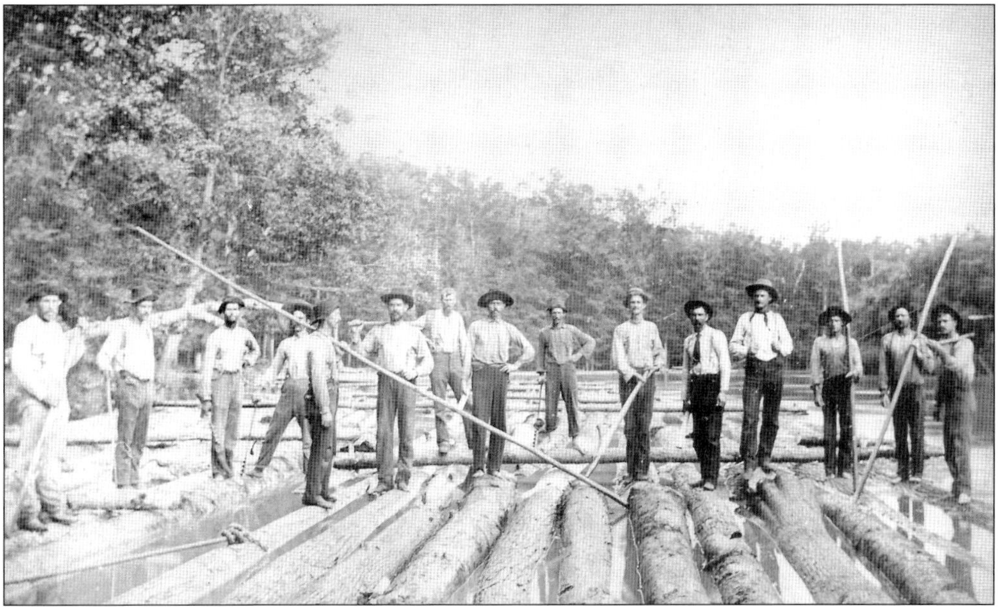

Most timber was cut in the Altamaha River swamps and fashioned into "timber rafts," like the one seen here. The timber was then rafted downriver to Darien, which was one of the world's leading exporters of pine from the 1870s until the first decade of the 20th century. Upon reaching Darien, the timber was sold, squared, and loaded into ships waiting in Doboy and Sapelo Sounds. (GTM.)

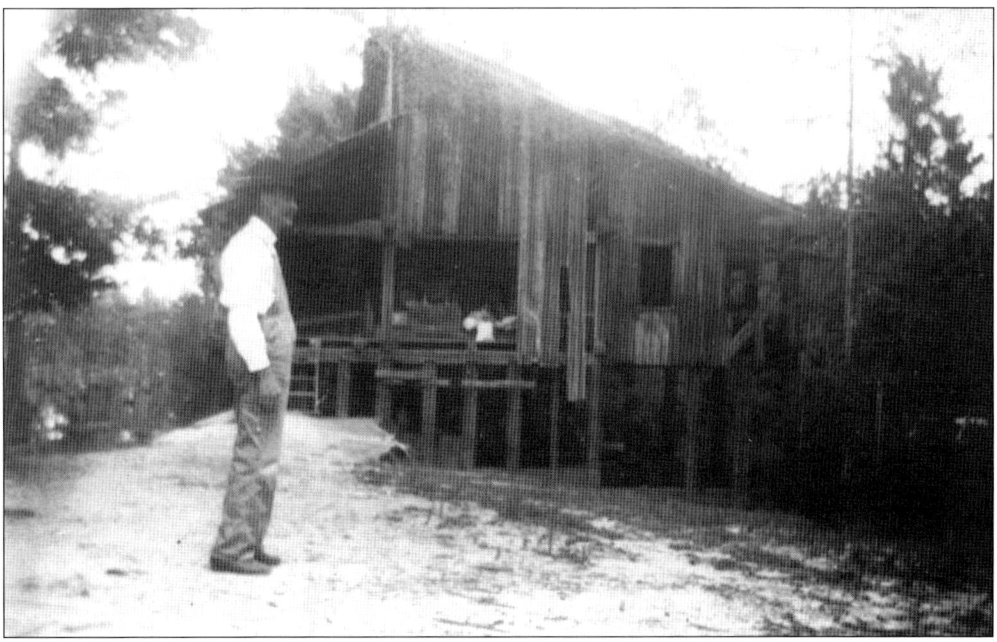

Charles Columbus Padgett is pictured around 1904 at one of his two gristmills on Watermelon Creek. This is likely the Water Mill, which featured a gristmill and sawmill on separate runs of the creek. Water Mill was built before the Civil War at Tison Crossroads on property presently occupied by Watermelon Creek Vineyard. The second, Lower Mill, was built in 1865 downstream near the present crossing of Highway 144. (GTM.)

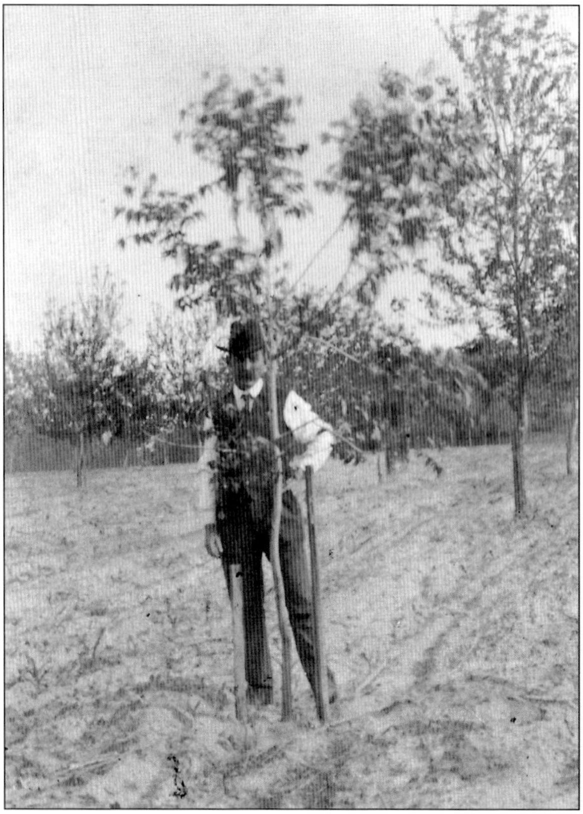

Prominent farmer John Martin Brewton, pictured at left around 1910–1915, pioneered the pecan industry in Southeast Georgia and North Florida. Georgia's first pecan boom lasted from around 1910 to 1925, and during that time, many orchards were planted by local farmers. Brewton planted his first trees in 1906; in 1925, the Brewton Pecan Company reported that it had shipped over 75,000 pounds of pecans from Glennville during the last season. Brewton also operated a large pecan nursery, pictured below, which supplied most of the early seedling trees to farmers in Tattnall and surrounding counties. As a result, many of the older pecan orchards in the area trace their lineage back to this nursery. The Brewton orchard—one of the oldest in the state—is still owned by his descendants on the road that bears his name. (Both, courtesy of Ann Keels Whiten.)

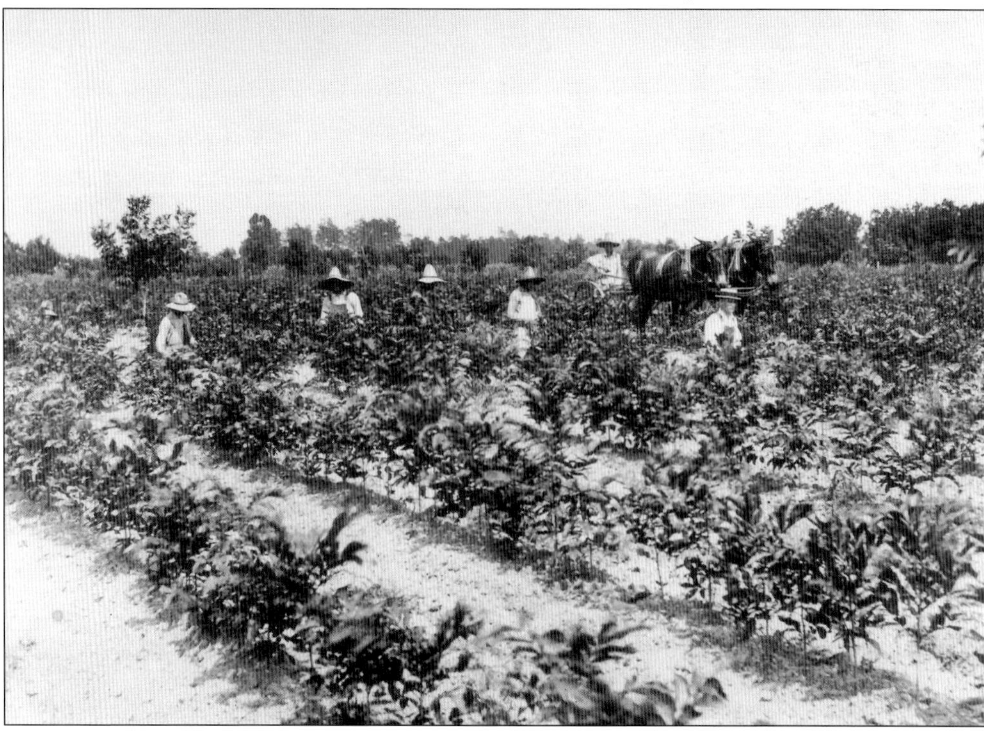

This photograph, taken around 1933, shows a typical Tattnall County barnyard scene at the farm of Byron G. Rogers, located east of Glennville. A child thought to be Rogers's daughter, Edna Belle, feeds ears of corn to the hogs. (Courtesy of Dylan Edward Mulligan.)

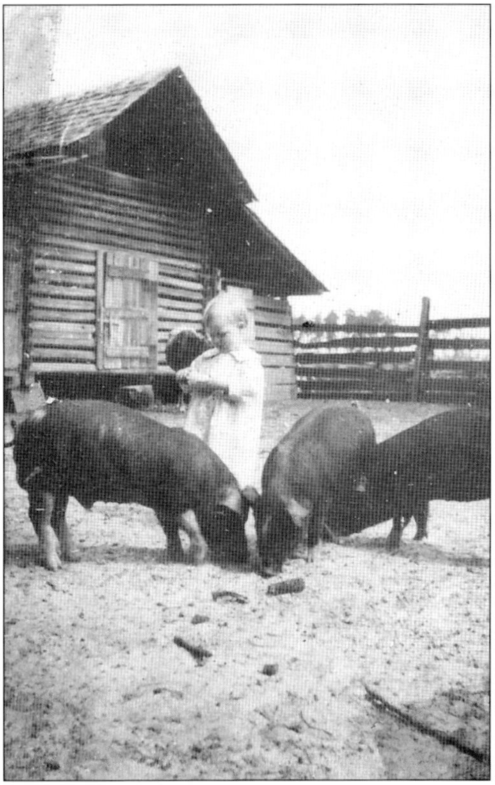

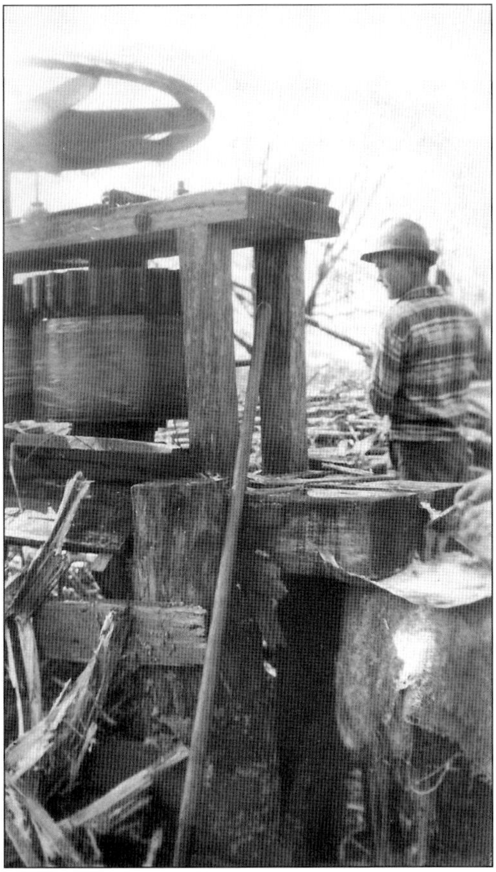

A common fixture on many larger farms was a sugarcane mill, like the one pictured here on the Rogers farm. In this late 1930s photograph, W.A. "Billy" Rogers feeds sugarcane into the mill's rollers, which were rotated by a log sweep hitched to a mule. The extracted juice was then taken to the adjacent boiler house to be cooked into syrup. (Courtesy of Dylan Edward Mulligan.)

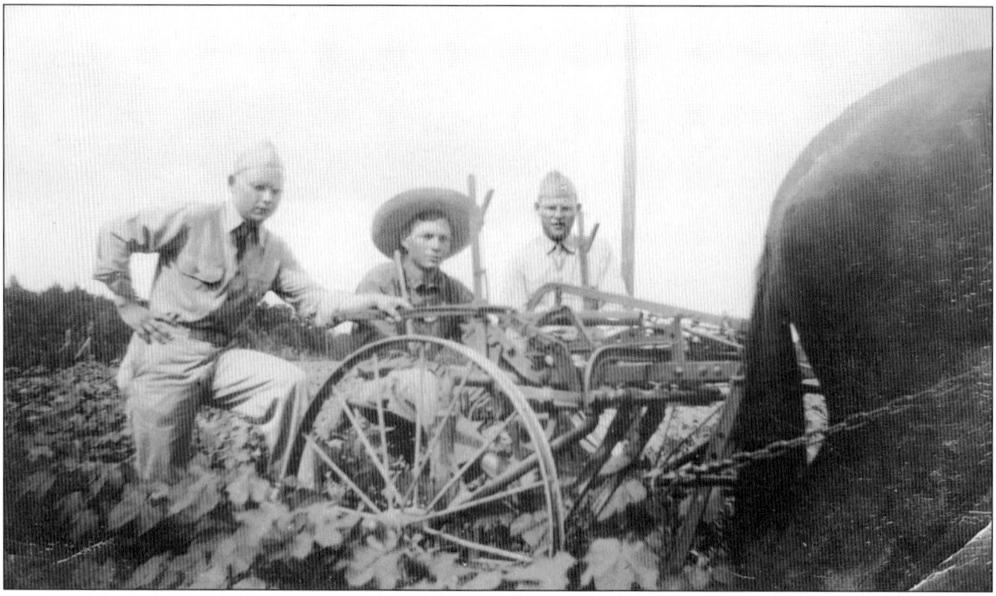

Pictured from left to right in 1942 are brothers Rupert, Earl, and Ruther Odom, with Earl seated on a plow pulled by a mule. (Courtesy of Janice Odom Steenken.)

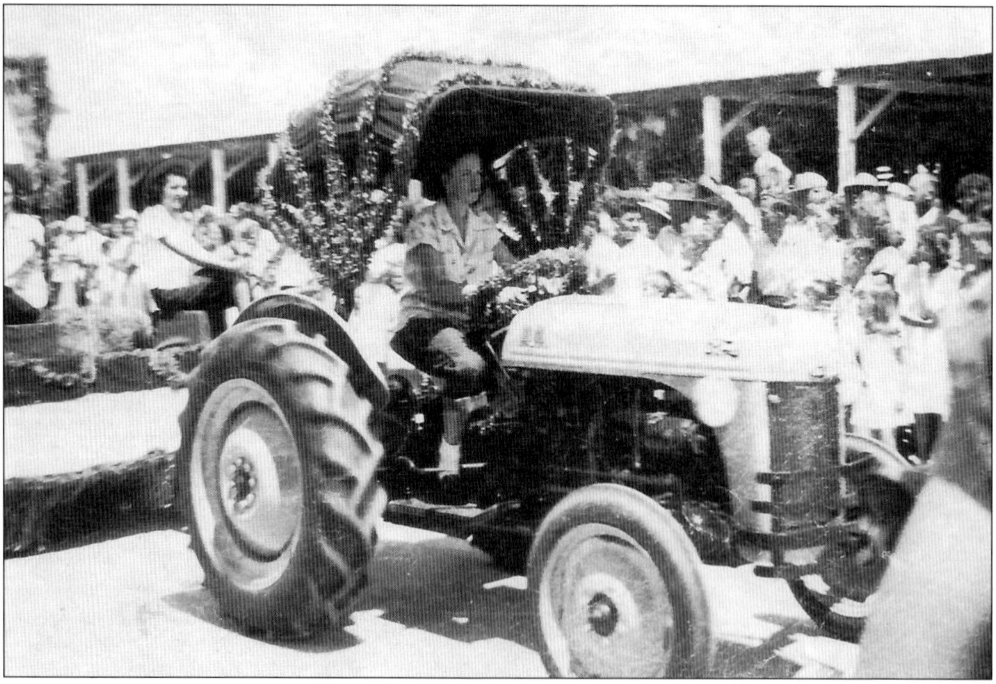

In 1939, Glennville farmer Byron Rogers attended a Ford Ferguson (Fordson) tractor demonstration at Henry Ford's Richmond Hill plantation. Rogers was so impressed that he went to a tractor dealer in Statesboro and purchased a 1939 Fordson 9N, which was the first rubber-tire tractor in Tattnall County. In 1942, Rogers purchased another Fordson and soon after abandoned his mule team, turning his large farm into the first fully mechanized operation in the Glennville area. In this early 1950s photograph, Edna Belle Rogers Mulligan—daughter of Byron and Julia Rogers—drives the 1939 Fordson in a tomato festival parade. (Courtesy of Dylan Edward Mulligan.)

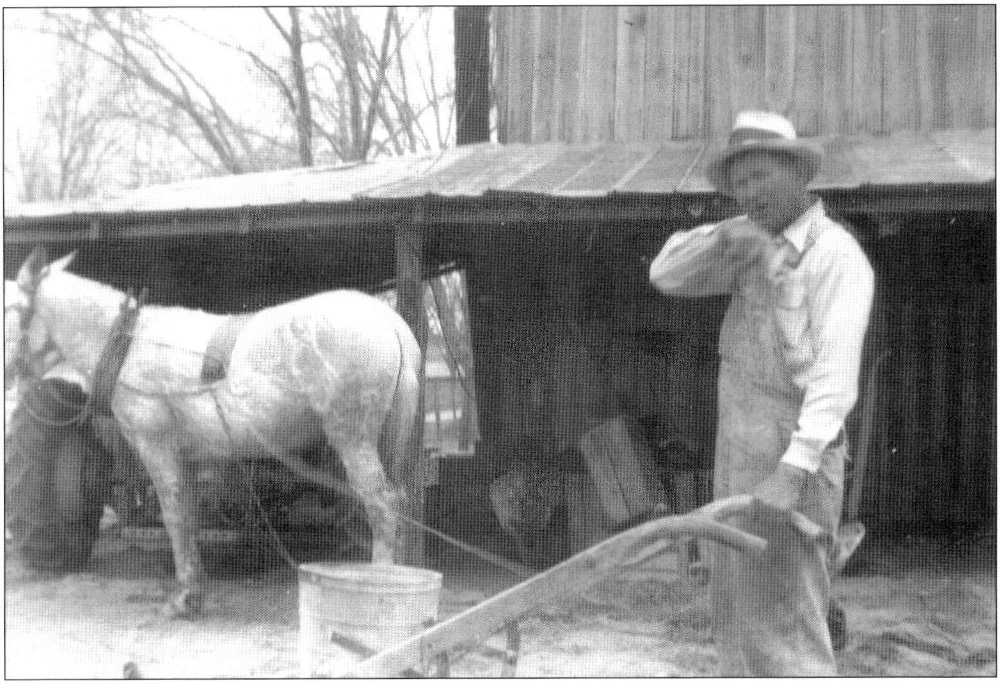

Pictured here around 1950 is prominent Glennville farmer Dan J. Dasher, standing behind a fertilizer hopper in front of his tobacco barn, which was located on the family farm southeast of town on Highway 196. In the background is a paradox of agriculture: Daisy the mule and a Ford tractor under the shed. In the 1950s, many farms still used both mules and tractors. (Courtesy of Julian Dasher.)

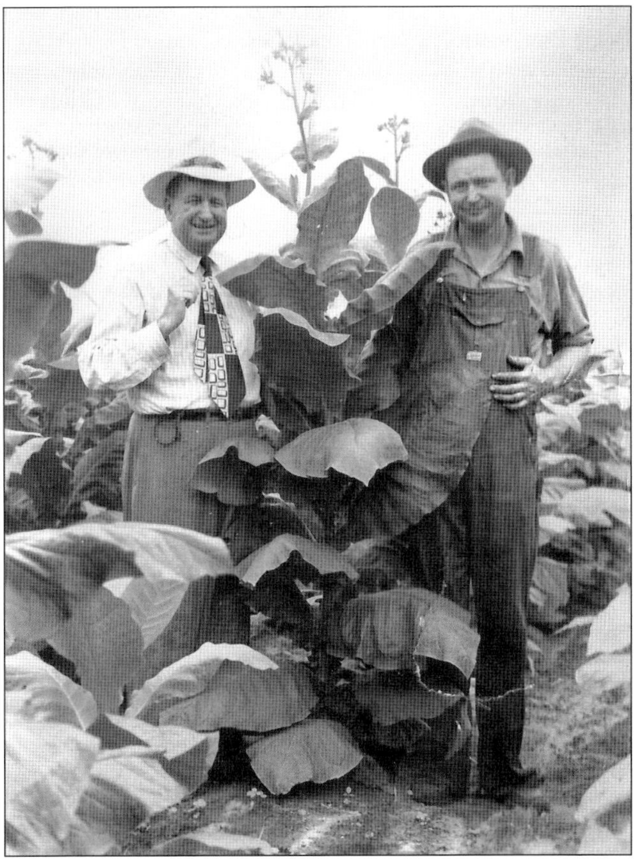

County extension agent Joe Johnson (left) examines the tobacco crop of Walter L. Dasher (right) in this early 1950s photograph. The Dasher farm was located east of Glennville off Highway 144 on Dasher Road. (Courtesy of G&R Farms.)

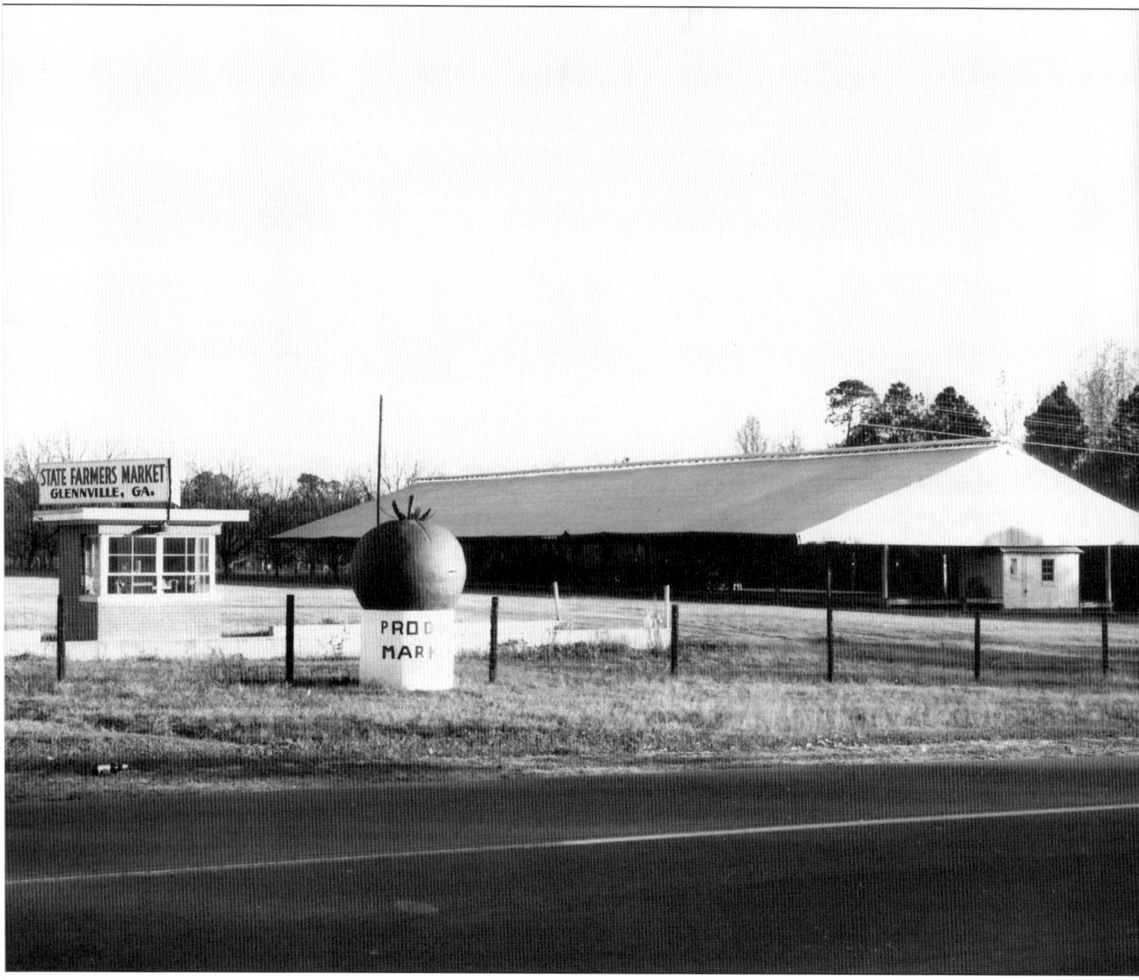

Glennville's second and present farmers' market was constructed in the early 1950s on Highway 301 South on land donated by Robert Clinton "Bob" DeLoach, father of Reese DeLoach, who owned the adjacent 301 Drive Inn. The giant metal tomato originally stood at First Baptist Church (as seen on page 104) and was moved in the 1940s to the old farmers' market on Highway 301 North. After the completion of the present market, the tomato moved again, as seen here in 1957. When built, the market featured two long sheds like the one pictured here. The above building was situated on the lower part of the property and is no longer standing; however, the other identical shed (not pictured) is still in use and stands just to the north, to the left of the tomato and weigh station. (Courtesy of the City of Glennville.)

Six

SOCIETY

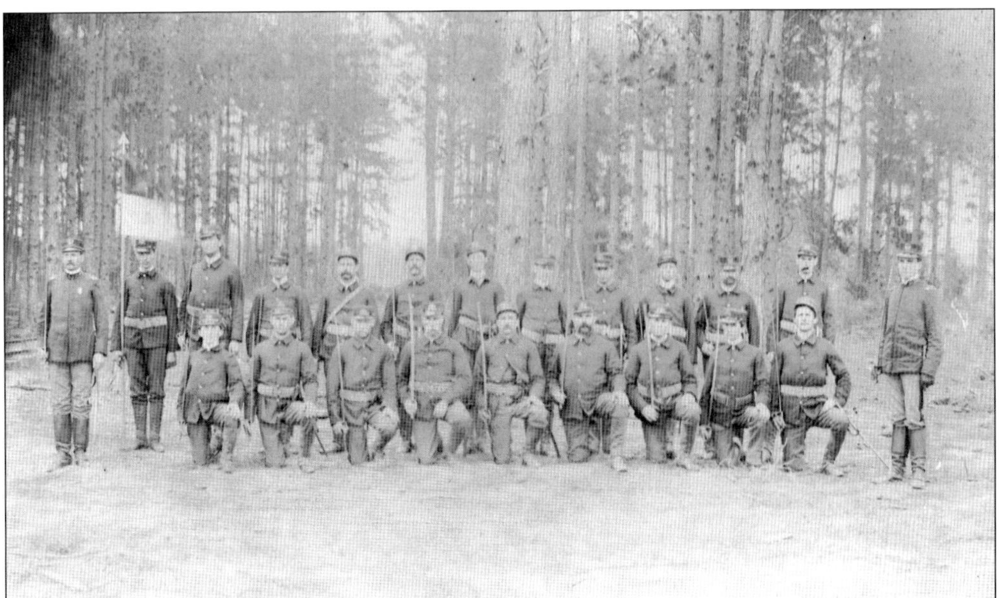

Much beloved in any community were its local militia units, such as the Meldrim Tattnall Guards pictured here around 1900. In addition to serving defensive purposes, the militias performed a variety of social functions, such as providing maintenance on roads and bridges, offering services for the underprivileged, and hosting cavalry balls and other events. John D. Bradley Sr. is kneeling at front left. (Courtesy of Richard Bradley Jr.)

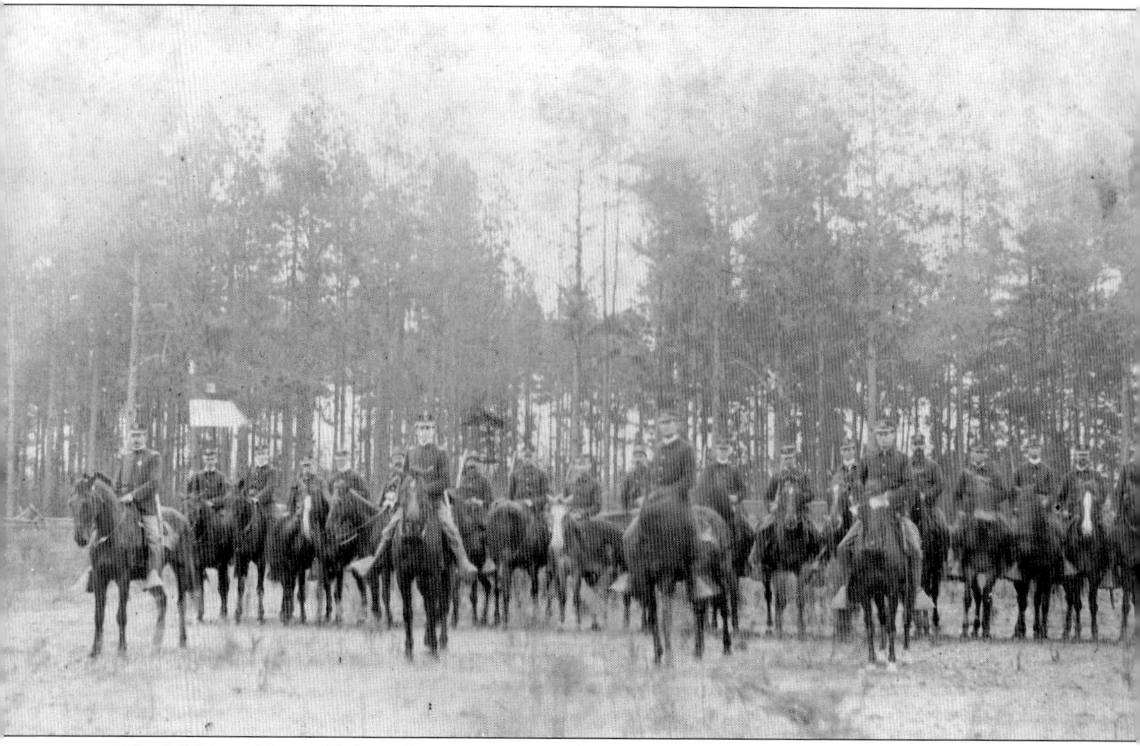

The Meldrim Tattnall Guards were organized in 1900 as Troop D, 1st Georgia Cavalry, and were named for the regiment's commander, Col. Peter W. Meldrim. The company was based at Hagan but also drew membership from Glennville and Reidsville. In this photograph, likely taken in 1900, the troop is mounted with sabers drawn, preparing for a practice charge. Third from left is a young John D. Bradley Sr., who was serving as captain of the troop by 1903. The various cavalry companies in the area held regular festivals, which included well-attended balls, drills, races, and "tilts." Tilting typically involved a mock charge and obstacle course in which a cavalryman had to aim the point of his saber through a small ring, and cut and slash straw-stuffed targets made to resemble humans. (Courtesy of Richard Bradley Jr.)

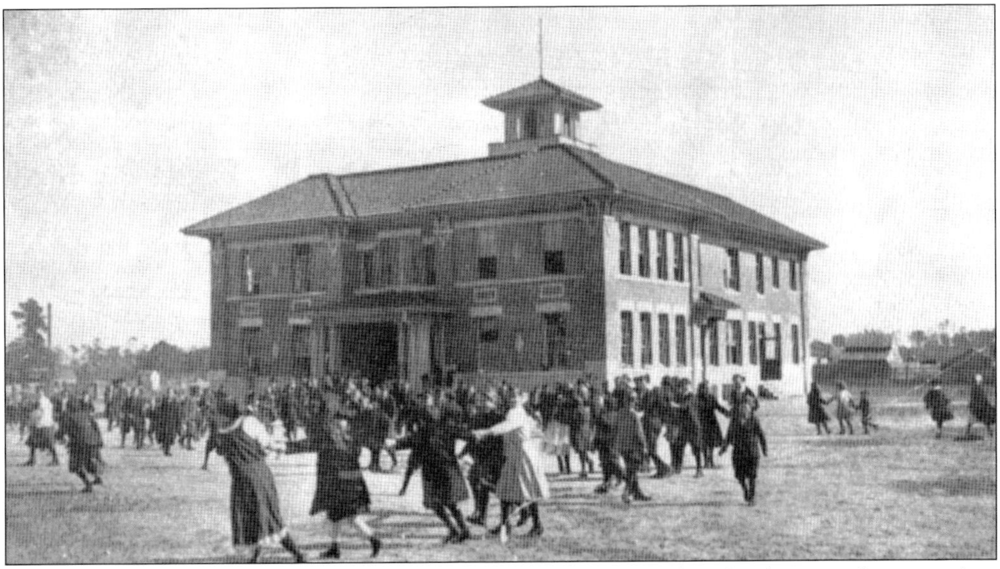

Central to community life for many decades was Glennville High School—in early years often referred to simply as Glennville School—pictured here in 1912 with a crowd of children playing in front. This building originally housed the entire Glennville school system until a new high school annex was completed in the early 1920s. At that time, this building was reserved for elementary and middle grades. (GTM.)

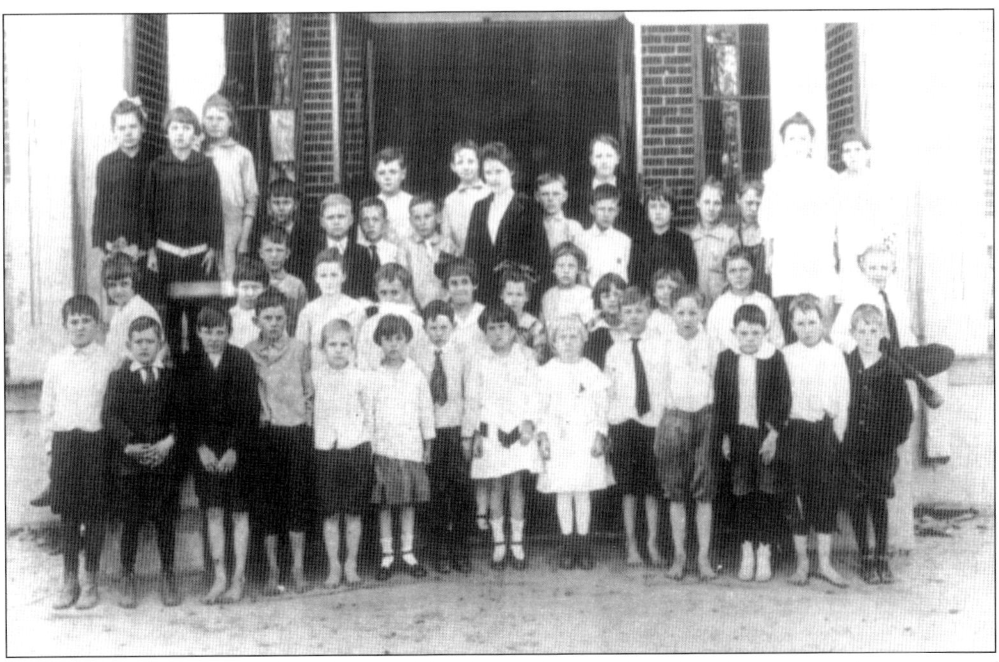

This photograph, dated March 30, 1917, shows the third grade class on the front steps of Glennville School. The teacher standing at center is thought to be Josephine Harvey, daughter of Superintendent J.M. Harvey. (GTM.)

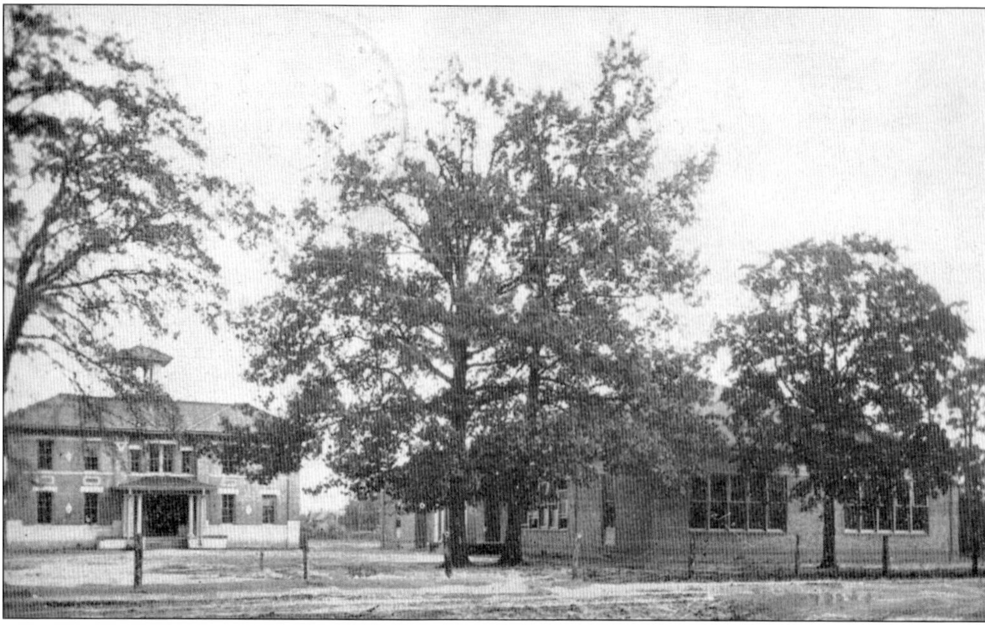

The 1924 postcard above shows the two-story elementary and middle school building on the left and the new, single-story high school annex on the right soon after its completion. This same building, shown below in 1956, would house Glennville High School until 1955, when a new high school campus was constructed on East Barnard Street. After 1955, the building pictured below became part of Glennville Middle School. (Above, courtesy of Brent Walker; below, courtesy of the Glennville Public Library.)

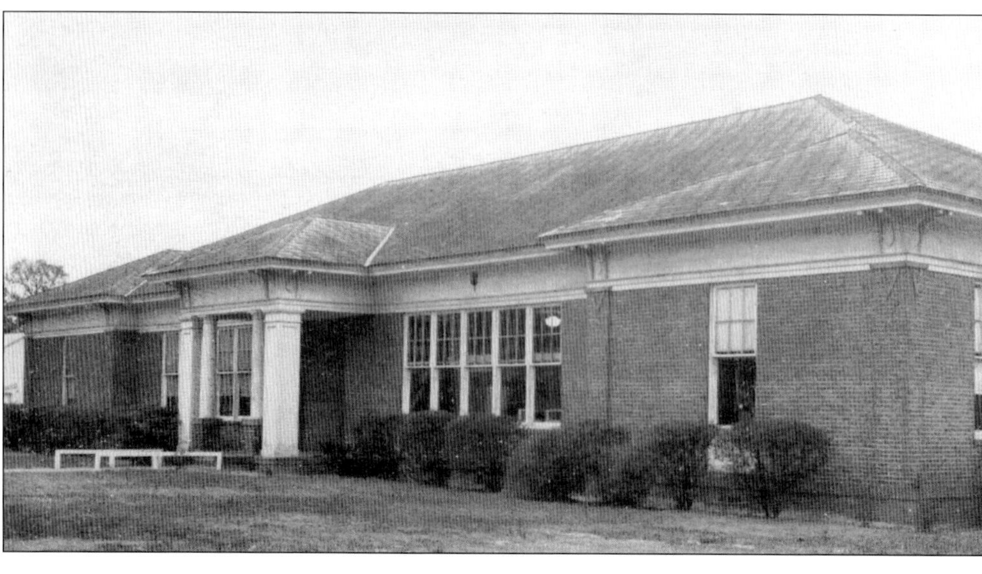

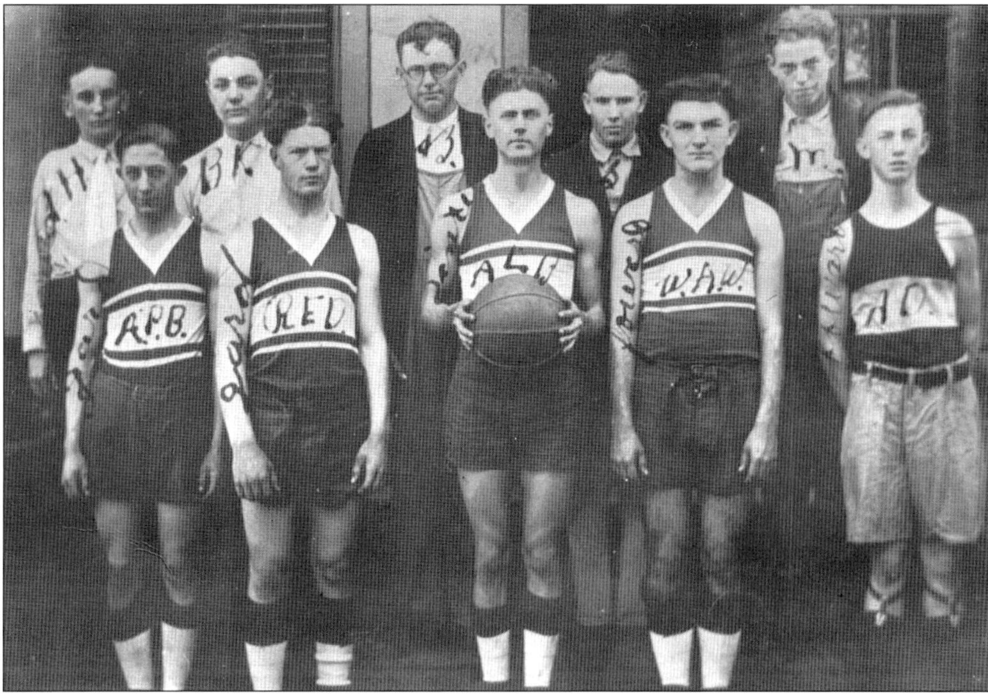

Pictured here in the early 1920s is the Glennville High School basketball team. From left to right are J.M. "Joe Boy" Hughes Jr., Alton Beasley, Barney Kicklighter, H.E. "Red" Kirkland, Ward Brannen, J.A. "Stevie" Bacon, Sam Groover, Ward Waters, Millard Waters, and Adriel Dubberly. (Courtesy of the Glennville Bank.)

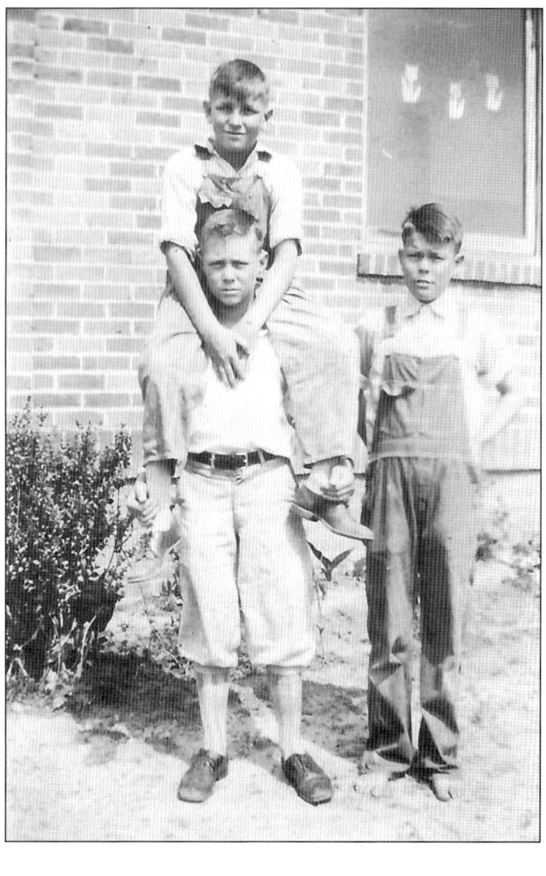

Pictured around 1932 in the Glennville schoolyard are Alfred Gordon Oliver Sr. (right) and Edward F. Mulligan Jr. on the shoulders of James R. Blitch. Gordon was the son of A.G. Oliver and Ruth Sikes Oliver, Ed was the son of E.F. "Ned" Mulligan Sr. and Laura Rogers Mulligan, and James was the son of Brantley D. Blitch and Nellie Everett Blitch. (Courtesy of Dylan Edward Mulligan.)

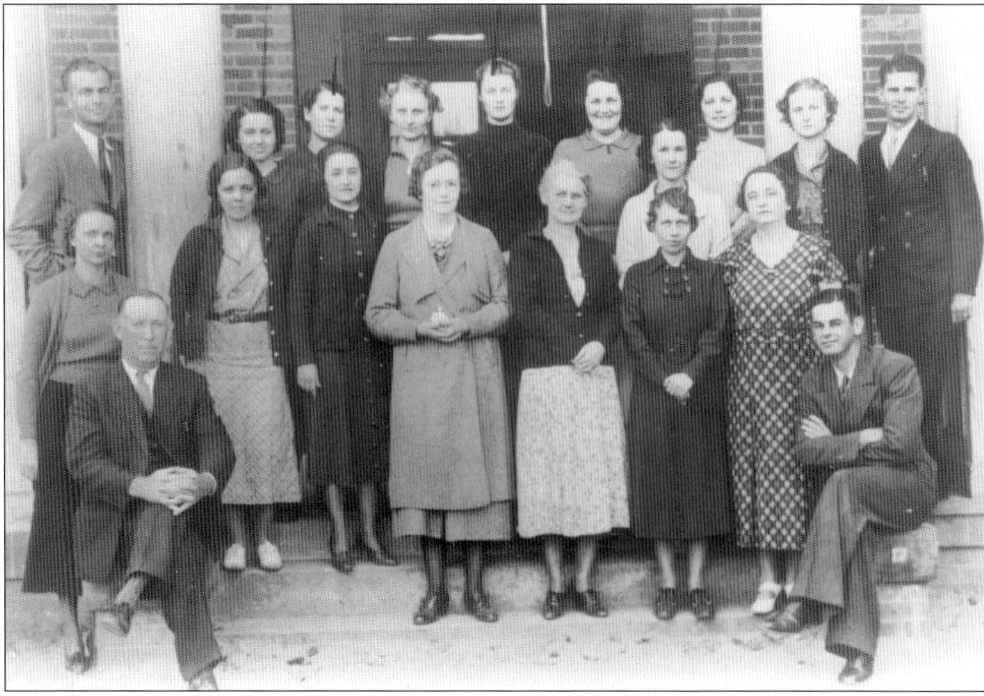

Pictured here around 1935–1936 is the faculty of Glennville High School. Seated are Superintendent Sam L. Gaskins (left) and Principal J.T. Alexander (right). Standing are, from left to right, (first row) Annie C. Zorn, Mabel Akers, Susie Collins, Amanda DeLoach, Donna Stanfield, Ethel "Doll" Rogers, and Myrl McCord; (second row) Johnie Hughes Kicklighter, Miss Dukes, Mary Gillingham Padgett, Mary Williams Wall, Miss Perry, Juanita New, Frances Hughes, Ruth Houston, Olivia Dubberly Hughes, and Deazy Rahn. (GTM.)

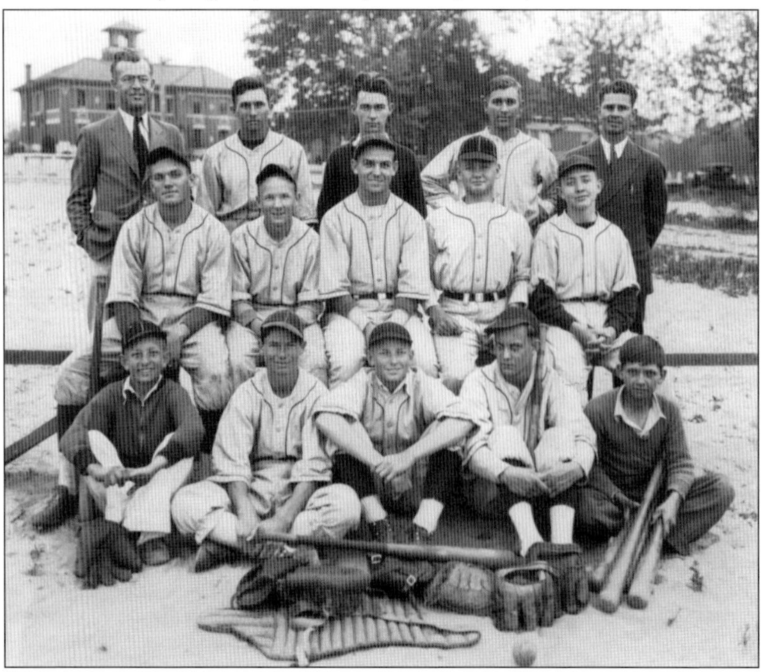

Pictured here is an early 1930s Glennville High School baseball team, with the school building in the background. (Courtesy of the *Glennville Sentinel*.)

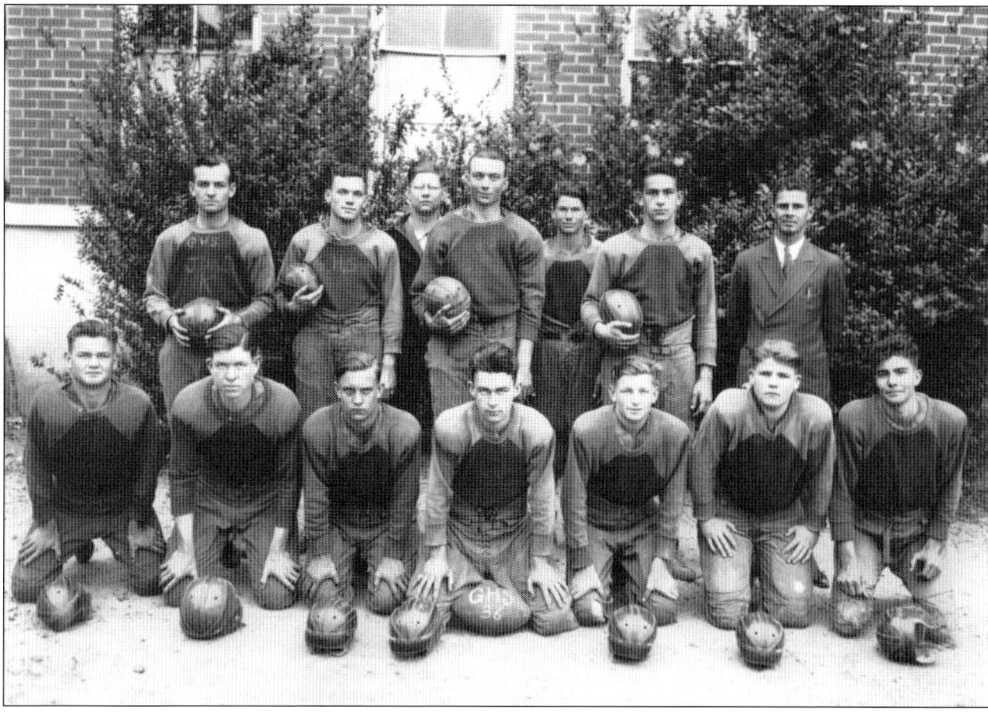

Pictured here is the 1936 Glennville High School football team in front of the school. From left to right are (first row) Jessie Sands, Persian Black, Junior Wilds, Edwin Waters, Ed Mulligan, Walter Strickland, and Quentin Kicklighter; (second row) Julian Kirkland, Harold Waters, Dean Minor, Talmadge Tootle, Cobb Purvis, George Hilliard, and Coach Deazy Rahn. (Courtesy of the *Glennville Sentinel*.)

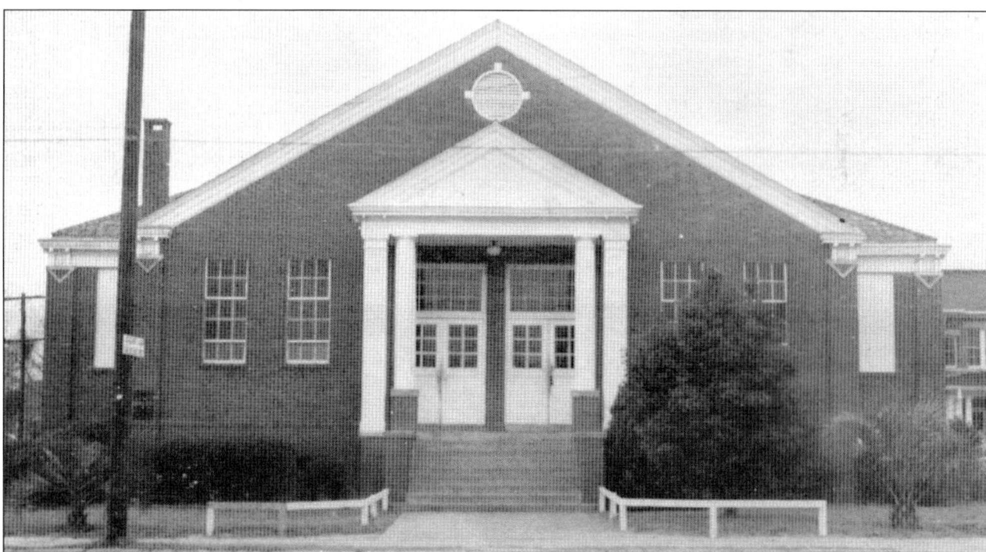
The Glennville City Auditorium, pictured here in 1956, was constructed adjacent to Glennville High School in 1939 as a project of the New Deal–era Works Progress Administration. The auditorium still stands at the corner of South Tillman and Bolton Streets and is the site of many public events throughout the year. (Courtesy of the Glennville Public Library.)

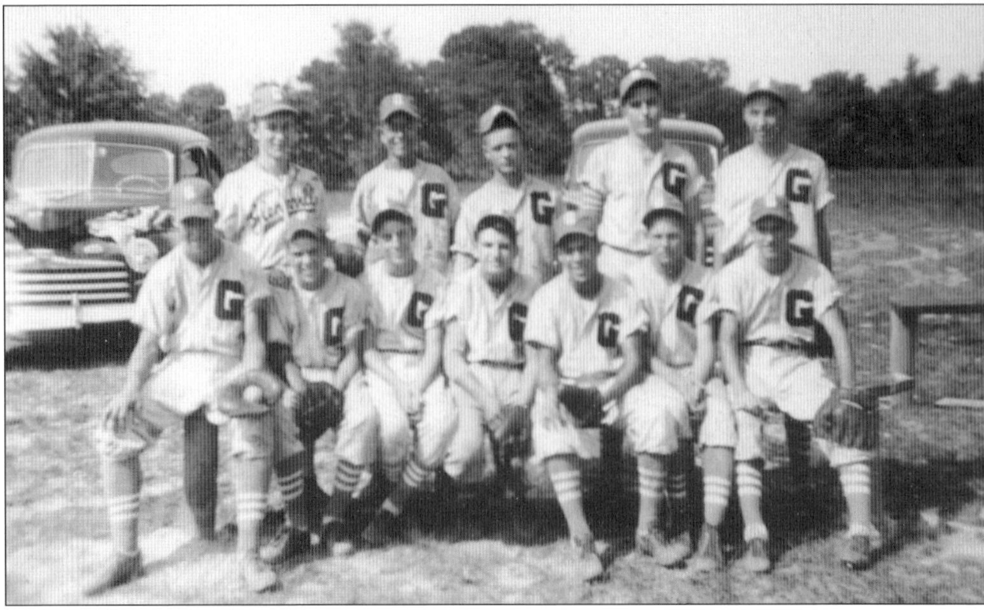

The Glennville High School baseball team is seen in this 1947 photograph. From left to right are (first row) James Tootle, Jared Durrence, Jesse Finch, Billy Lee, Mike "Dodo" Gutierrez, Theus Purvis, and Bobby Kicklighter; (second row) Wendell Todd, Jerry Rogers, John D. Kicklighter, Bill Rustin, and Jerry Kicklighter. (Courtesy of Bobby Kicklighter.)

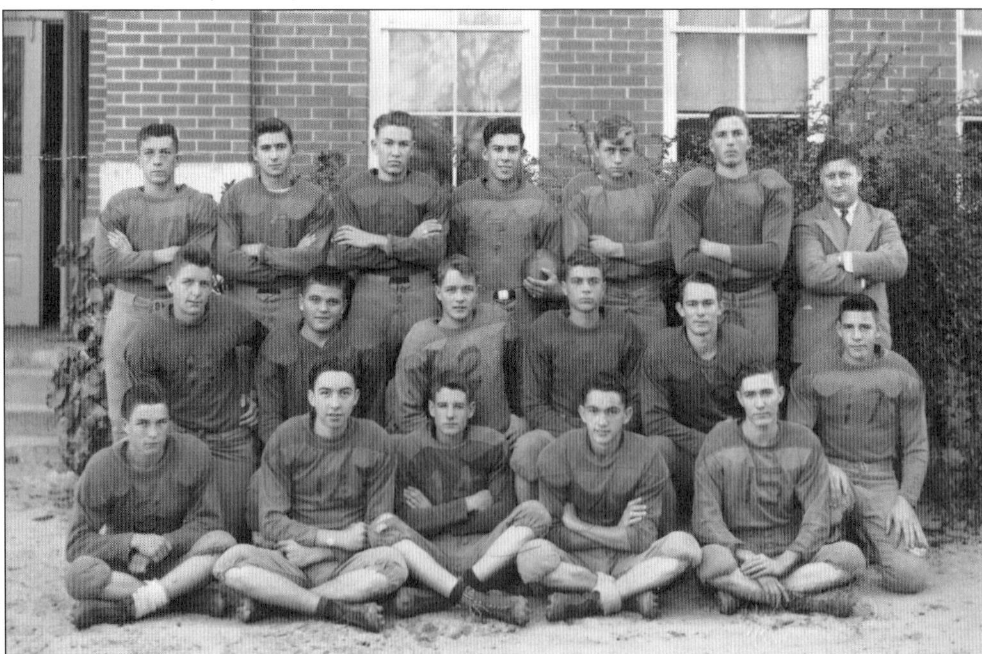

Pictured here is the 1948 Glennville High School football team. From left to right are (first row) Billy Brewton, Jerry Kicklighter, Claude Yarbrough, Bobby Kicklighter, and Colvis Leggett; (second row) Pat Stanfield, Billy Phillips, John D. Kicklighter, Jared Durrence, Wendell Todd, and Billy Easterling; (third row) Jesse Finch, Dan Dubberly, Charles Stewart, Mike "Dodo" Gutierrez, Bob Driggers, Bill Rustin, and Coach J.D. White. (Courtesy of Bobby Kicklighter.)

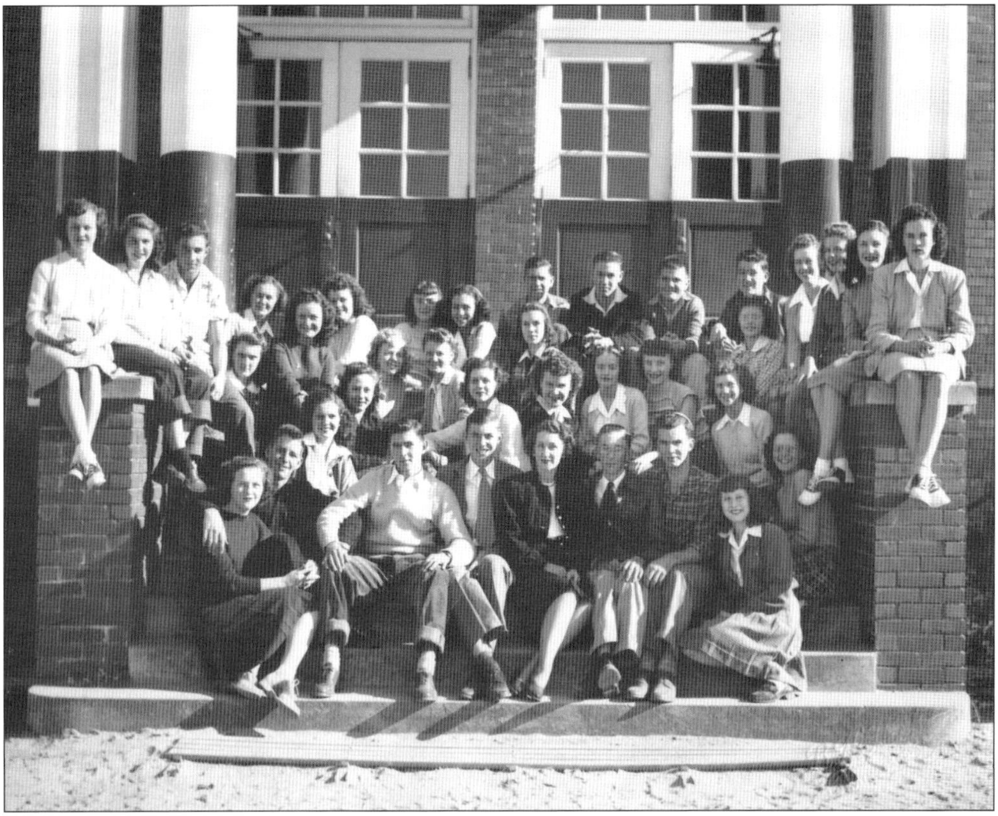

In this 1948 photograph, members of the Glennville High School Beta Club pose on the front steps of the city auditorium. (Courtesy of Dylan Edward Mulligan.)

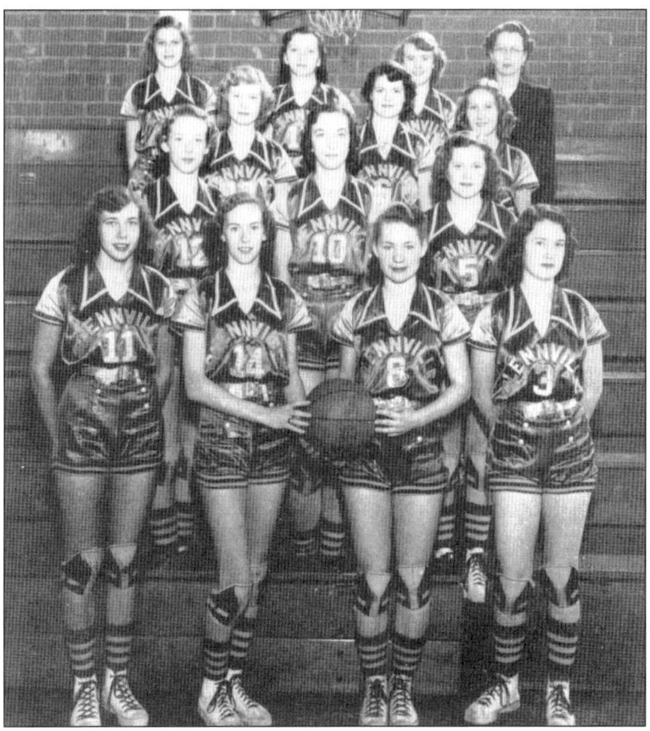

The Glennville High School girls' basketball team claimed the state championship in 1952. From left to right are (first row) Ann Futch, Ann DeLoach, Lela Jane Blocker, and Dianna Smith; (second row) LeGay Durrence, Melba Weitman, and Geraldine Lee; (third row) Lawanda Driggers, Shirley Jones, and Lou Beth Cammack; (fourth row) Betty Moody, Nelda Weitman, Retha Nell Barrow, and Coach Emily DeLoach. (Courtesy of the Glennville Public Library.)

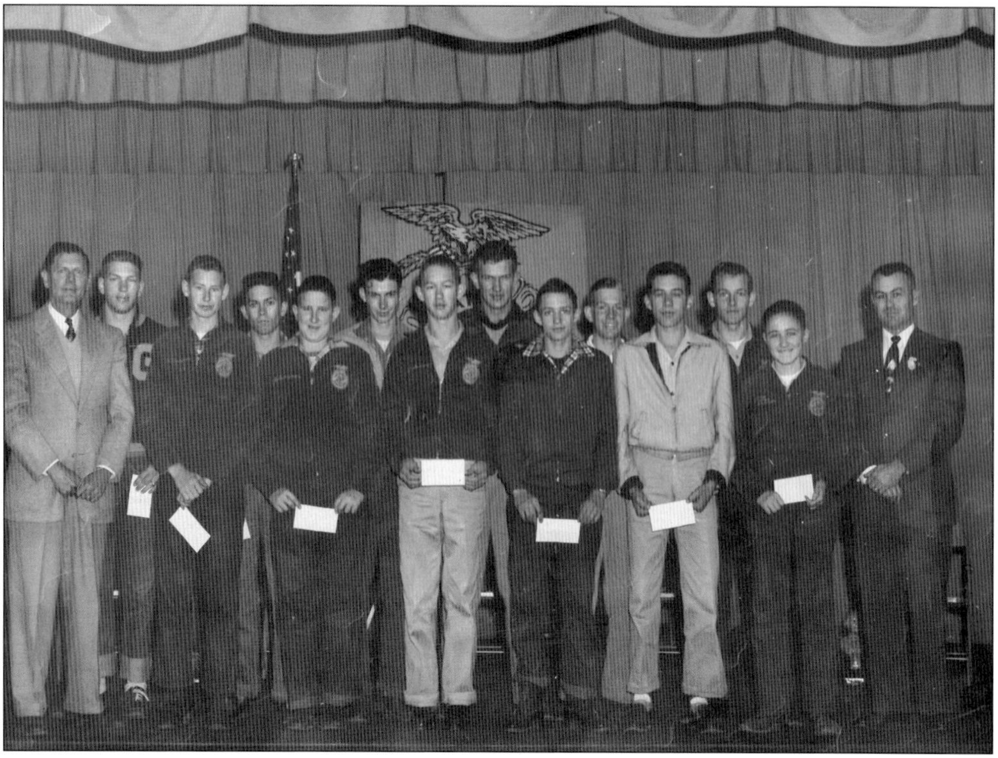

Seen here around 1954–1955 is the Glennville High School Future Farmers of America. From left to right are Glennville Bank president J.A. "Stevie" Bacon, Ferrell Bland, Merlie Thompson, Bobby Weitman, J.B. Durrence, Derrell Kicklighter, Robert Surrency, Jerrell Baker, Talmadge Purcell, J.I. DeLoach, Oren Driggers, Odean Thompson, Jerry Dutton, and Jonathan "Jake" Kaney. (Courtesy of the Glennville Bank.)

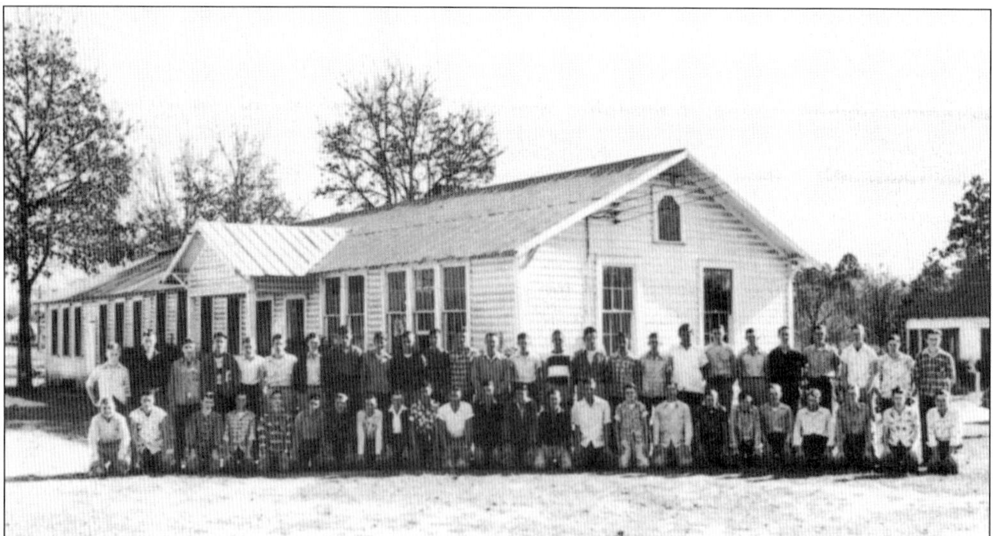

The Glennville High School agriculture building, pictured in 1950, stood directly behind the school on the now vacant lot between Howard, Bolton, and South Baker Streets. (Courtesy of the Glennville Public Library.)

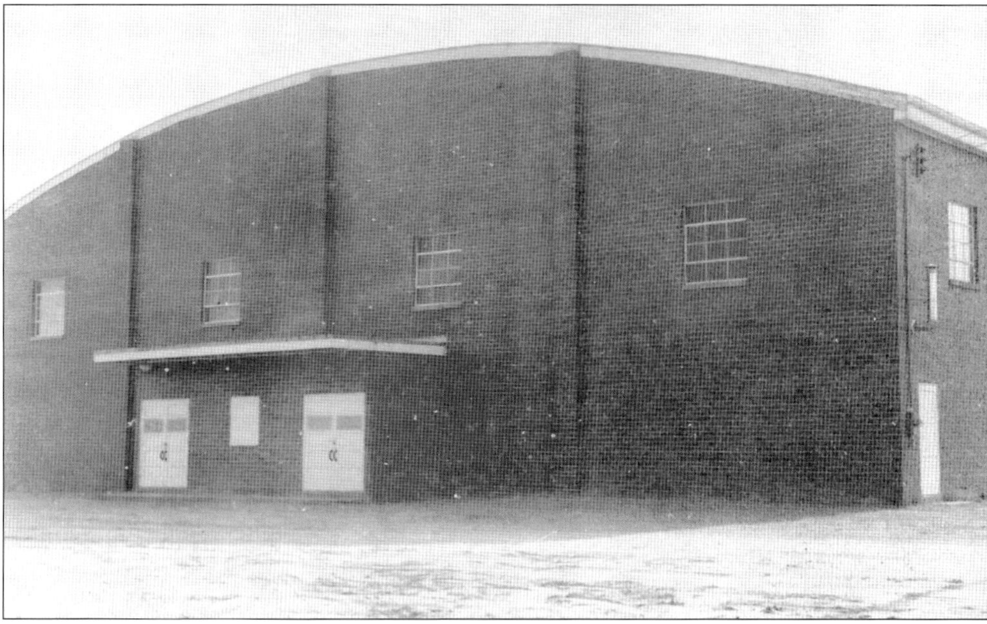

The Glennville High School gymnasium, pictured here in 1956, was built in 1953–1954 by the City of Glennville and, in addition to being used as a gymnasium, was also initially used as the local armory. This building still serves as the gymnasium of Glennville Middle School. The adjacent football field was built in 1952. (Courtesy of the Glennville Public Library.)

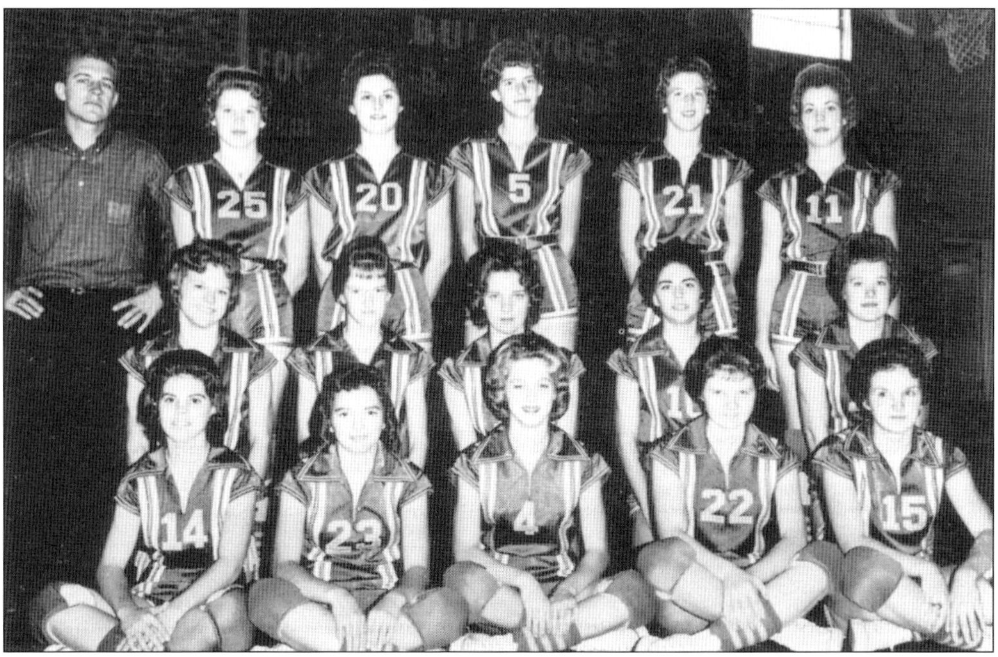

The Glennville girls' basketball team won the state championship in 1962. From left to right are (first row) Janet Sheffield, Bonnie Dubberly, Sue Durrence, Sandra Akins, and Beth Akins; (second row) Sharon Kicklighter, Katha Waters, Carolyn Blocker, Brenda Kicklighter, and Annette Branch; (third row) Coach Carlton Walton, Eve Strickland, Faye Jenkins, Gwendolyn Waters, DiAnne Durrence, and Anda Geiger. (Courtesy of the Glennville Public Library.)

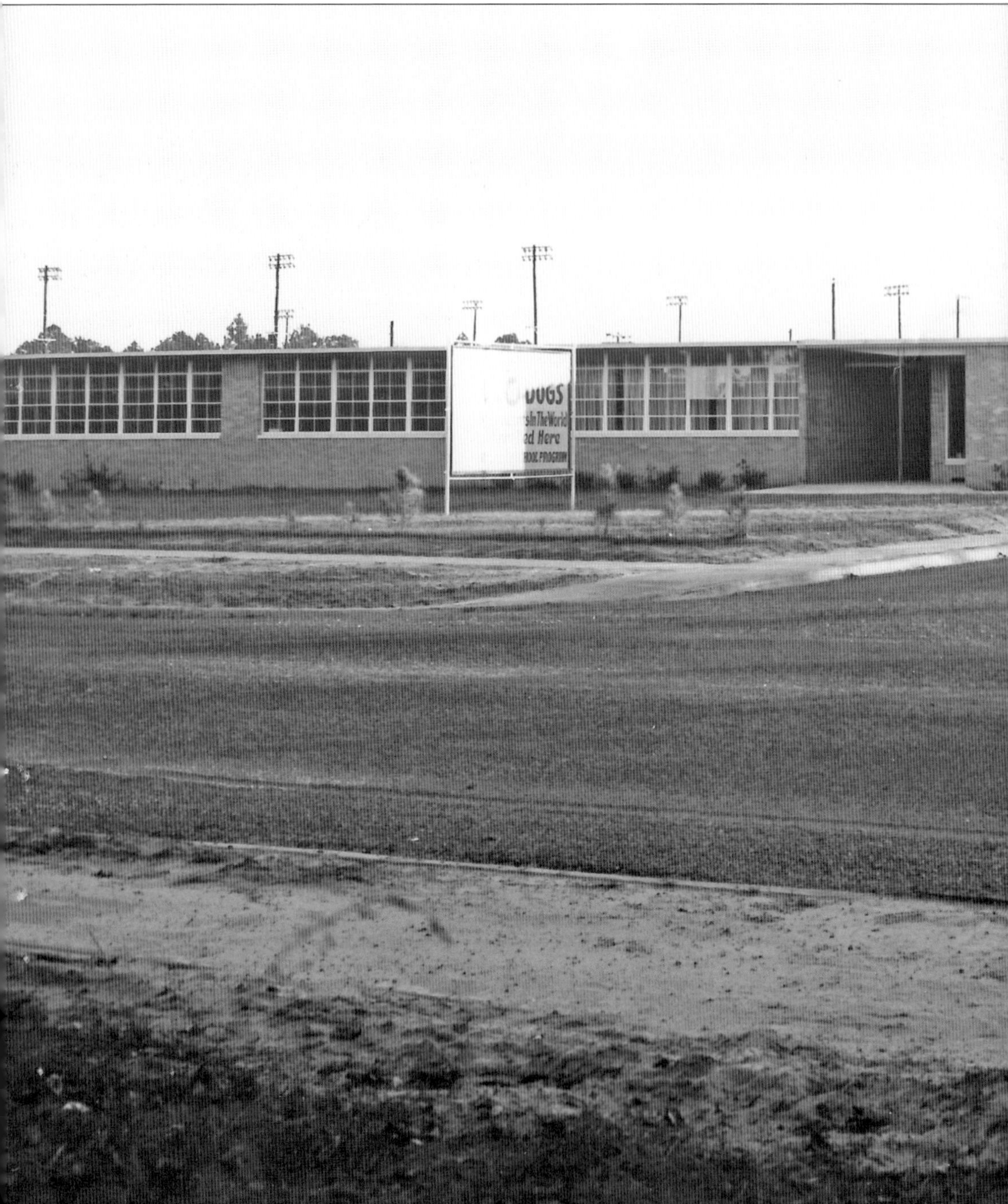

Between 1946 and 1952, the Ogeechee League—a semiprofessional baseball organization—was active in Southeast Georgia. One of the league's teams was the Glennville Athletics, comprised of local men and retired professional players. The team traveled and competed against Metter, Vidalia-Lyons, Millen, Statesboro, Jesup, Sylvania, Waynesboro, and others. The Glennville Athletics dressed in gray wool uniforms and were paid a salary ranging from $200 to $1,000 a

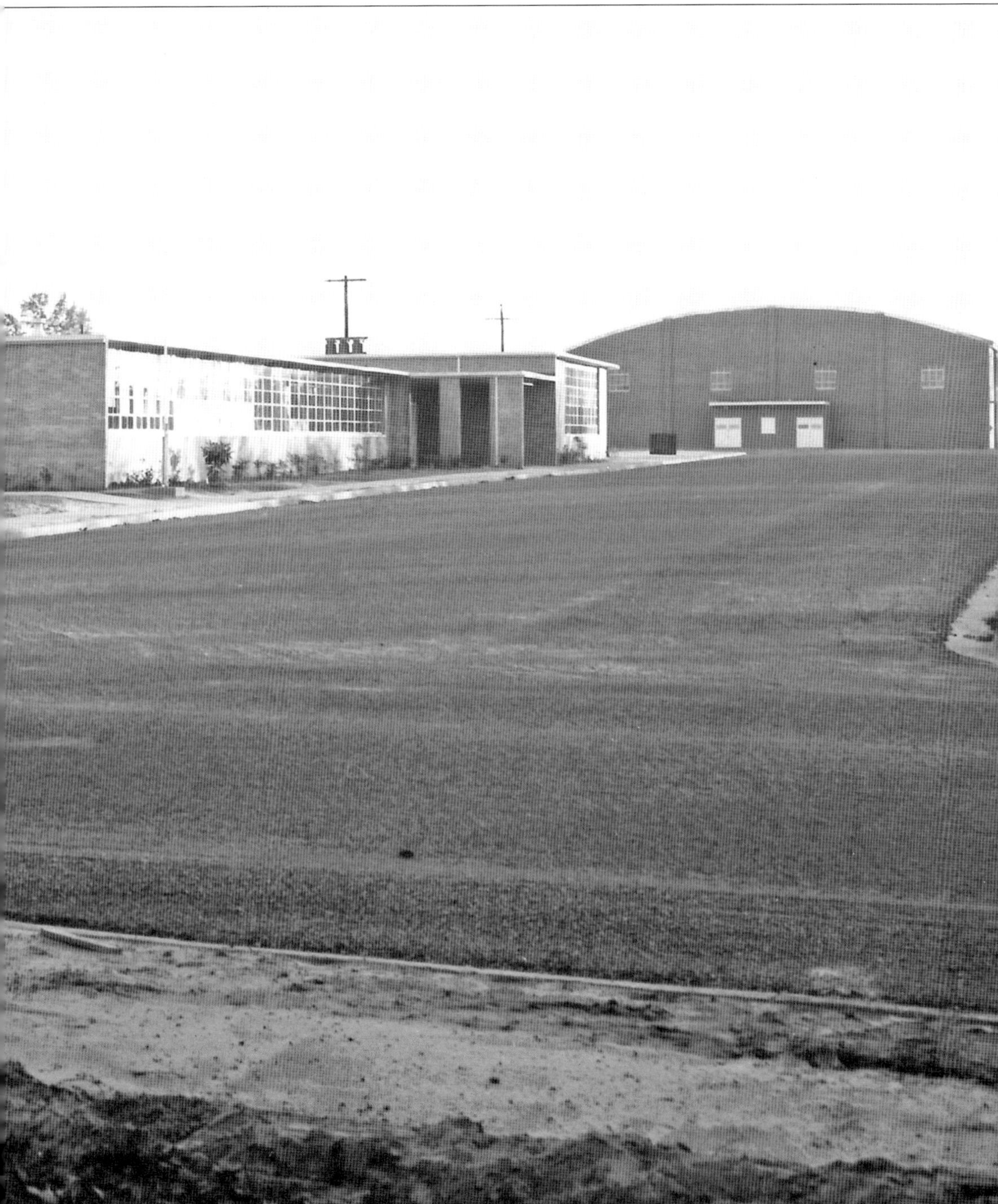

month. Their stadium was demolished to make way for the new Glennville High School building, built in 1955 and pictured here in 1957. Glennville High School remained in this building until 1993, when the county schools were consolidated into Tattnall County High School. This building subsequently became Glennville Middle School, which it remains today. (Courtesy of the City of Glennville.)

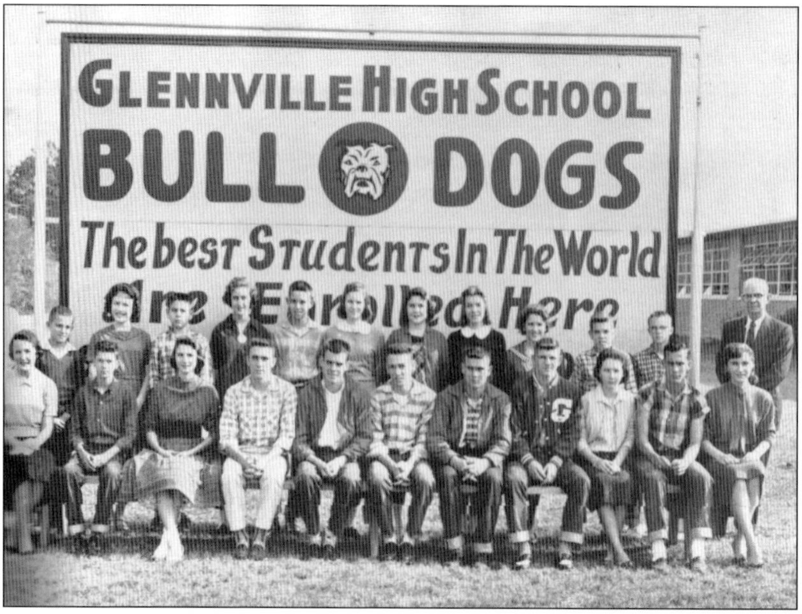

Pictured here around 1959 is the Glennville High School student council in front of the new high school. (Courtesy of the Glennville Public Library.)

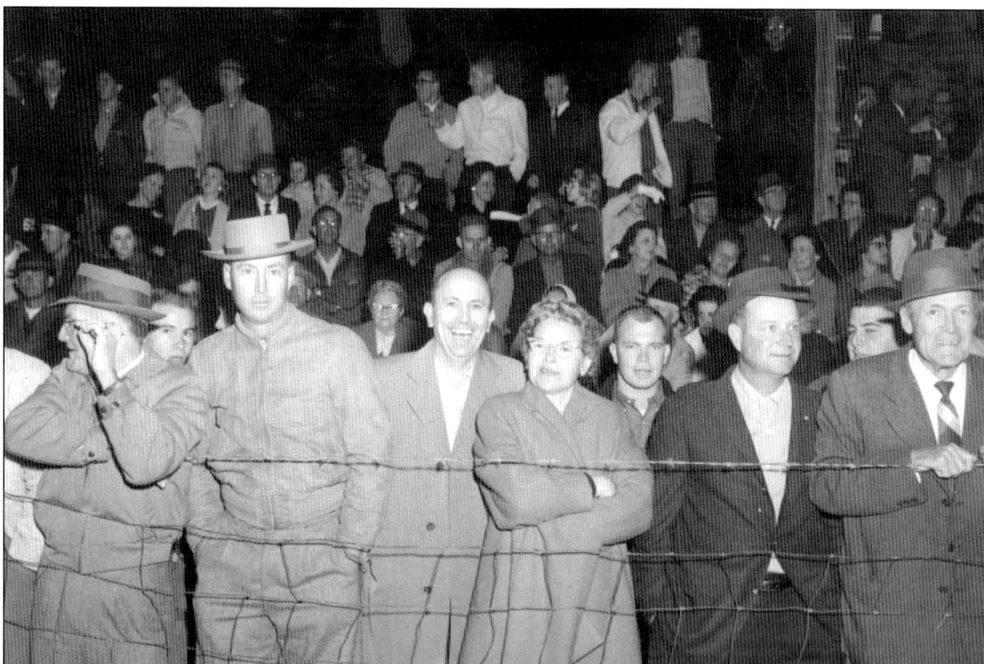

Glennville High School football games were always well-attended, typically with standing room only. Standing from left to right in this early 1960s photograph are Billy Purcell, Edwin DeLoach (background), Mack Baxter (wearing hat), Mayor Charlie Rowland, Susie Rowland, Aubrey Sikes Jr., unidentified, and Ray Smith. Among those in the stands, in no particular order, are Billy and Louise Howard, S.E. and Madera Smith, Dub and Mary Ellen Rogers, Gerald and Pam Dasher, Dan and Betty Dubberly, Bruce and Vera Dubberly, Marvin and Eleanor Perkins, Princeton Pirkle, Jimmy Beasley, Gene Dasher, Shelton DeLoach, Jimmy McCurdy, James Smith, Linda Strickland, Linda Brewton, Joan Smith, Herbert Holton, and Jerry Dutton. (Courtesy of Willie Bland.)

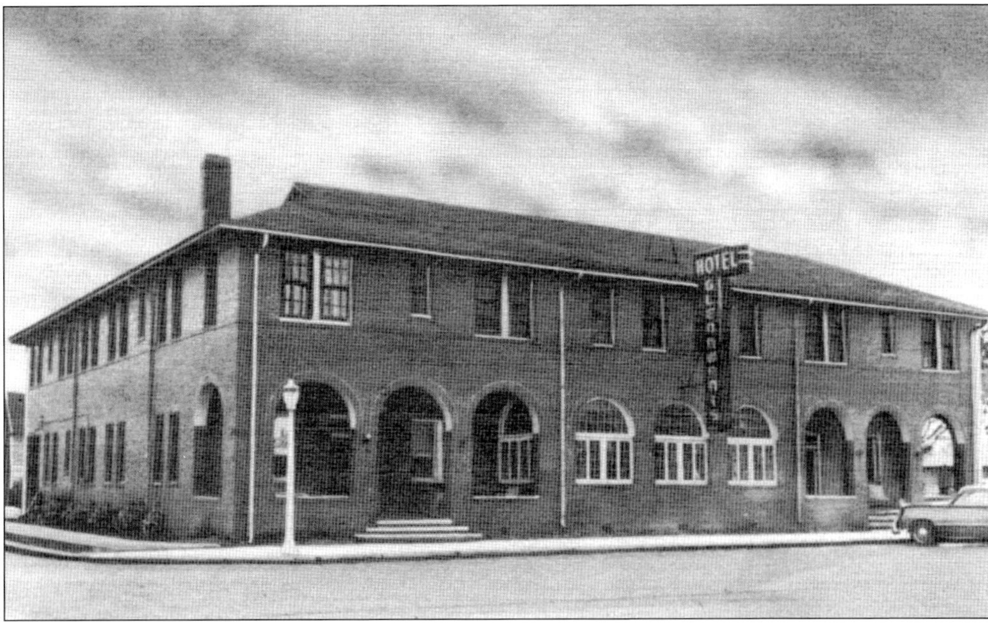

The Glennwanis Hotel, built in 1926, was the center of much social activity throughout the 20th century. In 1947, the hotel opened a dining room that served breakfast, dinner, and supper. (Courtesy of Brent Walker.)

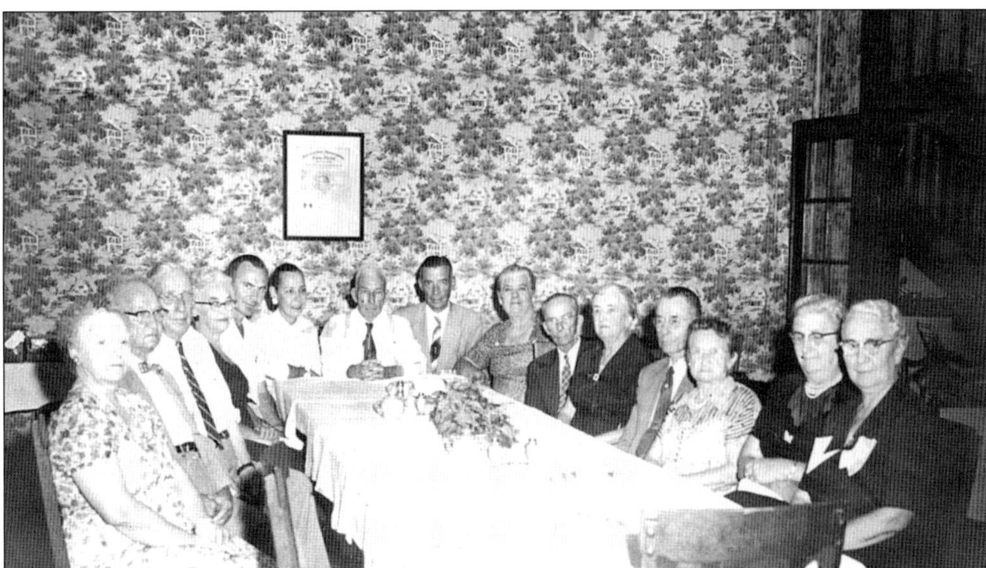

This photograph was taken in the Glennwanis Hotel dining room in 1960 at an 87th birthday party for Dr. Algernon Columbus Colson. From left to right are Ida Tootle, Mr. Dasher (Hal Mann's father-in-law), Dr. J.M. Hughes Sr., Edna Tootle, Dr. Charles H. Drake, Mrs. Colson (Dr. Colson's daughter-in-law), Dr. A.C. Colson, Col. John Colson (Dr. Colson's son), Maggie Colson, Judge Cleveland L. Cowart, Lillian Kennedy, Ozzie Davis, Mrs. Davis (Marvin Girardeau's mother), Jim Easterling "Aunt Jim" Dubberly, and Minnie Banks. (Courtesy of the *Glennville Sentinel*.)

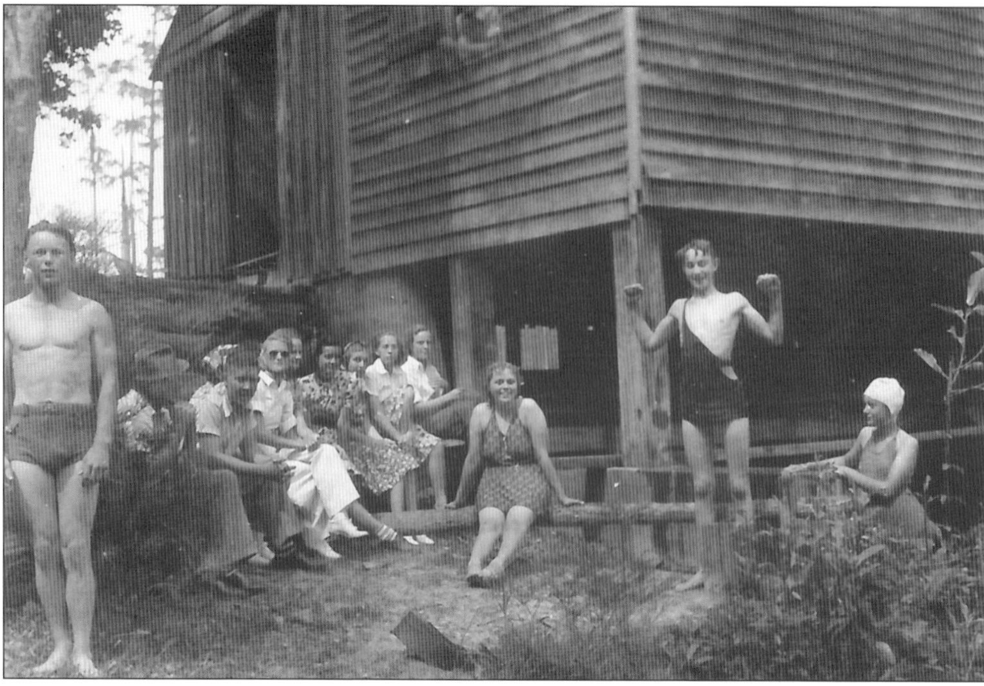

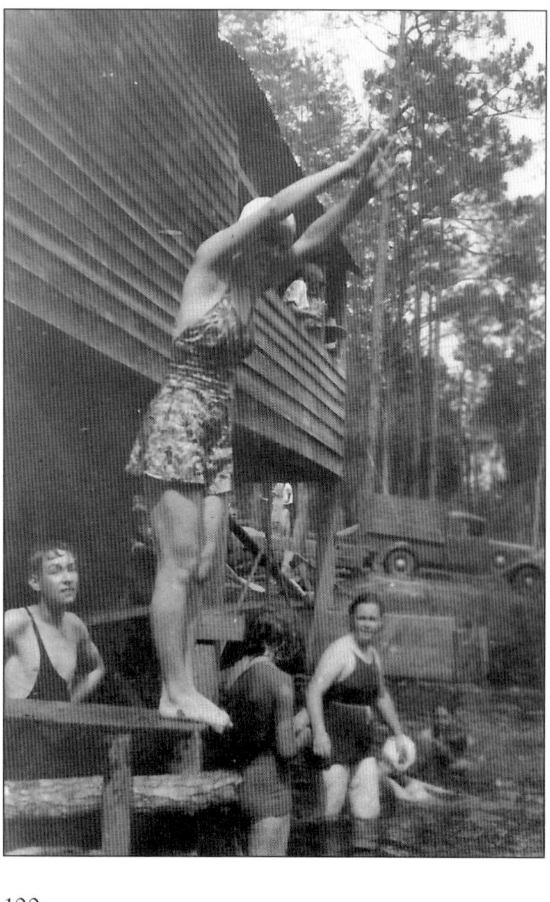

Groover's Mill, seen above and at left in the 1930s, was located several miles north of Glennville off Highway 250 and was operated for many years by Willie Groover. The mill was a favorite among local teenagers and families, who frequently congregated there on weekends to picnic and swim. (Both, courtesy of Rebecca Mulligan.)

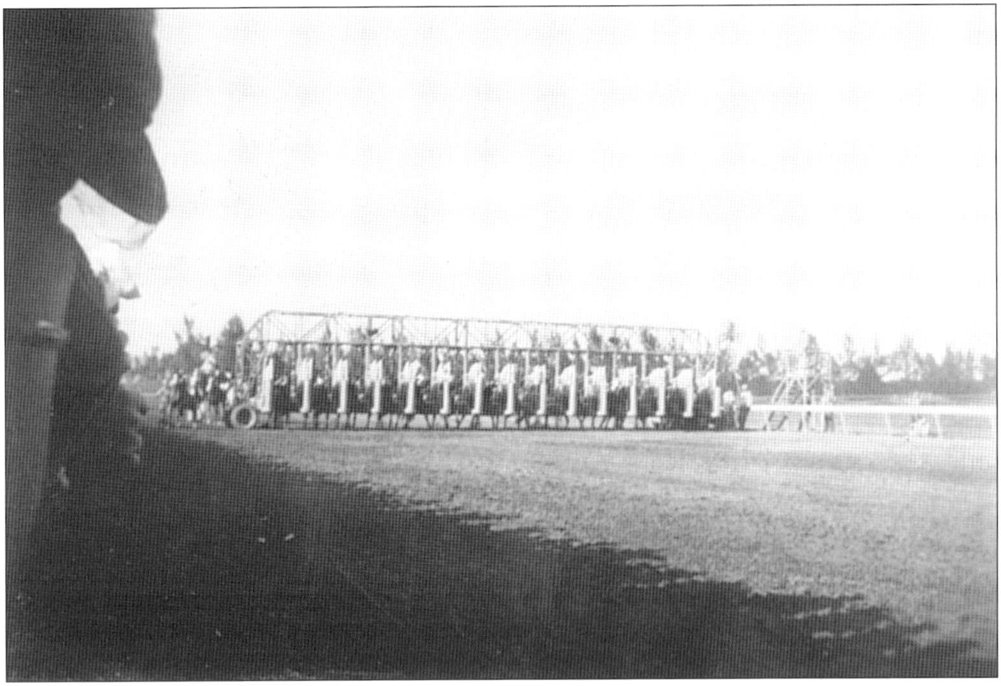

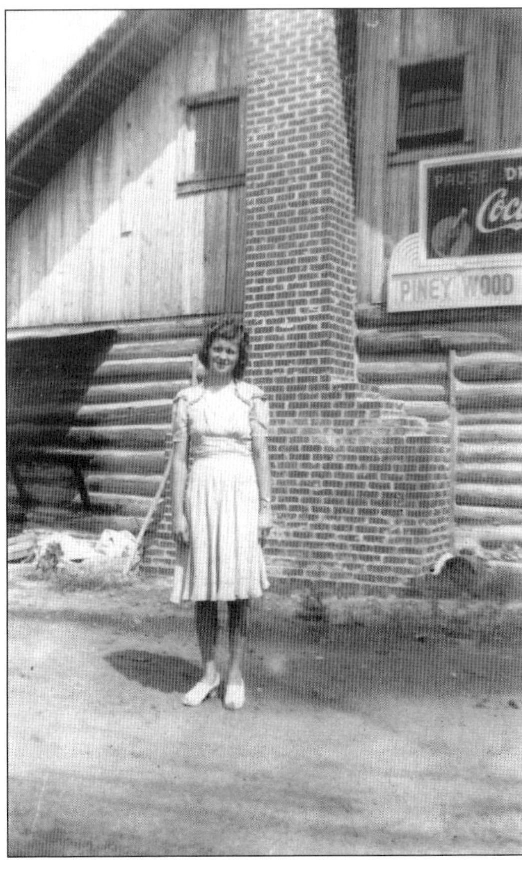

Horse racing in Tattnall County traces its origins to the cavalry races held by the Liberty Guards at their secondary drill ground and racetrack near Ebenezer Church. Piney Woods Race Club was established in 1938 and stood on the north side of the Glennville-Reidsville Highway near Mendes Road (then Racetrack Road). Four major races were held annually at Piney Woods: the tomato festival race in May and races on Memorial Day, the Fourth of July, and Labor Day. The stands at Piney Woods held 400 spectators, and the races were always highly anticipated by both locals and out-of-state visitors. Pictured above is the starting gate at the racetrack, and at right is Edra Baker outside the clubhouse at Piney Woods, which was later owned by the Glennville Veterans of Foreign Wars after the races ceased. (Above, courtesy of the *Glennville Sentinel*; right, courtesy of the Glennville Bank.)

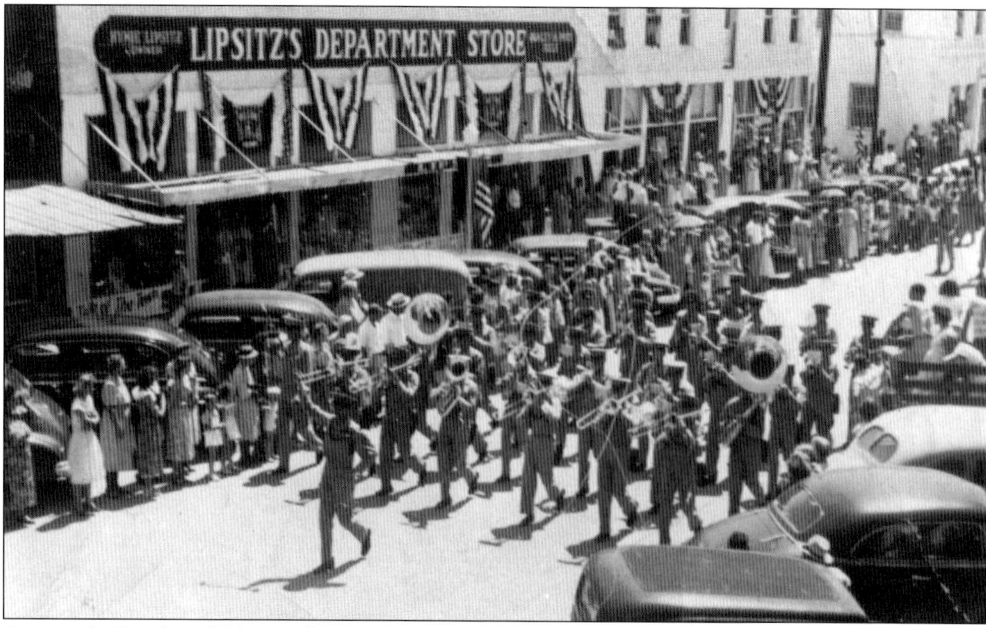

During the heyday of Glennville's tomato industry, an annual tomato festival and parade was held. The first such festival was held in 1938 and continued until 1941, when it was halted by World War II. The festival was reinstated in 1949 and continued until 1954. This photograph was taken around 1949–1950 and shows Barnard Street facing east toward Caswell Street. (GTM.)

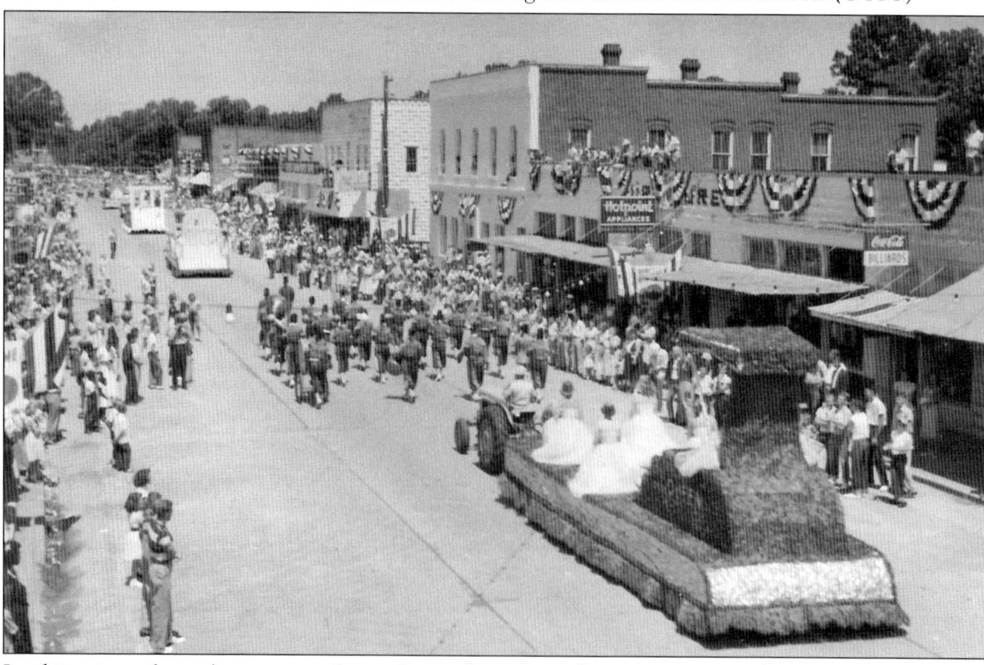

In this view of another tomato festival parade, notice the ever-present Shriners oriental band, followed by the tomato queen and her court. Also notice the spectators watching from the roof of H.E. Danner Furniture Company, adjacent to the Glennville Bank. This photograph was likely taken in 1953 or 1954 from the second floor of the Pal Theater by future mayor Charlie Rowland. (Courtesy of Judy Rowland Bland.)

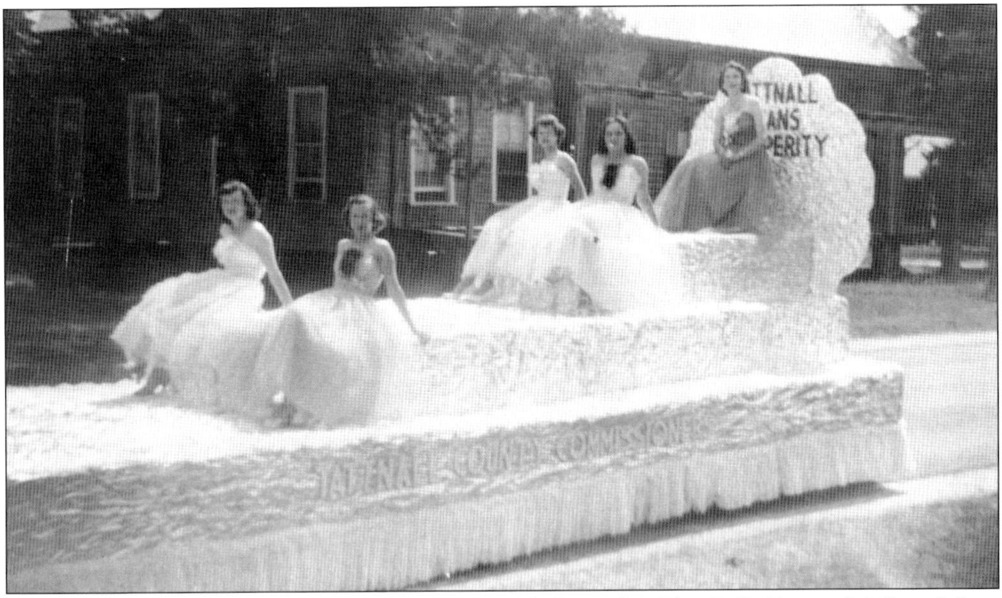

Pictured in the 1953 tomato festival parade are, from left to right, Edna Belle Rogers (Mulligan), Lois Kicklighter (Curry), Shirley Jones (Folsom), Betty Rhodes (Kicklighter), and Marian Stubbs. In the background is the J.J. Barnard house at the corner of Barnard and Herrington Streets. (GTM.)

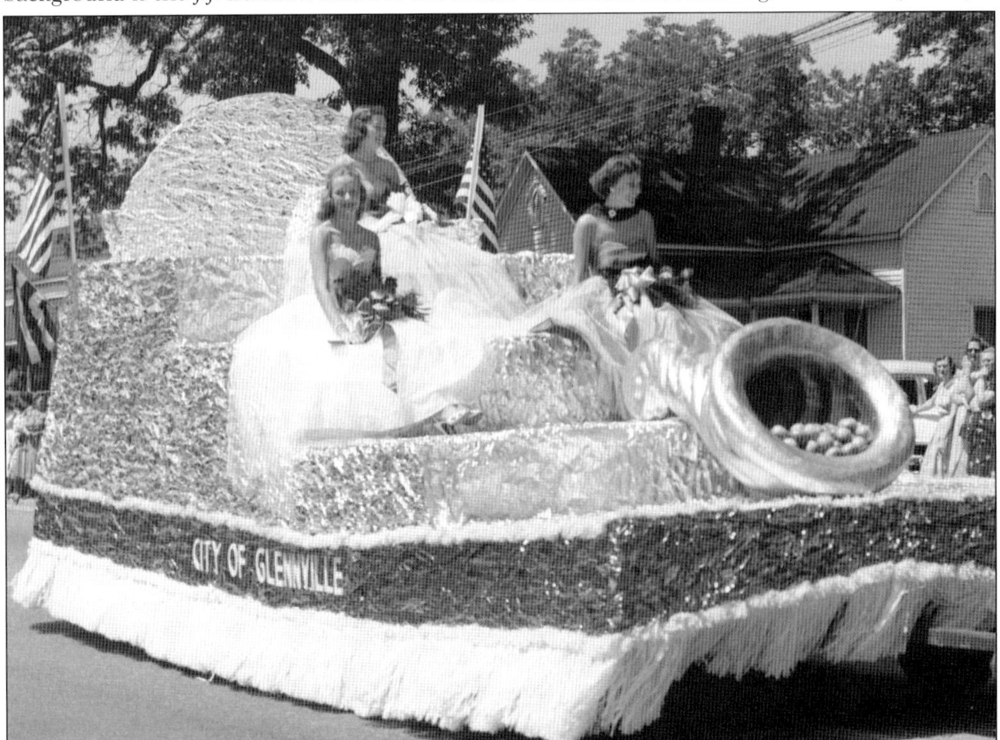

Shown here in the early 1950s is tomato queen Wilsmith Brannen (top) and her court, Melva Crummey Durrence (bottom left) and Edna Allen Folsom (bottom right). (Courtesy of the City of Glennville.)

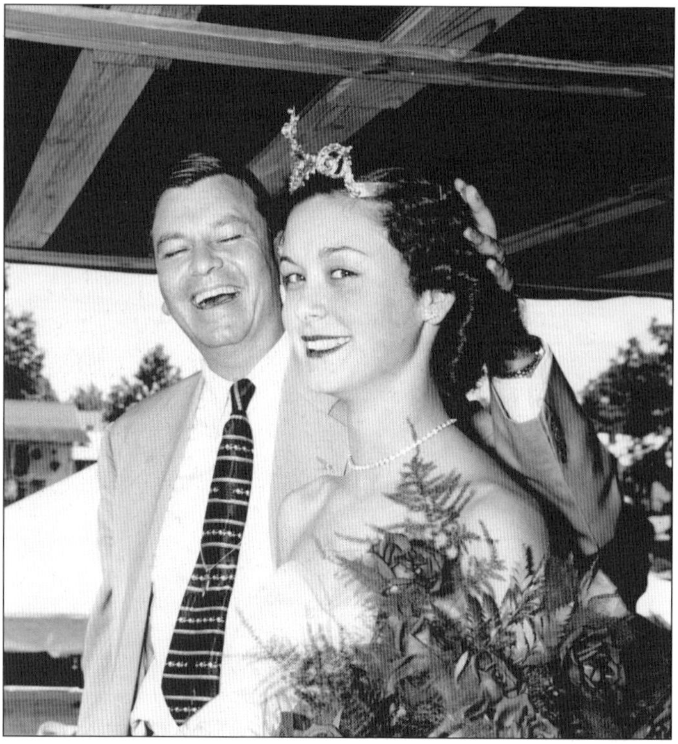

In 1954, Gov. Herman Talmadge (left) crowned Glennville's last tomato queen, Carolyn Durrence Dixon (right). It was the end of an era, as tomatoes began to lose their importance to the local economy when better varieties were discovered in Texas. The tomato was replaced by the sweet onion, which increased in popularity and had its own festival beginning in 1976. (Courtesy of the Glennville Bank.)

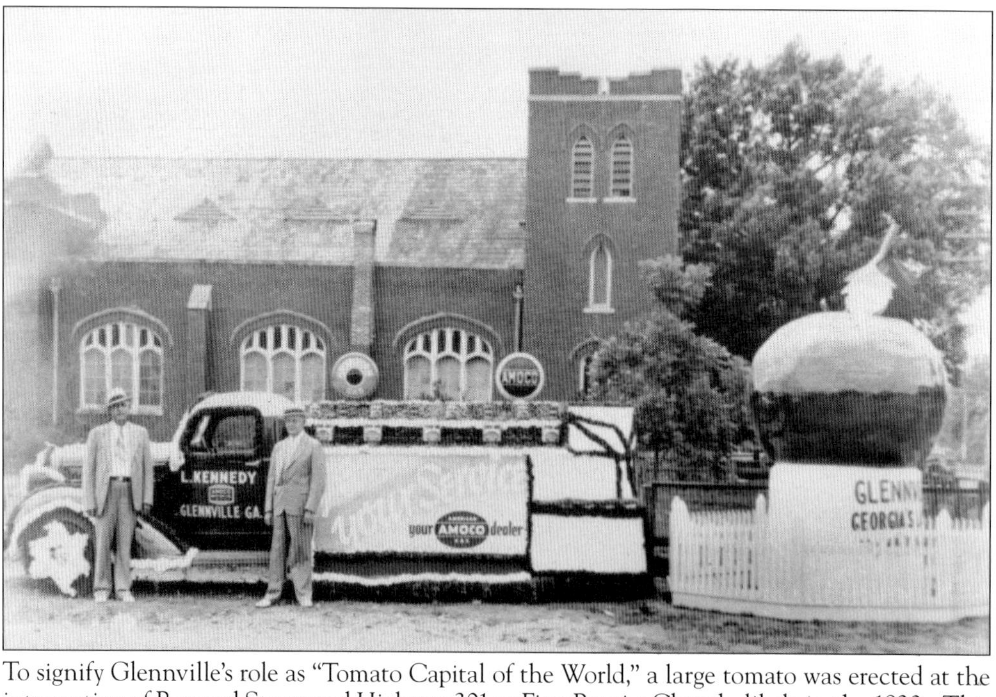

To signify Glennville's role as "Tomato Capital of the World," a large tomato was erected at the intersection of Barnard Street and Highway 301 at First Baptist Church, likely in the 1930s. This same tomato was later moved to the farmers' market on Highway 301 North and then to the new market on Highway 301 South. Lucious Kennedy, owner of a local Amoco station, stands on the left. (Courtesy of John Michael Kennedy.)

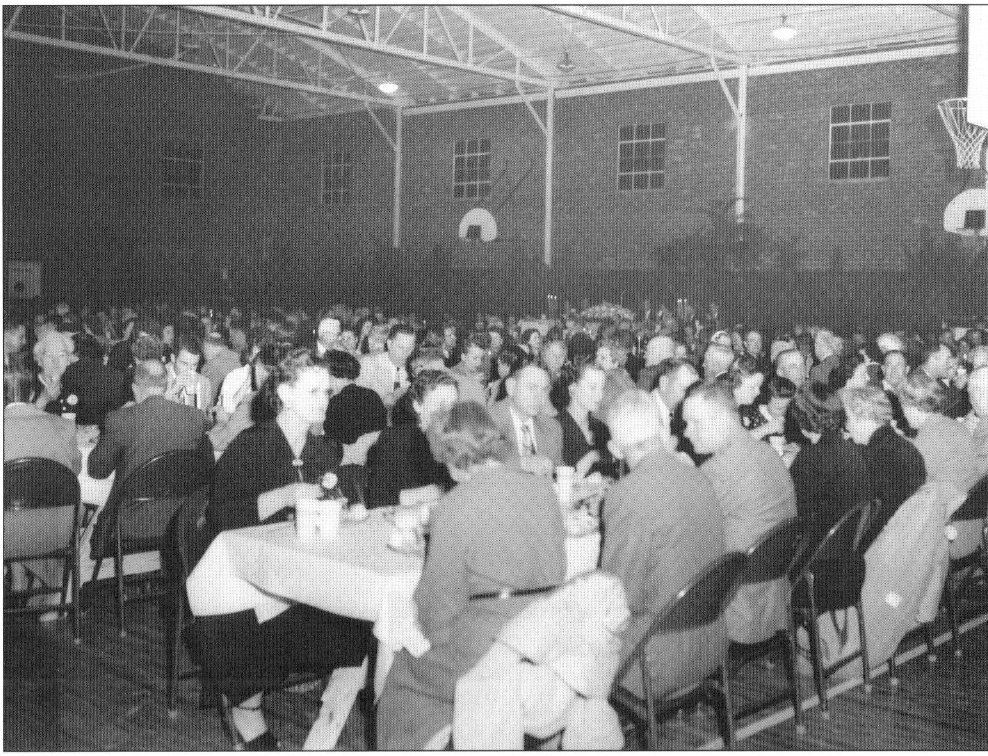

The Glennville Bank celebrated its 50th anniversary with a large party in the Glennville High School gymnasium, shown here on January 12, 1955. The gymnasium was frequently host to a variety of civic functions and dances. (Courtesy of the Glennville Bank.)

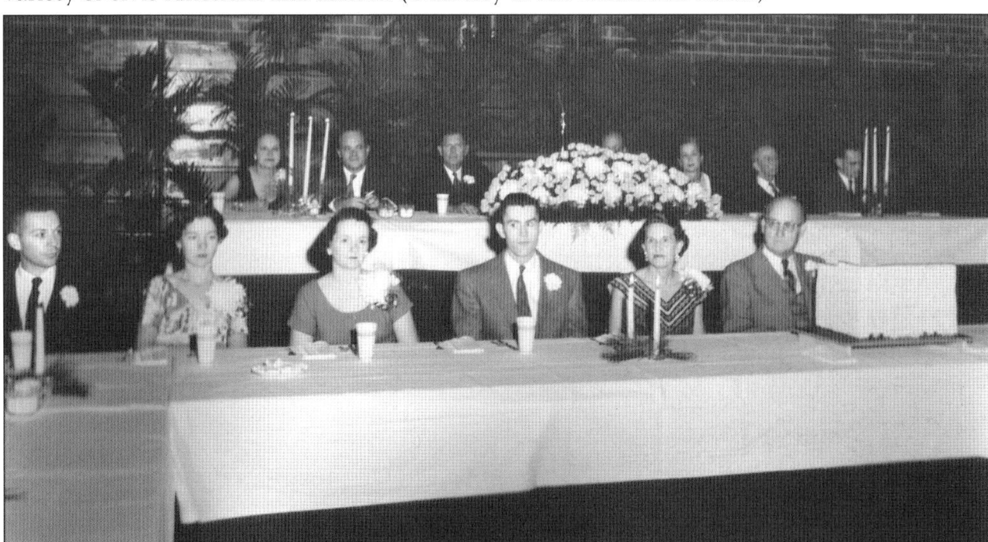

Seated at the table are participants in the Glennville Bank's 50th anniversary. From left to right are (first row) W.F. "Billy" Durrence Sr., Ruby Jo Durrence, Anne Rogers, Jack A. Rogers, May Seckinger, and J.B. Seckinger; (second row) Lynette Bacon, Mills B. Lane Jr., J.A. "Stevie" Bacon (bank president), Jean D. Kicklighter (behind the flowers), Doris Beasley Kicklighter, Judge Cleveland L. Cowart, and unidentified. (Courtesy of the Glennville Bank.)

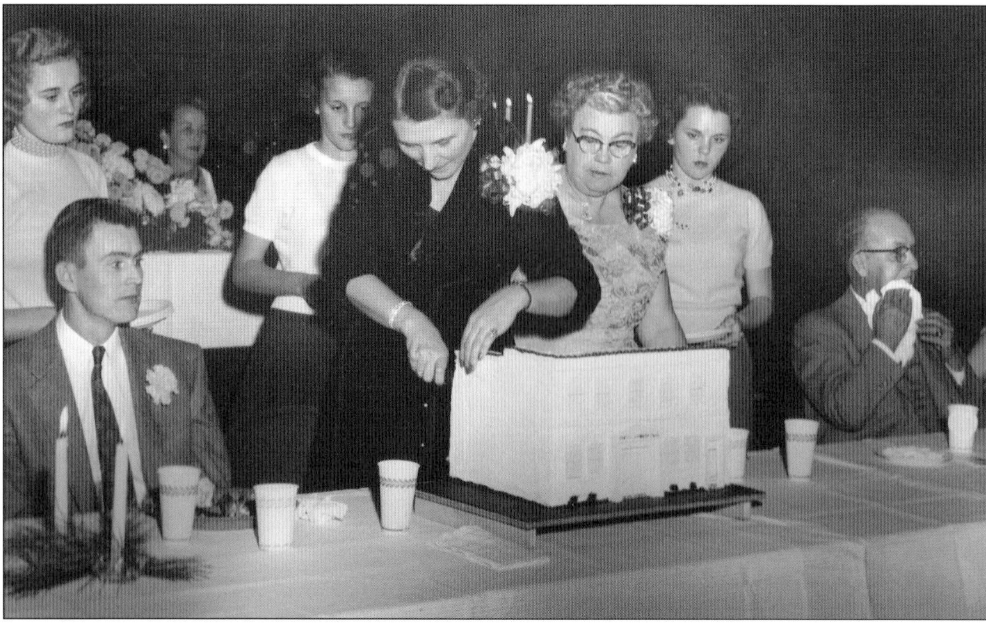

Photographed here is the cutting of a Glennville Bank cake on the bank's 50th anniversary celebration. From left to right are Gail Odom, Jack A. Rogers (seated), Doris Beasley Kicklighter (seated in the background), Jane Lewis, Gladys Waters (cutting the cake), Julia Banks, Carol Cowan, and J.B. Seckinger (seated). (Courtesy of the Glennville Bank.)

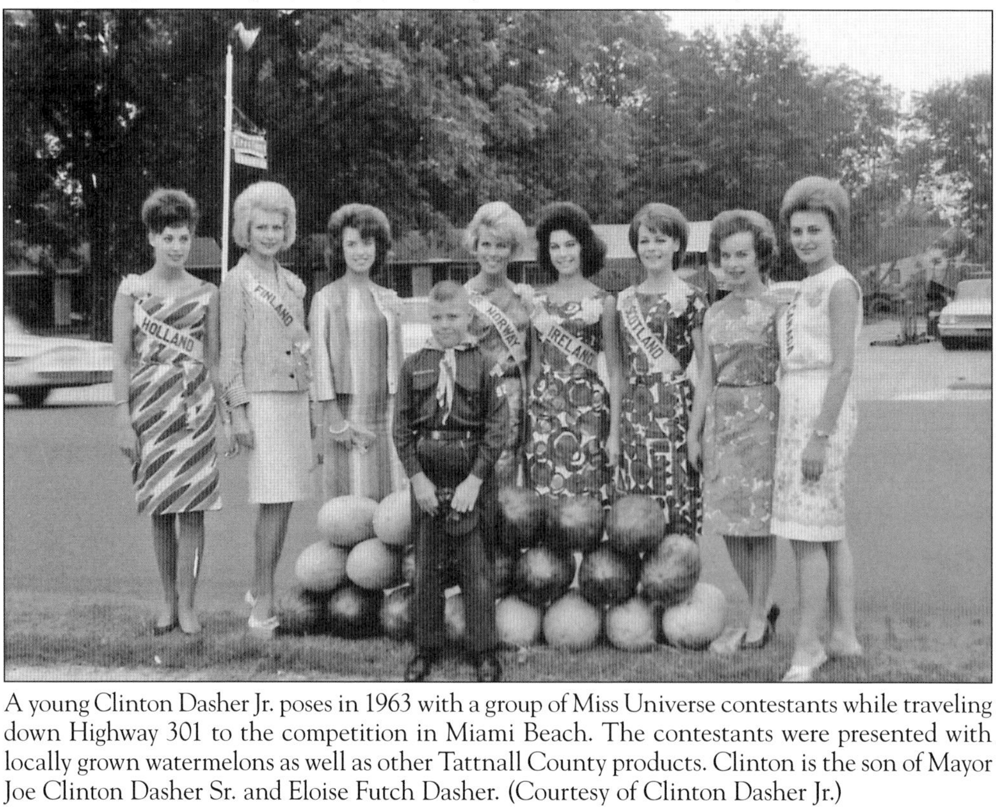

A young Clinton Dasher Jr. poses in 1963 with a group of Miss Universe contestants while traveling down Highway 301 to the competition in Miami Beach. The contestants were presented with locally grown watermelons as well as other Tattnall County products. Clinton is the son of Mayor Joe Clinton Dasher Sr. and Eloise Futch Dasher. (Courtesy of Clinton Dasher Jr.)

Seven

PEOPLE AND PLACES

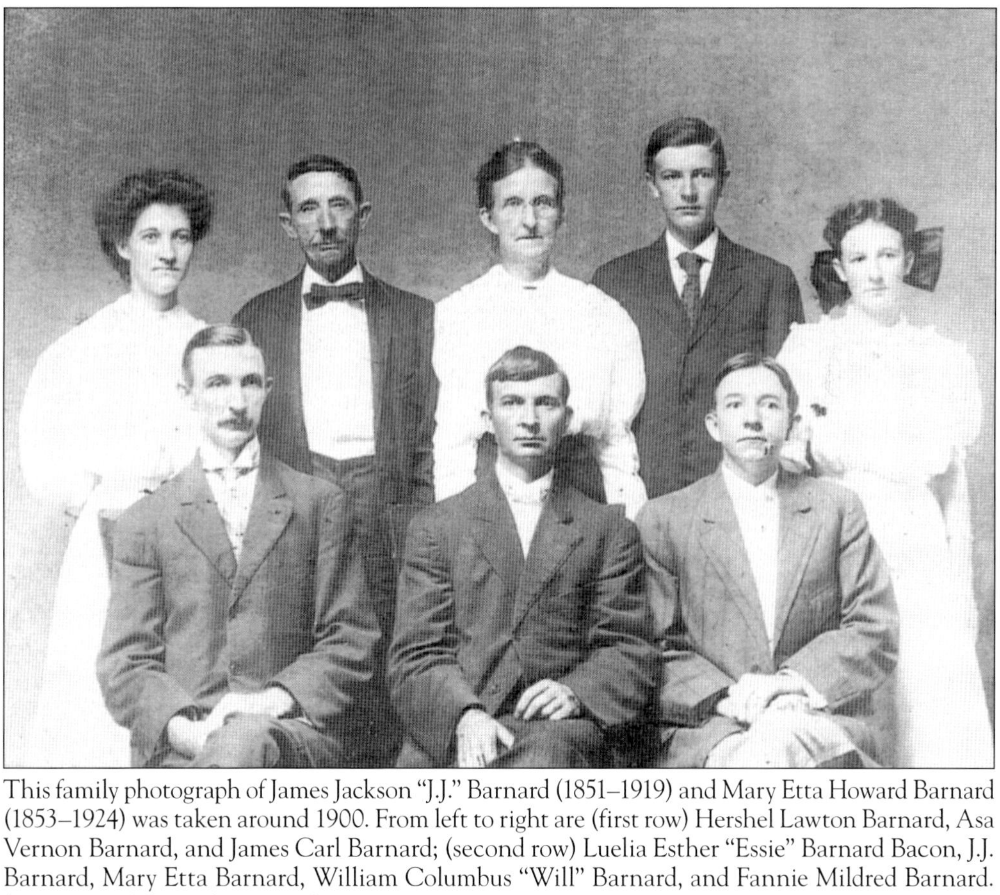

This family photograph of James Jackson "J.J." Barnard (1851–1919) and Mary Etta Howard Barnard (1853–1924) was taken around 1900. From left to right are (first row) Hershel Lawton Barnard, Asa Vernon Barnard, and James Carl Barnard; (second row) Luelia Esther "Essie" Barnard Bacon, J.J. Barnard, Mary Etta Barnard, William Columbus "Will" Barnard, and Fannie Mildred Barnard. (Courtesy of Juan Thompson.)

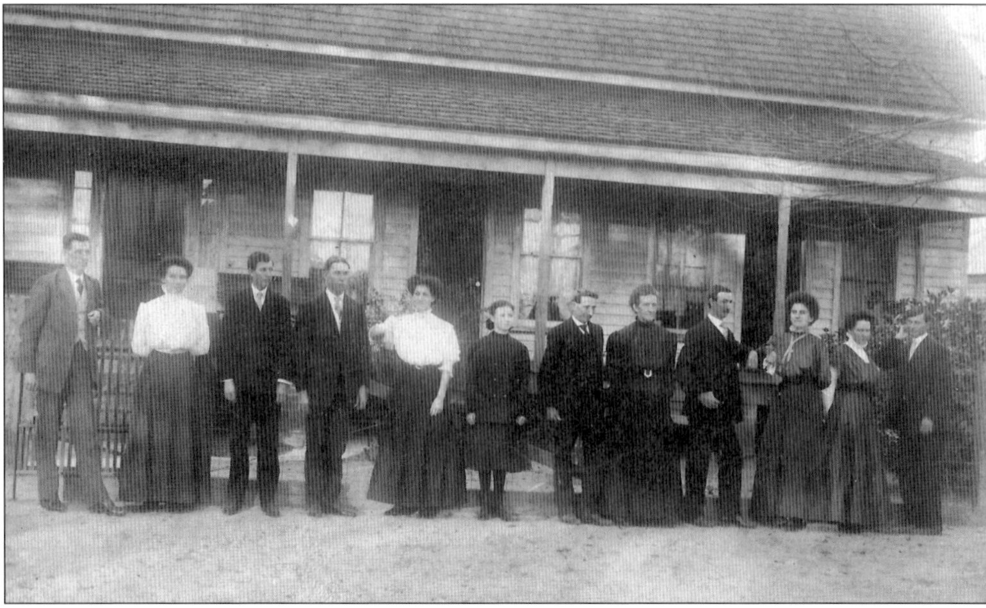

J.J. Barnard was one of early Glennville's most beloved and prominent citizens. When the town's street system was formally organized in 1902–1903, Barnard Street was named in his honor, and Marietta Street was named for his wife, Mary Etta. Members of the Barnard family stand here in front of the Barnard home, which still stands at the northeast corner of East Barnard and Herrington Streets, across from the present Glennville Middle School. The front porch pictured here once faced Barnard Street. From left to right are Clevie Barnard, Ola Barnard, Will Barnard, Edwin H. "Hawk" Bacon Jr., Essie Barnard Bacon, Fannie Barnard, J.J. Barnard, Mary Etta Barnard, Lawton Barnard, Mannie Barnard, Mamie Barnard, and Vernon Barnard. (Courtesy of Juan Thompson.)

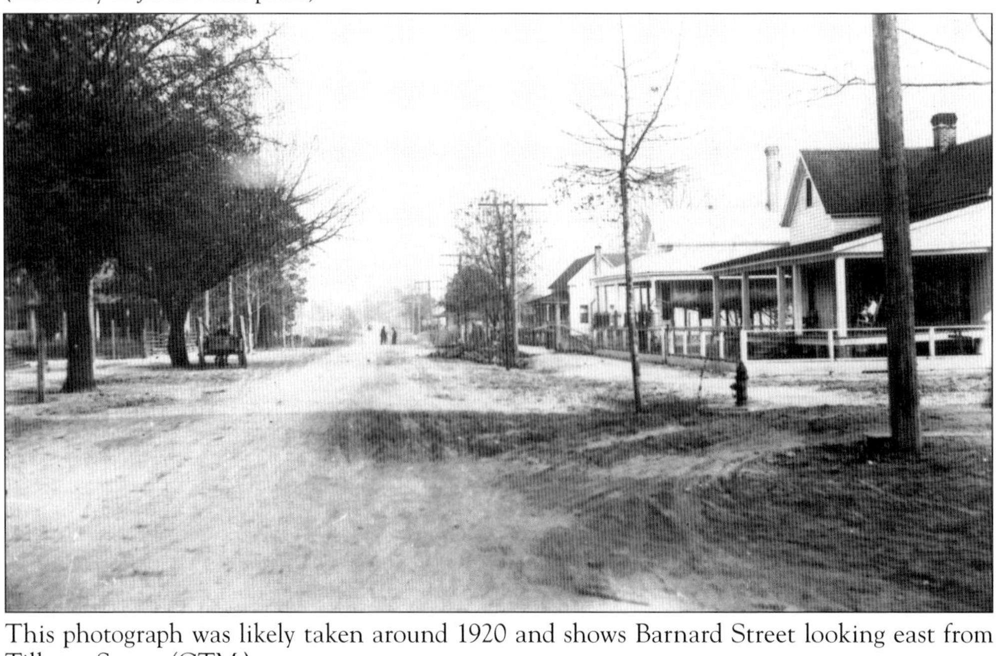

This photograph was likely taken around 1920 and shows Barnard Street looking east from Tillman Street. (GTM.)

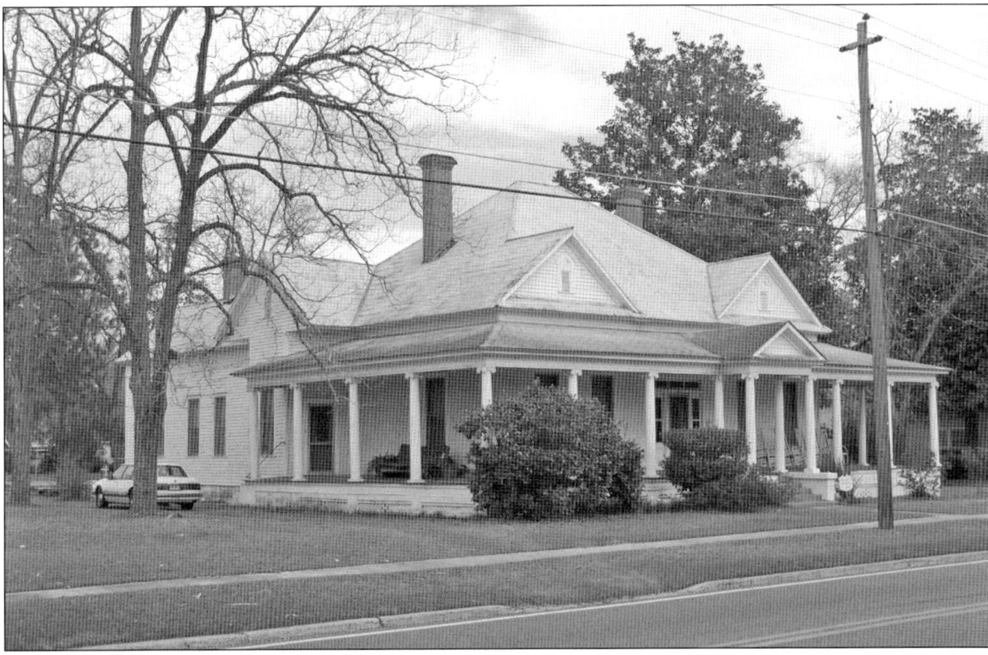

The Holland-Kirkland house, located at the corner of Barnard and Henry Streets, was built around 1902 by Jim Holland and was sold to Dr. G.W. Tootle sometime before 1922. In 1923, it was purchased by James E. and Minerva Bacon Kirkland. It is presently owned by their son Junior and his wife, Vonceil Beasley Kirkland. (Courtesy of Dylan Edward Mulligan.)

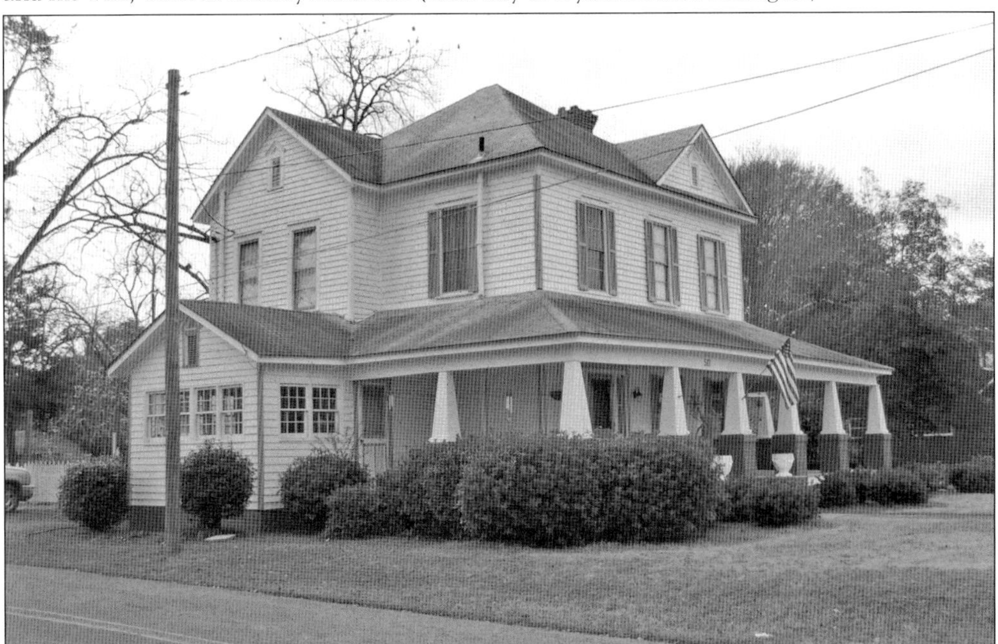

At the corner of Barnard Street and Cowart Avenue, the Cowart house was built in 1912 by Judge Cleveland Lamar "C.L." Cowart and his wife, Danella Shuptrine Cowart. Their two sons, Carroll Lamar and Dan Shuptrine Cowart, both practiced law and served as judges like their father. Dan and Vivian Weitman Cowart moved into the house in 1949. (Courtesy of Dylan Edward Mulligan.)

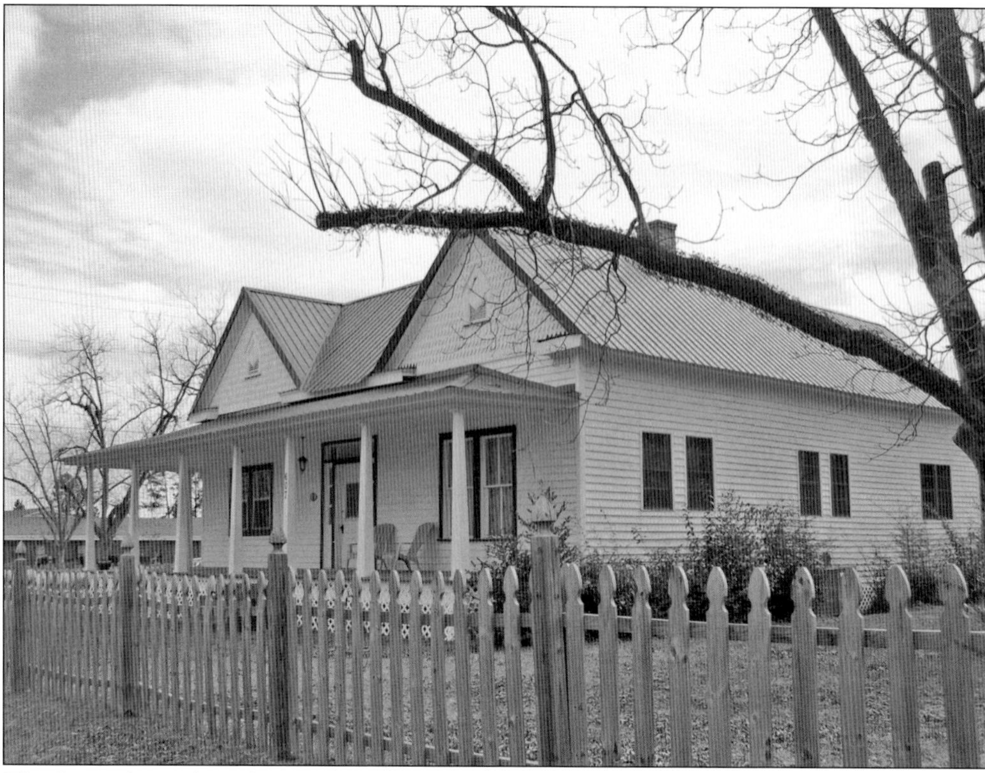

This home, located on the southwest corner of Barnard and Herrington Streets, was built before 1910 by J.J. Barnard for his daughter Esther and her husband, E.H. "Hawk" Bacon Jr. Bacon managed the sawmill of Dr. G.W. Tootle a few blocks west of this house. (Courtesy of Dylan Edward Mulligan.)

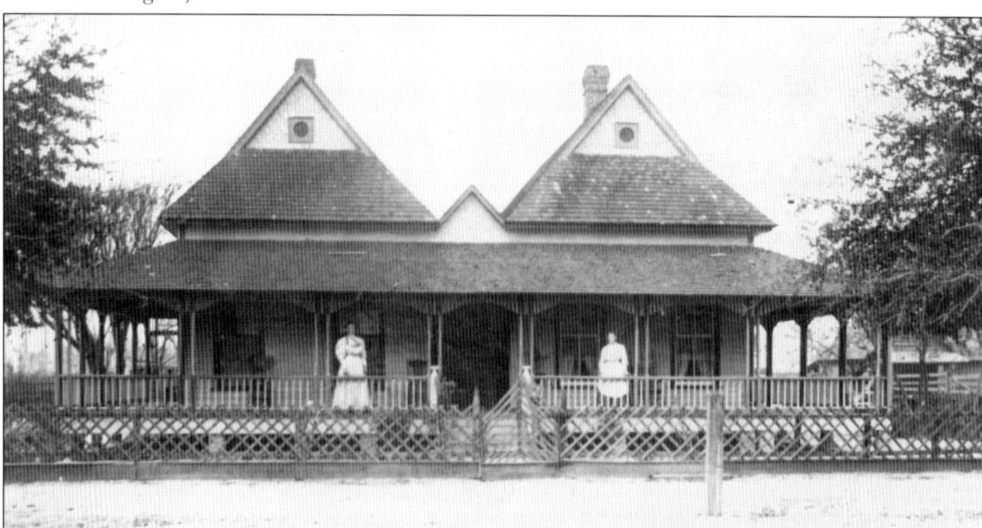

This house, pictured in 1906, was built around 1902 at the northeast corner of Barnard and Tillman Streets by Dr. George W. Tootle and his wife, Lennie Jenkins Tootle. Tootle was one of Tattnall County's leading physicians for many decades. He was the father of J. Slater Tootle, whose modern residence was later built on this site. (Perkins.)

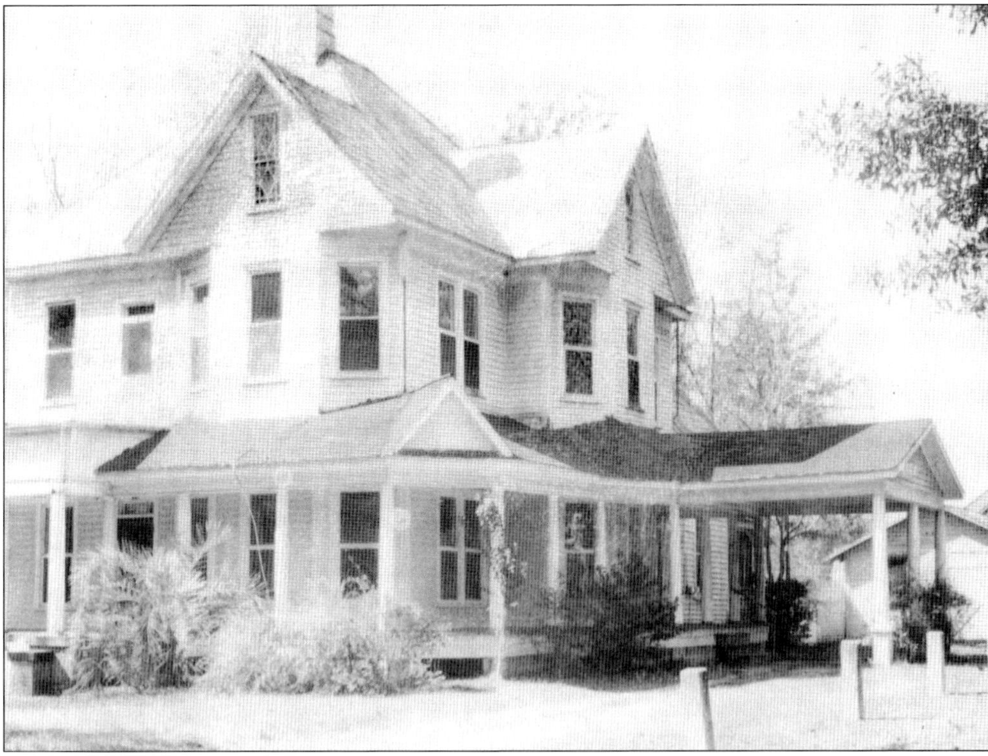

This house was built around 1900 on the west side of North Caswell Street by Dr. J.M. Hughes Sr., who sold it to Jewish merchant Joe Lipsitz around 1916. Lipsitz then sold the house to Leila Easterling Kicklighter around 1921. In 1959, Jack A. Rogers purchased the home and had it dismantled, using bricks from the chimney to construct his new home on the same site. (Courtesy of Anne Lewis Rogers.)

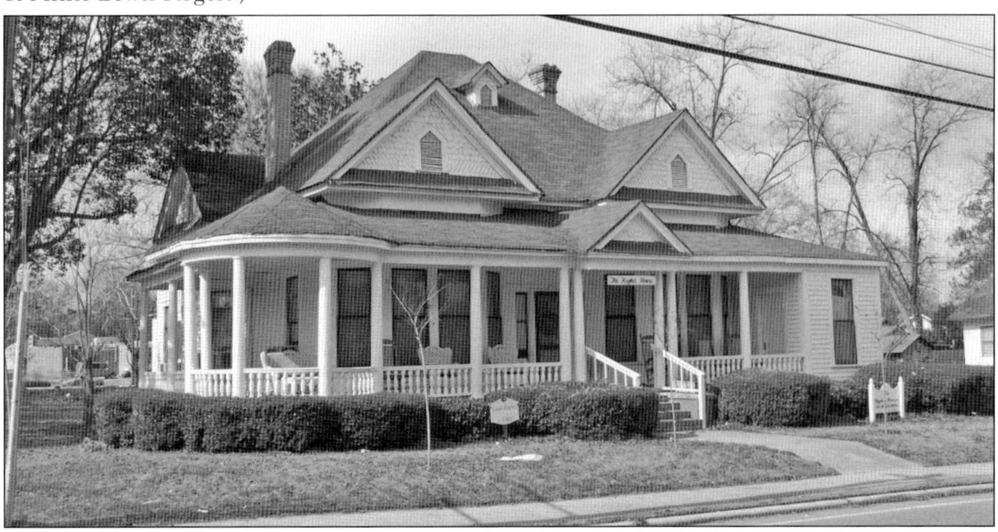

The Hughes house, located on Caswell Street just north of Barnard Street, was built in 1905 by Asa DeLoach for his daughter, Eula DeLoach Coates. In 1927, the home was purchased by Dr. J.M. Hughes Sr. Hughes, like Tootle, was one of Glennville's most beloved medical doctors. The home is presently owned by Jerrell and Bobby Baker. (Courtesy of Dylan Edward Mulligan.)

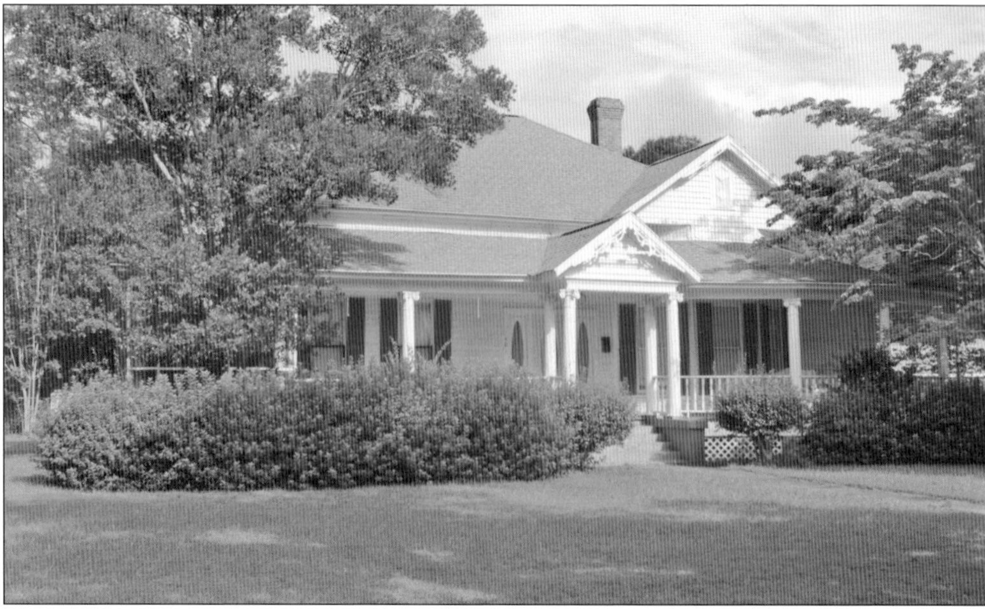

The Kicklighter house, located on the northwest corner of North Caswell and China Streets, was built in 1915 by Samuel Jasper Kicklighter and Eva Stanfield Kicklighter. S.J. Kicklighter was a prominent businessman, and his house was one of the finest ever constructed in town. It featured intricate interior and exterior woodwork as well as a Tiffany chandelier from Chicago. (Courtesy of Dylan Edward Mulligan.)

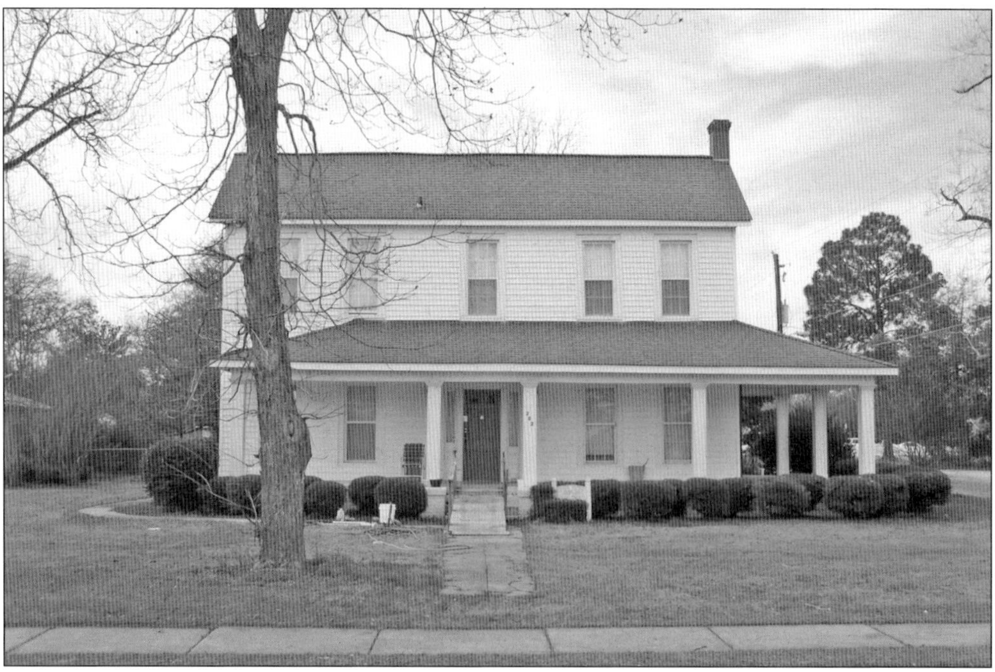

The Mann-Dixon house, located at the southwest corner of South Tillman and Institute Streets, was built in 1914 by Martha Vianna "Anna" Easterling Mann, widow of Dr. Willie Henry Mann. Around 1924, Anna sold the house to Claude Dixon, whose family lived there for many years. (Courtesy of Dylan Edward Mulligan.)

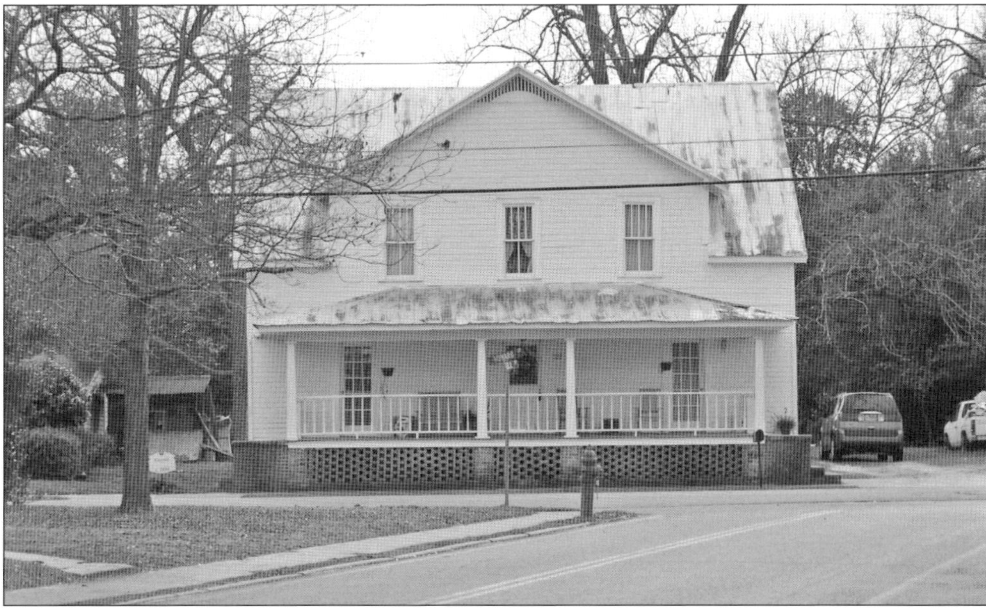

The Caswell house, located on Howard Street at the end of Caswell Street, was built in 1894 by John B. Caswell, for whom the street is named. It was purchased in 1916 by George Woodcock and in 1963 by Buel Barnard, who lived there until his death in 1986. Barnard's daughter Miriam and her husband, Logan Porter, have owned the house since 1989. (Courtesy of Dylan Edward Mulligan.)

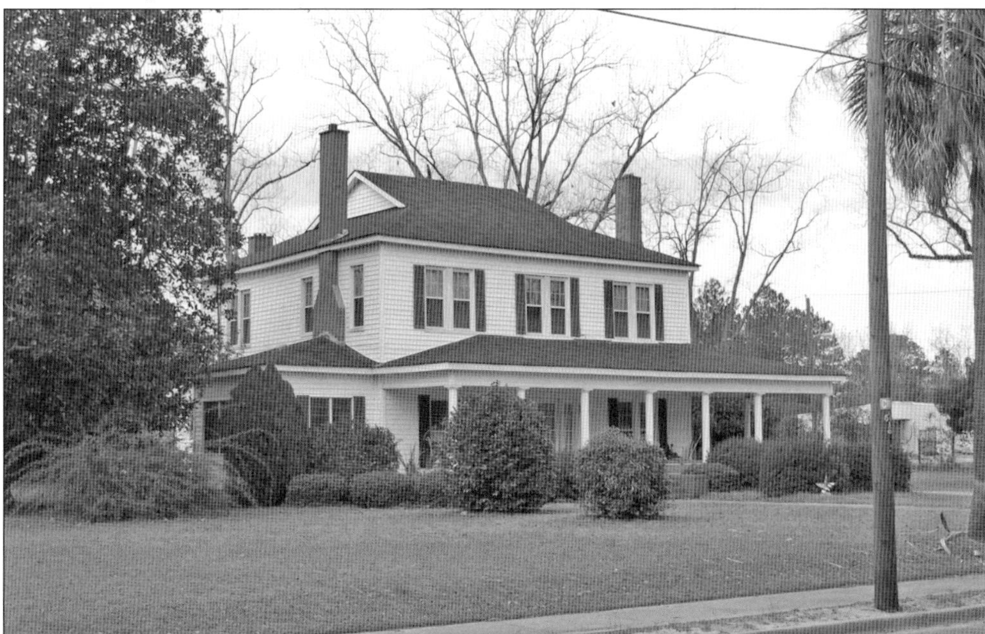

The Williams-Grice house, located on North Church Street, was thought to have been built sometime before 1914 by A.J. Williams, a local carpenter and early ice salesman. In the mid-1920s, the house was purchased by Judge Joseph Thomas Grice, a prominent lawyer and early historian. (Courtesy of Dylan Edward Mulligan.)

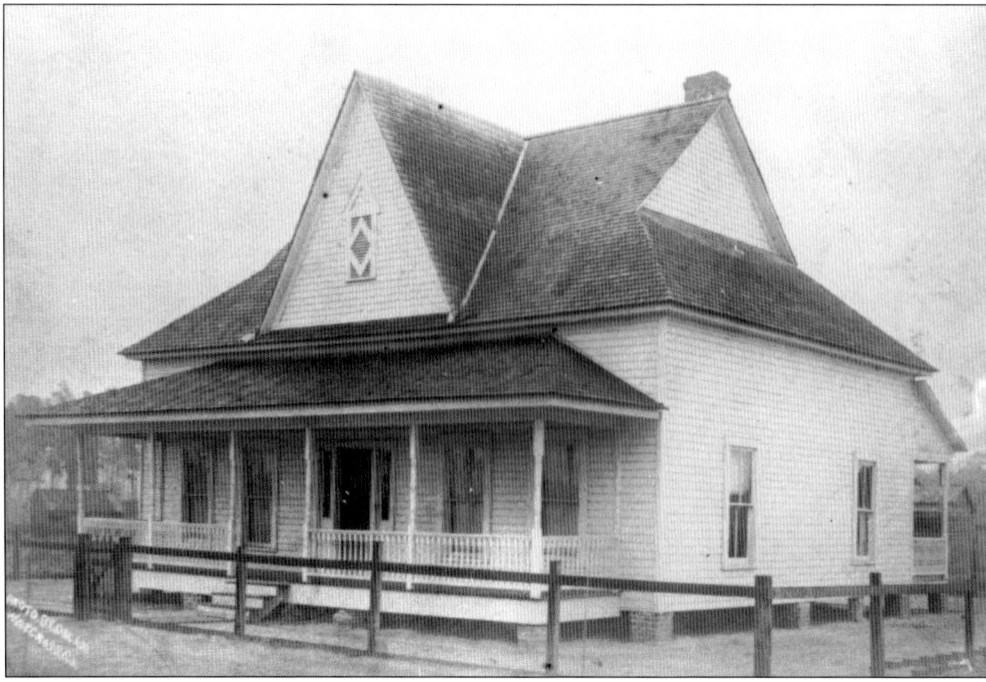

This house stood on the west side of South Church Street. It was built around 1906, when this photograph was taken, by G. Ransom "Rance" Anderson and Mamie Anderson, whose son Bill and his wife, Susie, later occupied the house. (Perkins.)

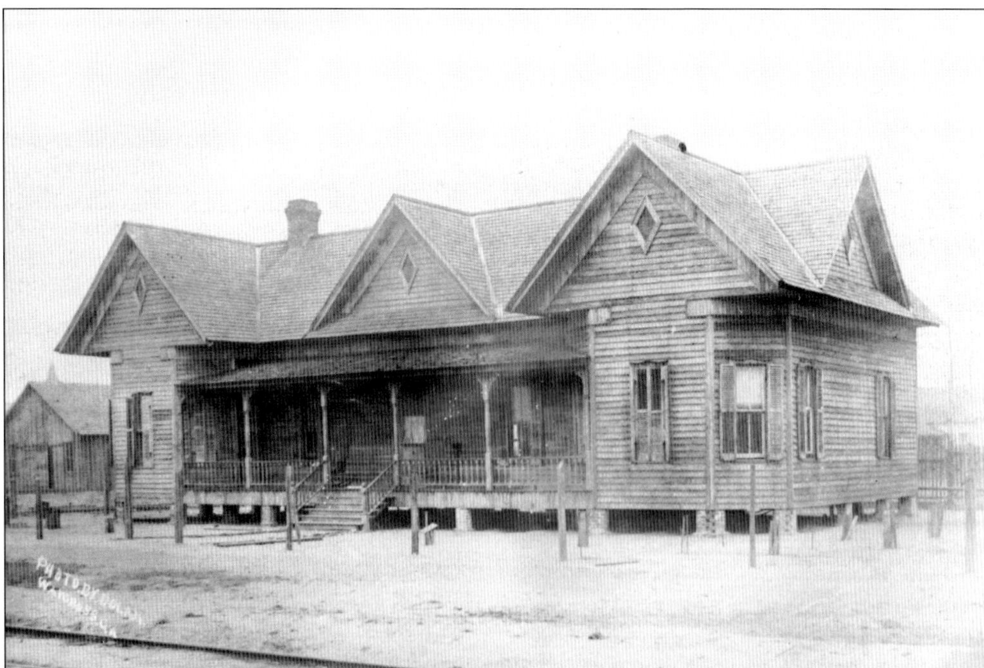

The exact location, date of construction, and ownership of this house remains unknown; however, its architectural design was unlike anything else constructed in Glennville. In this 1906 photograph, the steeple of the Methodist church can be seen at back left. (Perkins.)

William F. "Bill" Durrence (1853–1940) was a son of John H. and Nancy Wilkinson Durrence and one of Tattnall County's leading citizens. W.F. Durrence was a large landowner, farmer, and businessman and was very involved in the early development of Glennville. He served as the second president of the Glennville Bank from 1908 until his death in 1940. (Courtesy of the Glennville Bank.)

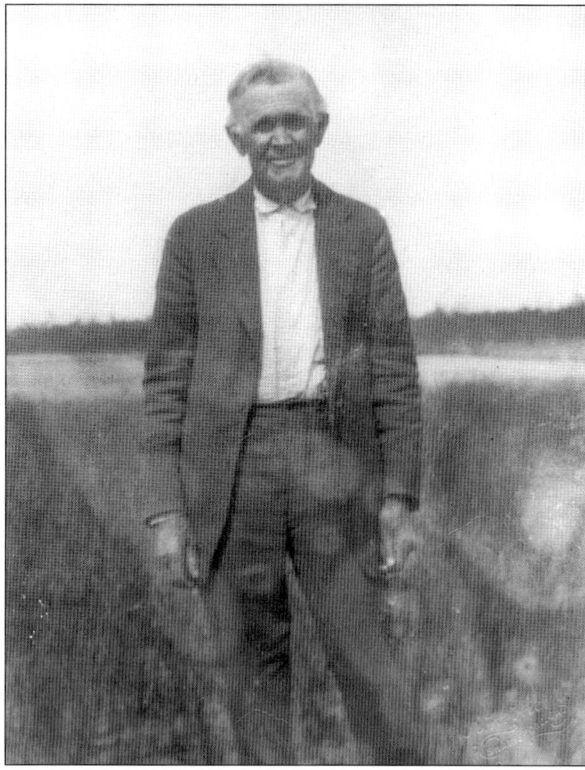

John Alton "Stevie" Bacon (1905–1999) served as the fourth president of the Glennville Bank from 1952 to 1974 and as chairman of the board of directors from 1974 until 1990. (Courtesy of the Glennville Bank.)

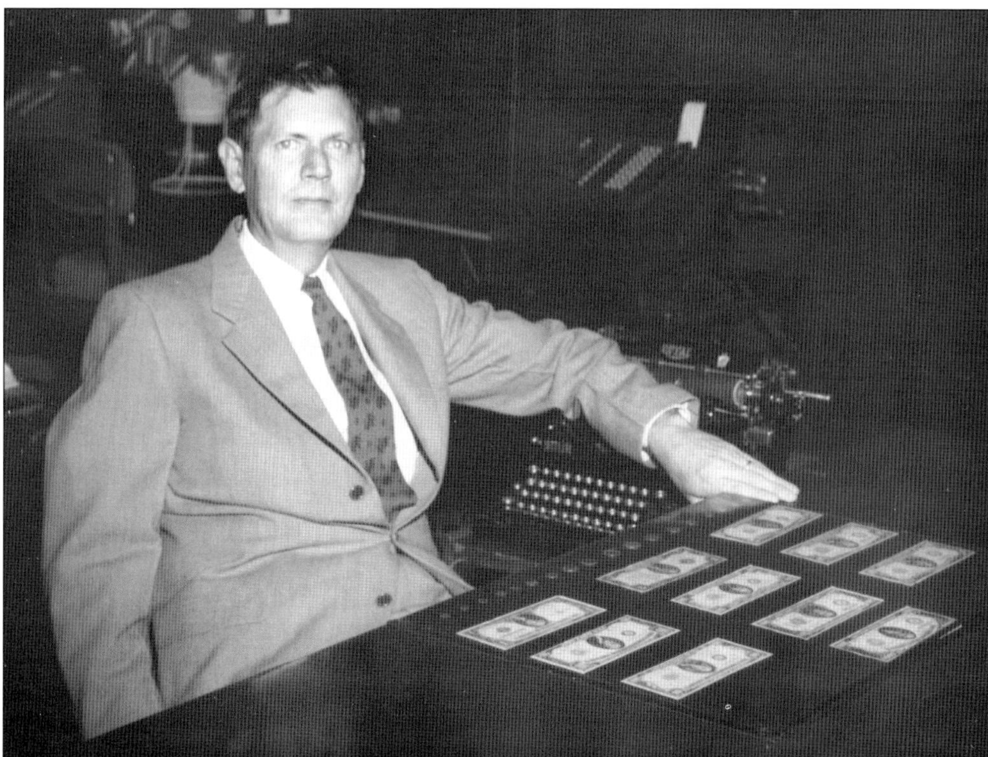

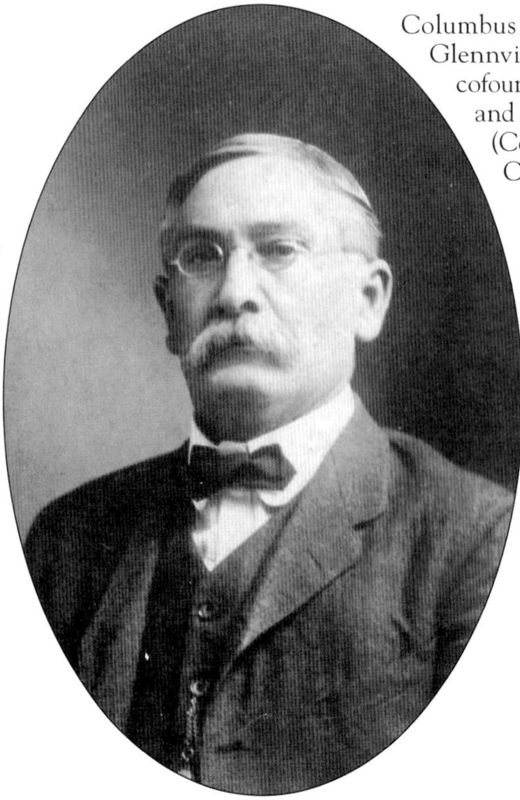

Columbus S. "Lum" Grice (1855–1933) was one of Glennville's leading merchants. In 1891, he helped cofound the Glennville United Methodist Church and donated the lumber to build the sanctuary. (Courtesy of the Glennville United Methodist Church.)

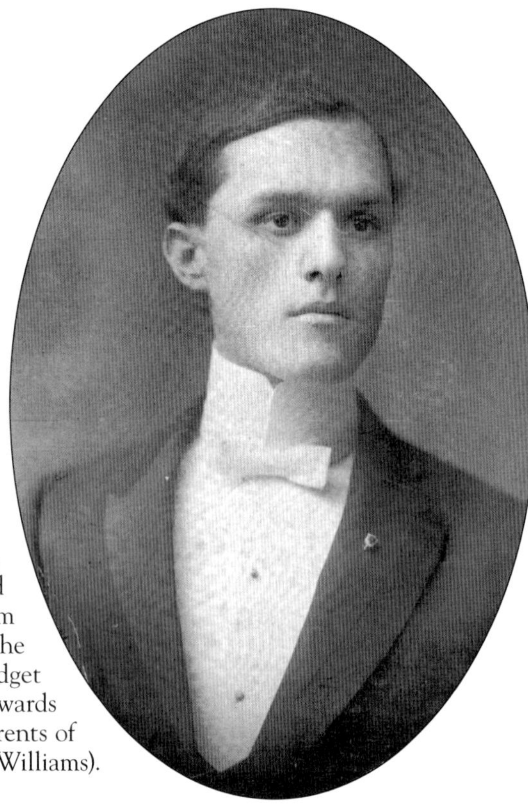

Mayor Dr. Shelton Orlando Edwards (1882–1947) was born in Daisy, which was founded by his father, T.J. Edwards. Arriving in Glennville in the early 1900s, S.O. Edwards was a prominent farmer and dentist and served as mayor of Glennville from 1920 to 1923. He was especially proud to be the first mayor to manage the city with no budget deficits. Edwards and his wife, Ola Grice Edwards (daughter of Columbus Grice), were the parents of Ann Edwards deTreville (later Ann Edwards Williams). (Courtesy of the City of Glennville.)

George M. Love (1823–1907) was a prominent farmer between Glennville and Mendes. When his neighbors began organizing a Primitive Baptist church in 1888, Love donated the land, and the church was named Love's Chapel in his honor. He is pictured here with two of his grandchildren thought to be Lon and Pearl, children of David and Loanzy Love. (Courtesy of Bobbette Dasher.)

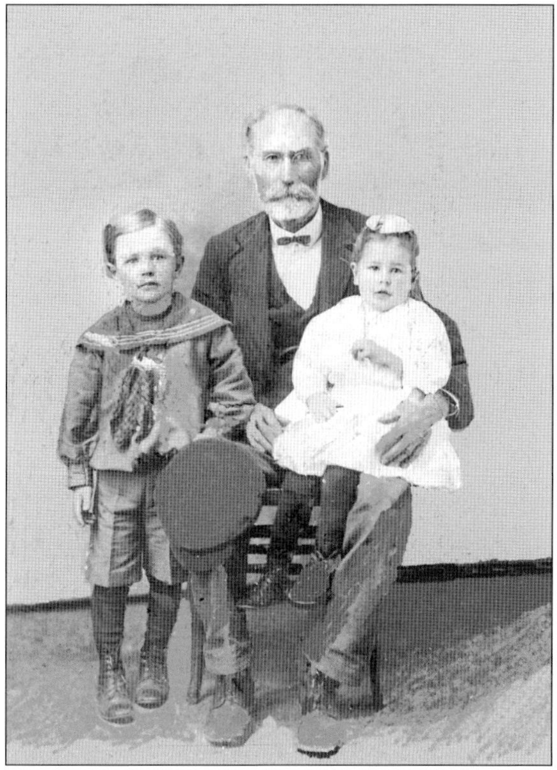

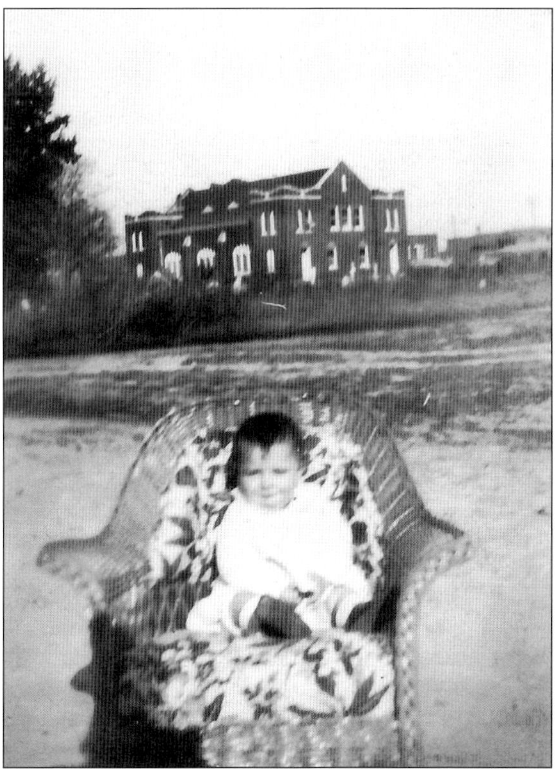

The back of First Baptist Church can be seen in the background of this photograph of Roger Rudolph Mulligan (1927–1928), the infant son of Edward F. "Ned" Mulligan Sr. and Laura Rogers Mulligan. The photograph was taken in front of the Mulligan home, which stood on the west side of South Church Street across from the present church parking lot. (Courtesy of Dylan Edward Mulligan.)

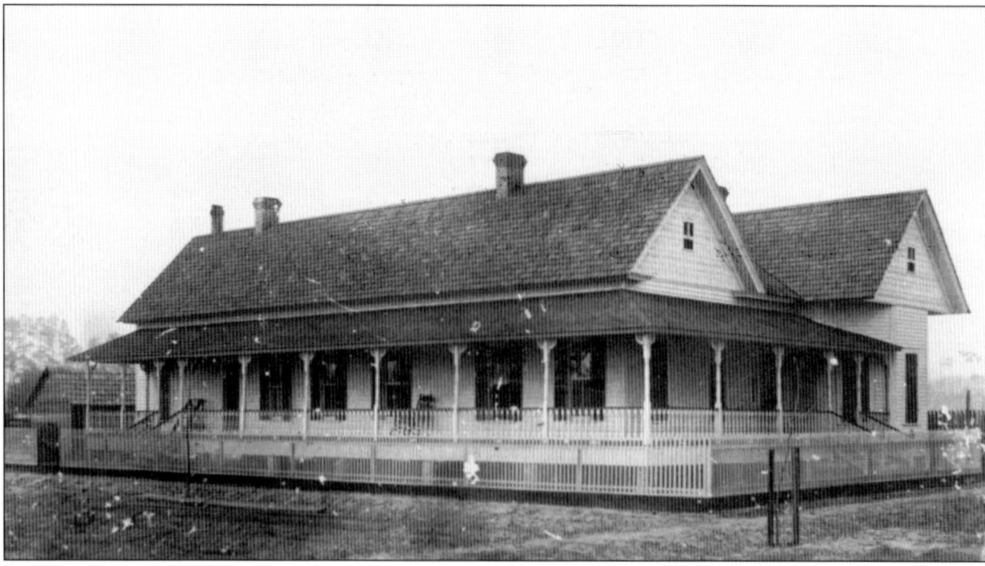

This house stood on the east side of Highway 301 South just north of the Free Will Baptist Church. Pictured here in 1906, it was divided into two separate duplexes. Over the years, residents included Rosa Hamilton, Jo Ann Padgett, Dr. Rogers, and the Brantley D. Blitch family. The home's last owner was Mary Kicklighter, wife of H. Prentice Kicklighter and daughter of Rosa Hamilton. (Perkins.)

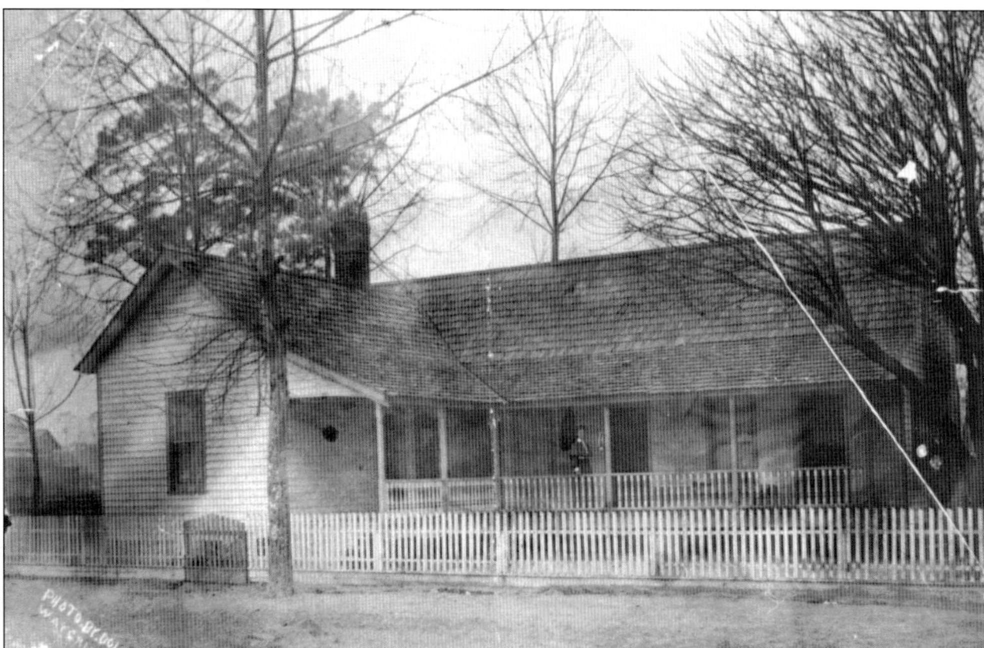

The Banks house, pictured here in 1906, stood on the west side of South Caswell Street across from Institute Street near the later location of First Citizens Bank. It was built around 1890 by Henry J. Banks, first president of the Glennville Bank. In the 1920s, the house was inherited by Banks's granddaughter Eunice Rogers, who in later years married Holmes Sands. The Banks house burned in the 1960s. (Perkins.)

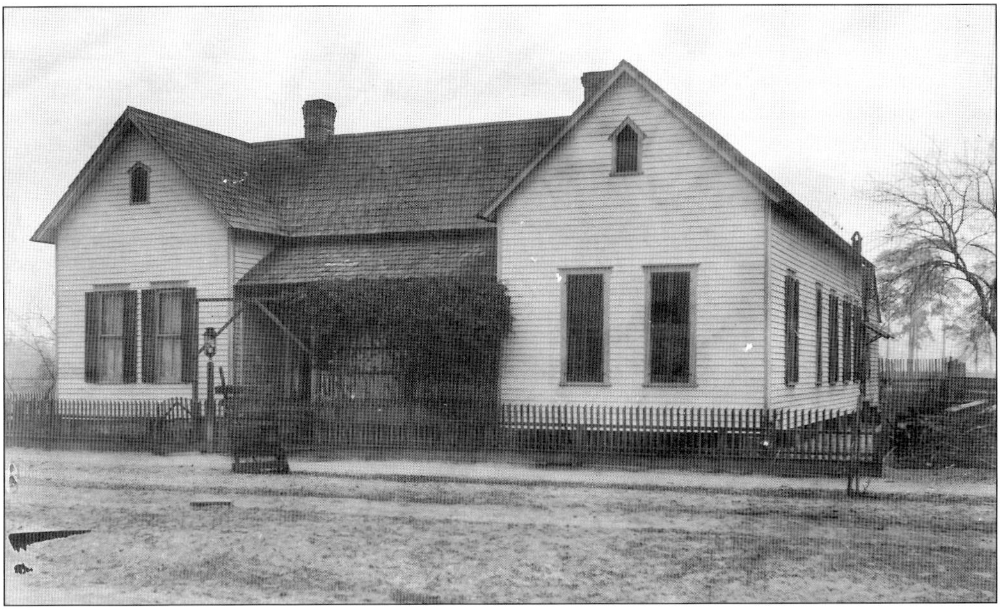

The Easterling house, seen here in 1906, was built on the northeast corner of South Caswell and Institute Streets around 1904 by the widow of James O'Neill Easterling, Martha Emily Howard Easterling, for whom Howard Street was named. Sometime after 1924, the house was sold to W.F. Durrence. In 1948, his widow, Viola James Durrence, sold the property to the Christian Church for use as a parking lot. (Perkins.)

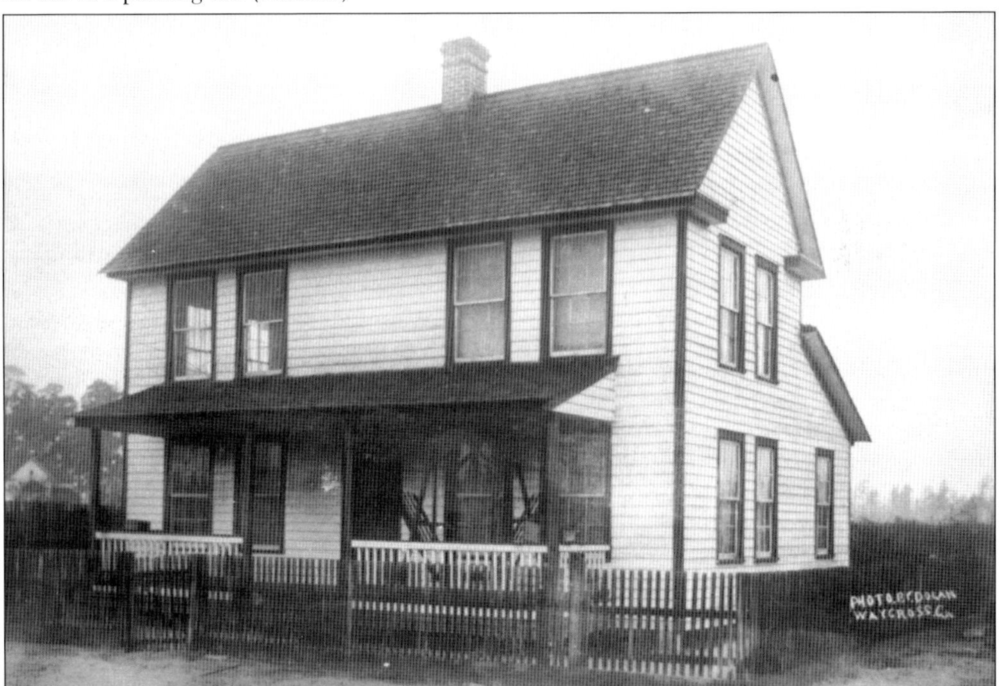

The Bolton house, located on the northwest corner of South Baker and Bolton Streets, is pictured here in 1906 and was thought to have been owned by Ora Bolton or a member of her family, who owned the entire block between Barnard, Tillman, Bolton, and Baker Streets. (Perkins.)

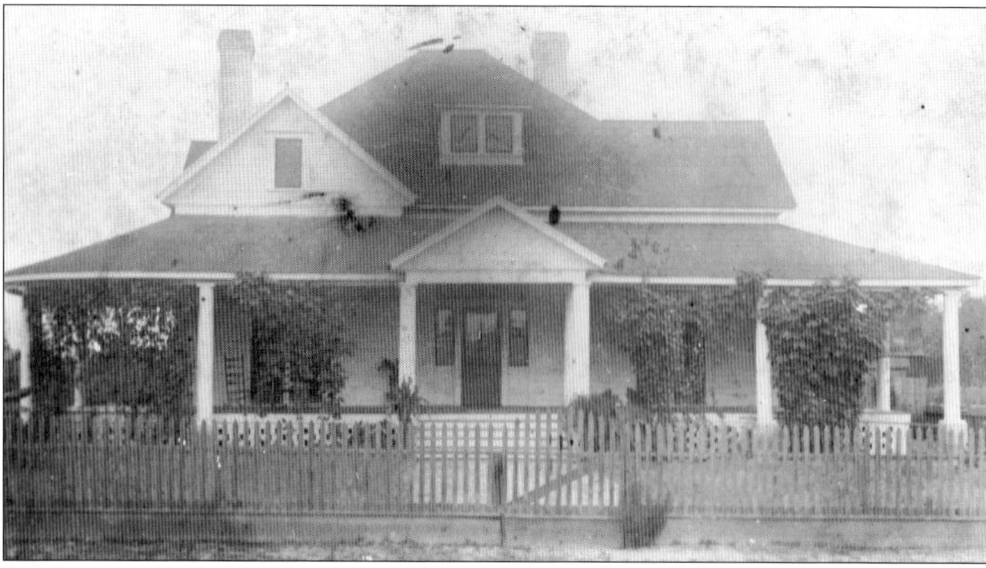

This house was built in 1908 at the southeast corner of North Caswell and China Streets by John D. Bradley Sr. Soon after, Bradley sold the home to the Tuten family, who owned the Savannah & Southern Railway. They in turn sold the house to John Beasley, and it was later owned by Curtis and Betty Burns. The house still stands, though unrecognizable after many modern renovations. (Courtesy of Richard Bradley Jr.)

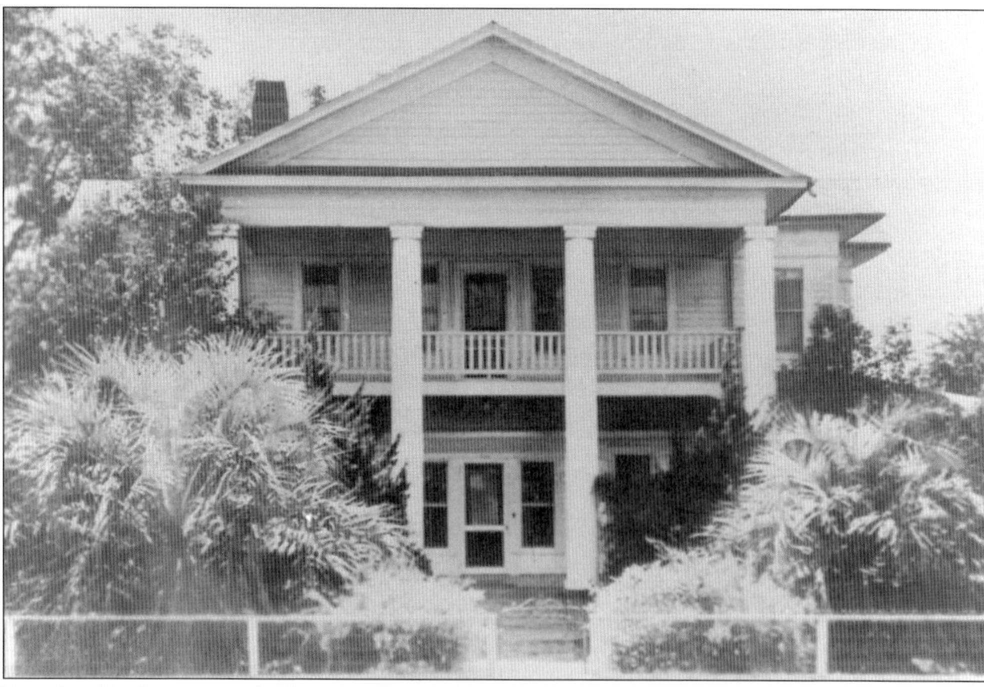

The Bradley house was built around 1893 by Jasper B. Seckinger and was originally a single-story home. In 1916, it was purchased by John D. Bradley Sr., who in 1932 conducted extensive renovations, adding the second floor and columns to give it its present appearance. One of Glennville's most recognizable landmarks, the Bradley house still stands on West Barnard Street between Church and Rushing Streets. (Courtesy of Brent Walker.)

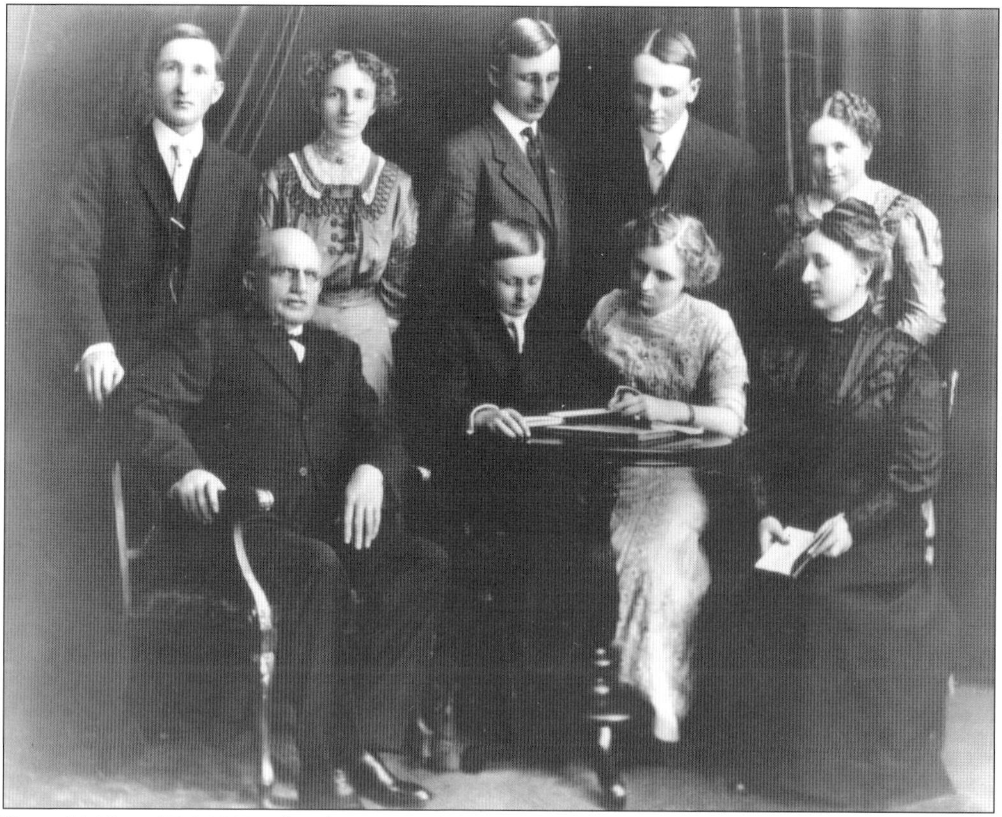

Daniel Milton "D.M." Bradley (1850–1925) of Hagan was the original owner of the Collins & Glennville Railroad and made substantial contributions to the development of Glennville. From left to right are (first row) Daniel Milton Bradley, Waldo Bradley, Jane Bradley, and Jane Matilda Brewton Bradley; (second row) John Daniel Bradley Sr., Rosamond Bradley, Daniel Marcus Bradley, William Daniel Bradley, and Bessie Fontaine Bradley. (Courtesy of the Glennville Bank.)

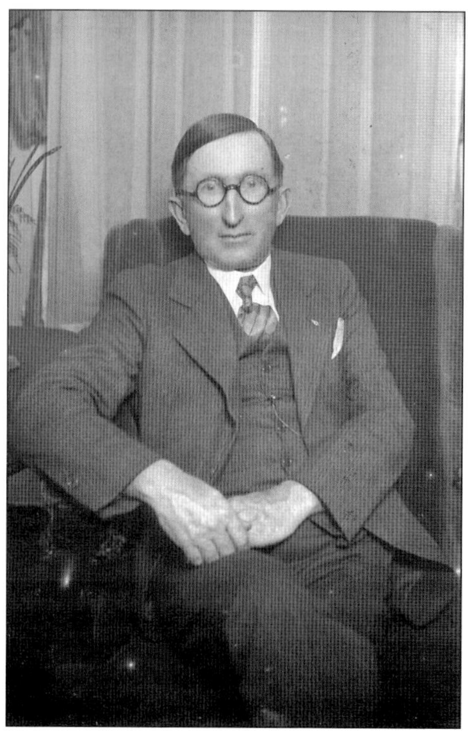

Capt. John Daniel "J.D." Bradley Sr. (1879–1963) was one of Glennville's leading citizens. The son of D.M. and Jane Matilda Brewton Bradley, he became president of the Collins & Glennville Railroad upon his father's death and served in that capacity until 1941. J.D. Bradley was an astute businessman, public servant, and philanthropist and was much beloved by the people of Glennville. (Courtesy of Richard Bradley Jr.)

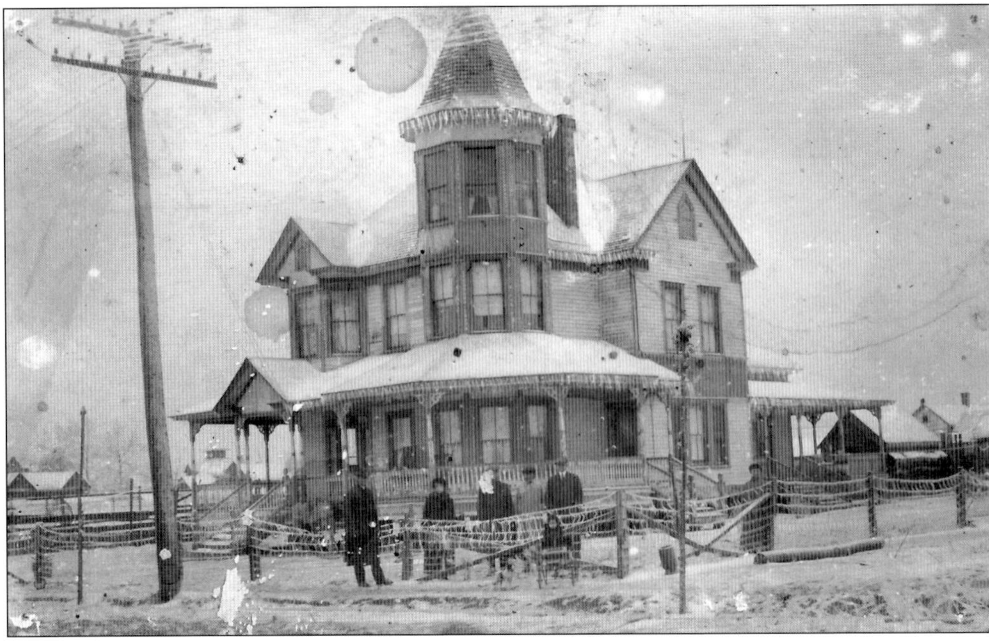

The Mann-Anderson house, pictured here in 1906, was built around 1900 by Dr. Willie Henry Mann on the west side of Morris Street between Charlton Street and Mendell Avenue. Following Dr. Mann's death in 1909, the home was acquired by Iva Anderson, who operated it as a florist shop. Following Anderson's death, his children converted the house into apartments. The home burned in 1955. (Courtesy of M. Eldred Mann.)

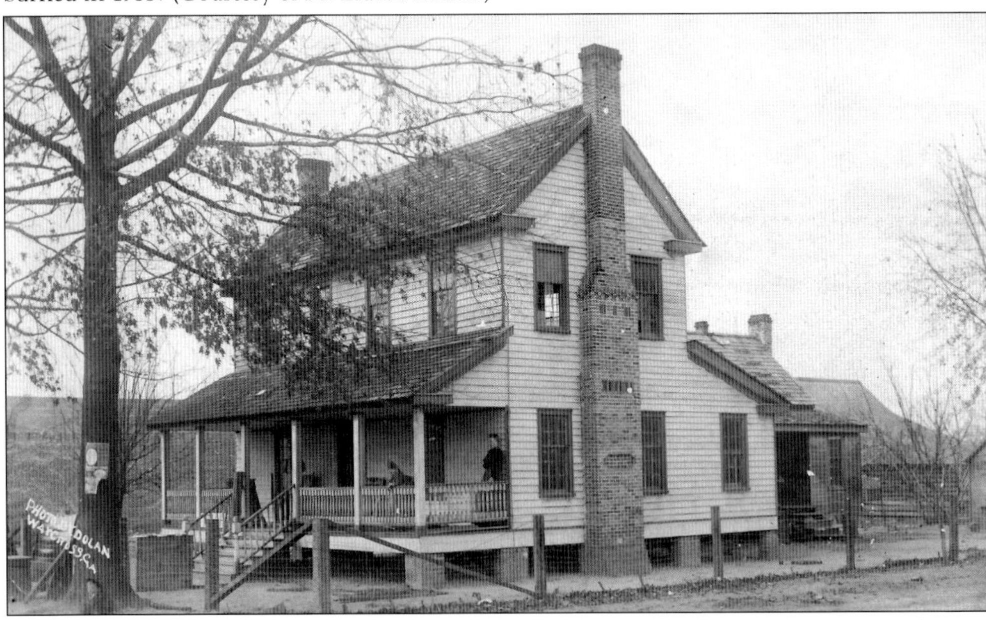

Details about this home, pictured in 1906, remain elusive. It was located on Barnard Street across from the Glennwanis Hotel and may have once belonged to the Surrency and Collins families. Later owners included Cordie Faircloth and Dr. A.C. Colson. At some point, the porch was removed and replaced with a drive-through filling station, as seen in the 1929 photograph on page 47. (Perkins.)

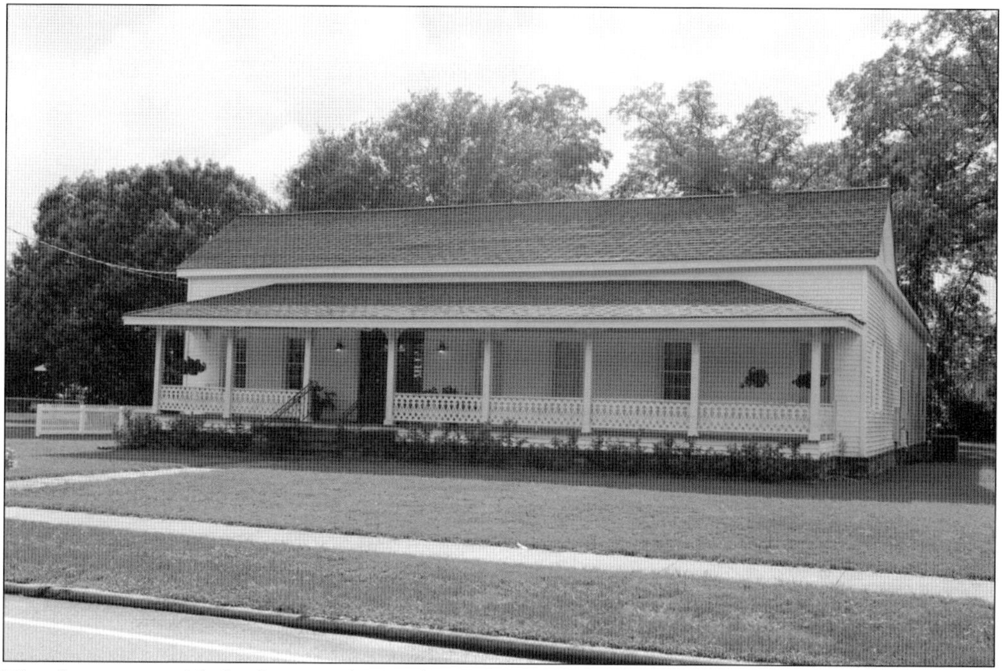

This house, possibly built around 1880 by Capt. Joseph D. DeLoach or his son Asa DeLoach, once stood on North Caswell Street just north of the Glennville Bank. Asa's daughter Netherae DeLoach Harvey lived in the house until her death in 1988. The house was later moved to its present location on North Caswell Street between China and Cedar Streets, where it serves as the law office of Hugh J. McCullough. (Courtesy of Dylan Edward Mulligan.)

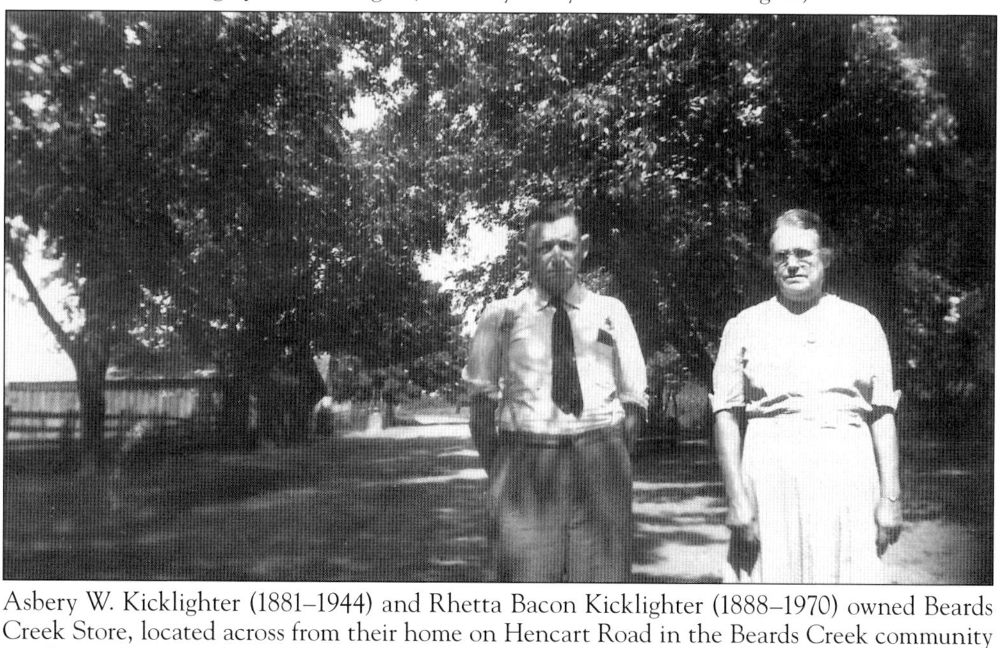

Asbery W. Kicklighter (1881–1944) and Rhetta Bacon Kicklighter (1888–1970) owned Beards Creek Store, located across from their home on Hencart Road in the Beards Creek community northeast of town. Their country store was a mainstay in the community and served countless families in the surrounding countryside. They are pictured here standing on Hencart Road in the 1930s. (Courtesy of Louise Griner Dasher.)

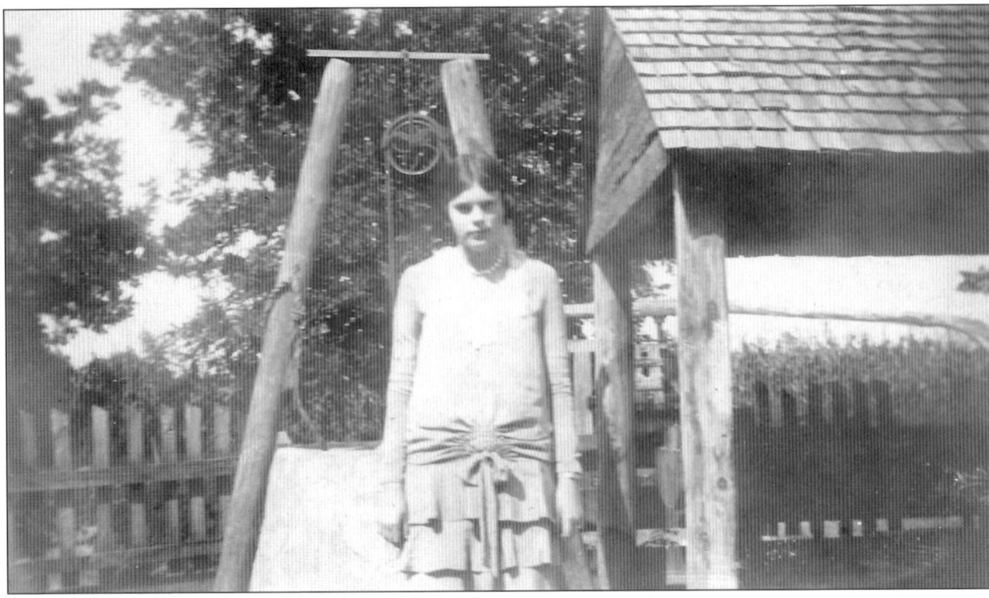

Jewel Kicklighter Griner (1914–2011), the daughter of Asbery and Rhetta Kicklighter, is pictured here around 1930 on the family farm in Beards Creek community. (Courtesy of Louise Griner Dasher.)

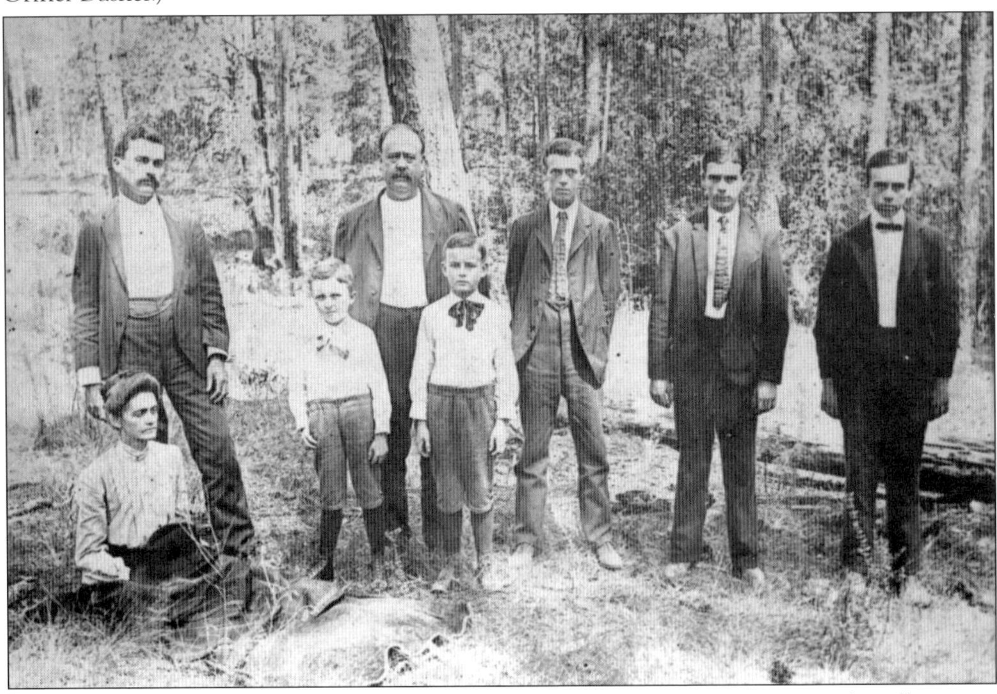

From left to right are Lennie Jenkins Tootle (seated), Dr. G.W. Tootle, J. Slater Tootle, Allen Jones Sands, J. Holmes Sands, Emery Arthur Sands, G. Olin Sands, and Clarence Kenneth Sands. Lennie Tootle was a sister of Georgia Jenkins Sands, deceased wife of Allen Sands. This photograph was taken around 1898–1900, likely near Mt. Pleasant ("Sand Hill") Methodist Church in the far eastern point of Tattnall County, now part of Fort Stewart. A "cat face" is cut into the pine tree in the background for turpentine. (Courtesy of Larry Jones Sands.)

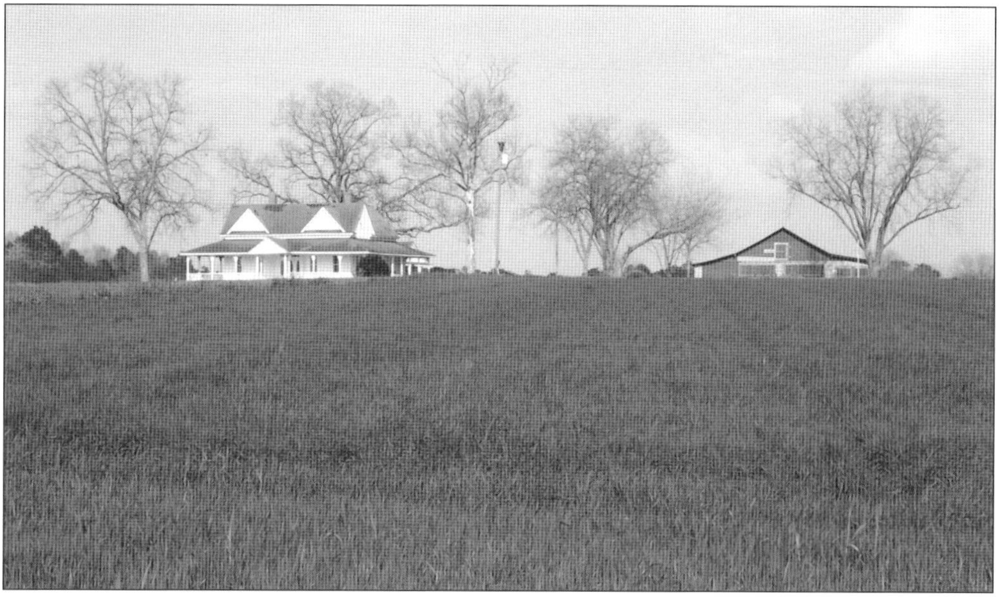

The Dasher house was built by Clarence Sands between 1910 and 1920, just east of town on a prominent hill overlooking Highway 144. The home was for a time owned by Henry Williams before being repurchased by the Sands family. In the early 1960s, the house was acquired by Walter and Winnie Fennell Dasher and is presently owned by their grandson, Heath Dasher. (Courtesy of Dylan Edward Mulligan.)

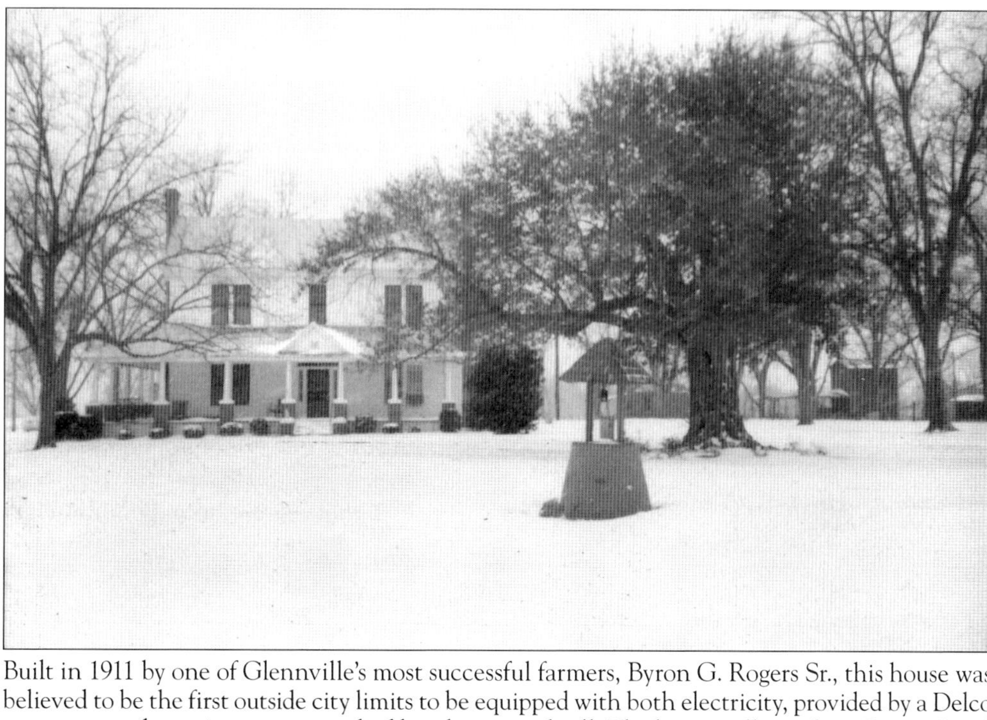

Built in 1911 by one of Glennville's most successful farmers, Byron G. Rogers Sr., this house was believed to be the first outside city limits to be equipped with both electricity, provided by a Delco generator, and running water, supplied by a large windmill. The house still stands on Rogers Road east of town and is owned by Byron and Julia Rogers's great-grandson Dylan Mulligan. (Courtesy of Dylan Edward Mulligan.)

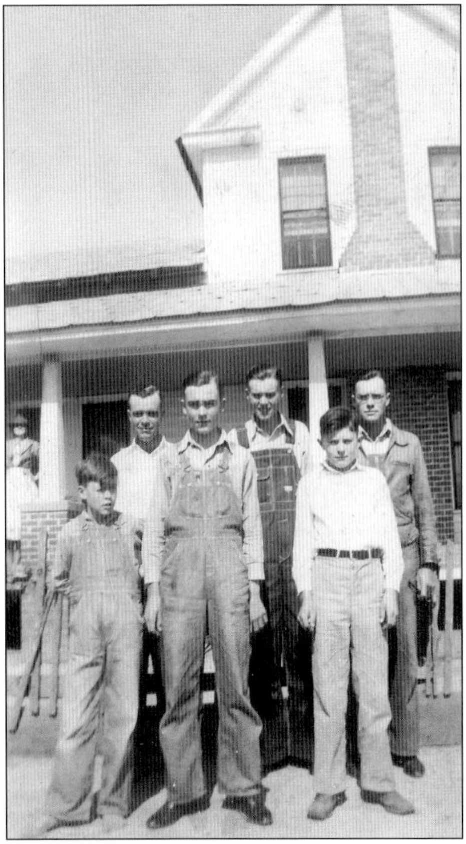

In this photograph from around 1935 are, from left to right, William Alex "Billy" Rogers, Dan Carlton Rogers Sr., Byron Green "B.G." Rogers Jr., Emory Lee Rogers, Jack Arthur Rogers, and Ira Wilson Rogers—sons of Byron G. Rogers Sr. and Julia Smiley Rogers. Julia Rogers stands on the porch of the Rogers home in the background. (Courtesy of Faye Moncrief Rogers.)

Pictured around 1910 are, from left to right, Byron Green Rogers Sr. (1889–1980), Mamie Lou Rogers Thompson (1897–1939), John Leroy Rogers (1888–1988), Julianne Ardelia "Annie" Rogers Cochran Ward (1892–1980), and Viola Virginia Rogers Long (1893–1970). They were children of Joshua Lawton Rogers and Florence Gay Rogers. (Courtesy of Josephine DeLoach Rogers.)

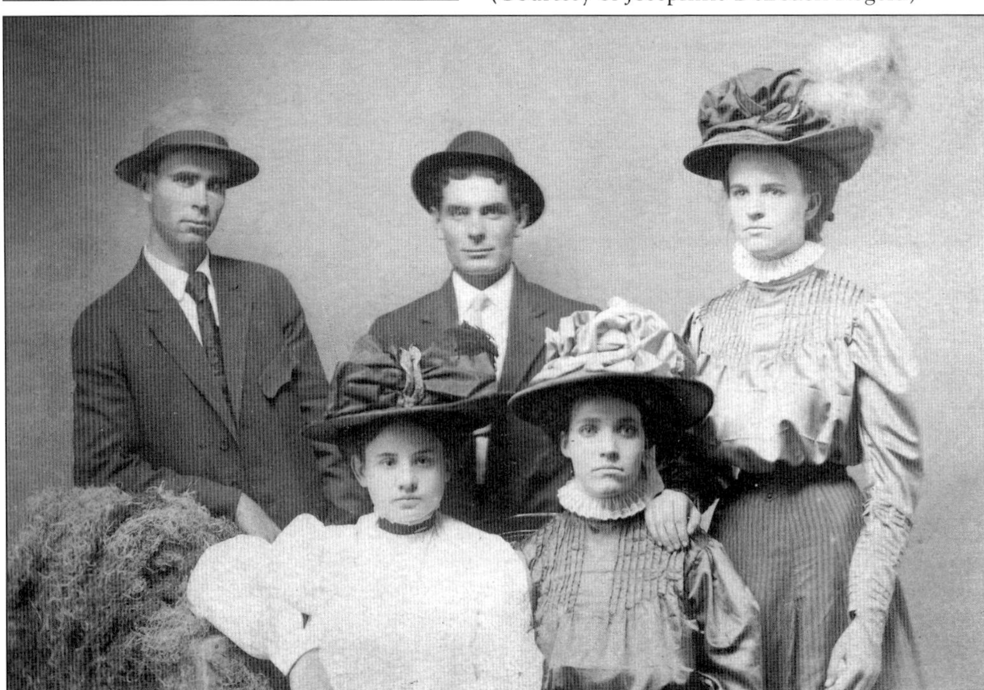

Glennville's greatest hero was Capt. Robert DeLoach (1918–1949), who served with great distinction as a fighter pilot during World War II. After the war, he was one of the Air Force's first jet pilots and was killed in action during a training exercise. He is pictured here shortly before his death with his baby cousin Susan Tootle and her grandmother Edna Tootle. (Courtesy of Bobby Kicklighter.)

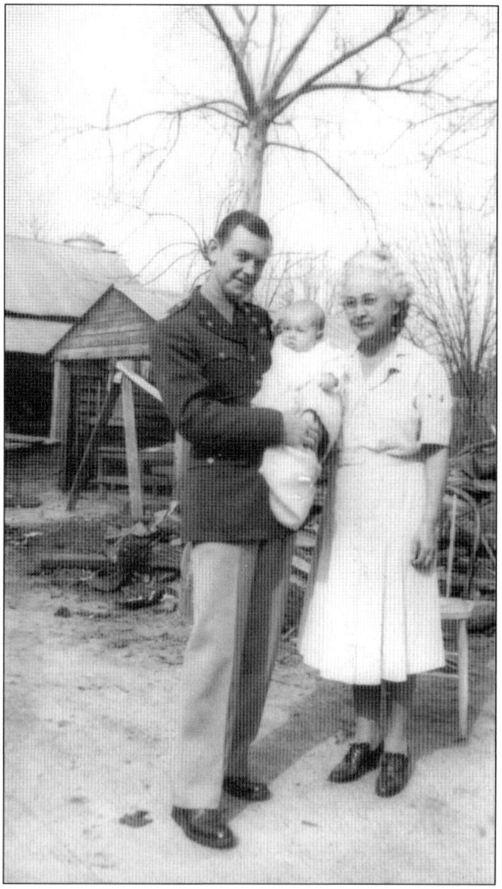

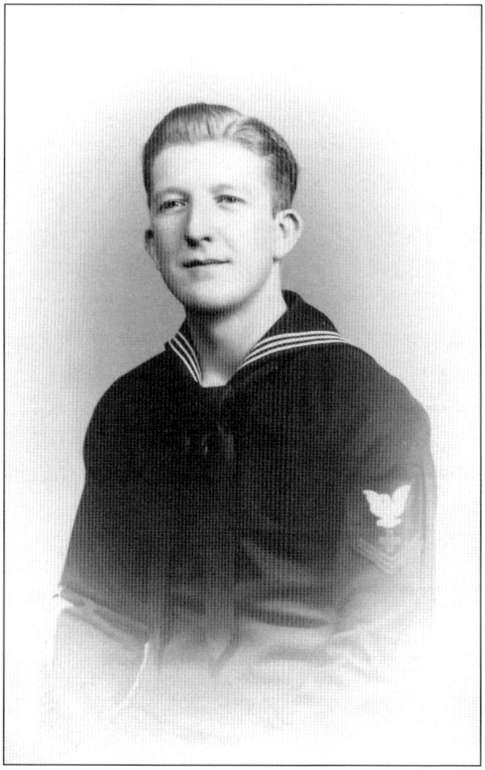

After serving in the Navy as a chief pharmacist's mate during World War II, Marvin L. Perkins (1919–1989) returned to his beloved Glennville, where he served in many public capacities and was employed with First Citizens Bank for 35 years. Perkins exhibited a great love for Glennville and its history and amassed an impressive collection of historical photographs, without which this volume would not have been possible. (Courtesy of Ann Perkins Gibbs.)

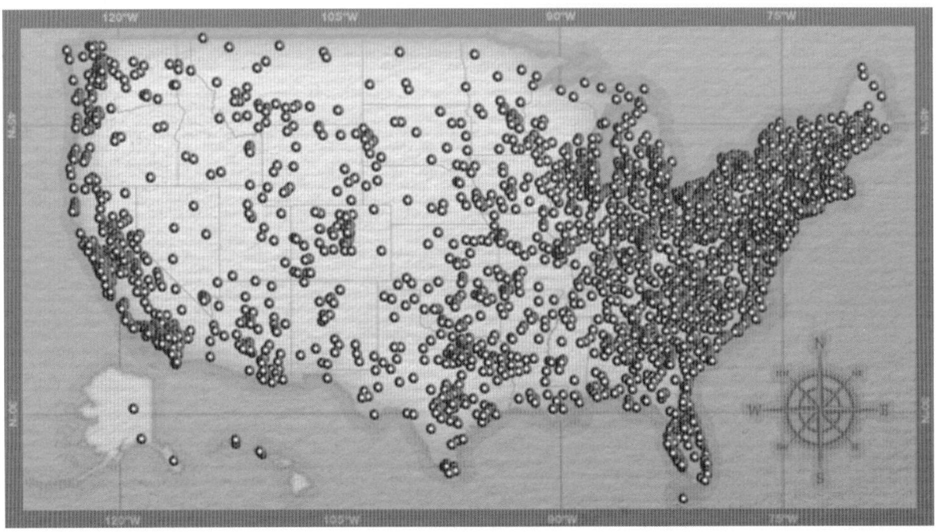